IS IT GOOD FOR THE JEWS?

ALSO BY STEPHEN SCHWARTZ

Spanish Marxism vs. Soviet Communism:
A History of the POUM (with Víctor Alba)

From West to East: California and the
Making of the American Mind

Kosovo: Background to a War

The Two Faces of Islam: Saudi Fundamentalism
and Its Role in Terrorism

Sarajevo Rose: A Balkan Jewish Notebook

IS IT GOOD
FOR THE JEWS?

The Crisis of America's
Israel Lobby

Stephen Schwartz

DOUBLEDAY
New York London Toronto Sydney Auckland

ACKNOWLEDGMENTS

I owe everything in the achievement of this work to my editor and friend Adam Bellow, assisted by colleagues Daniel Feder and Chris Fortunato. But I would be remiss in not also thanking Seth Lipsky and J. J. Goldberg of the *Forward*, who published my work, and my friends Ronald Radosh and Fred Siegel, who helped with some details. *Il consigliere* Richard Torre also deserves his customary recognition. And finally, a nod to Léo Malet, who showed the way. Nevertheless, I alone am responsible for all opinions, as well as any errors or infelicities, in this book.

Washington-Dubrovnik-Amsterdam-Warsaw-Jerusalem
2004–2006

PUBLISHED BY DOUBLEDAY

Copyright © 2006 by Stephen Schwartz

Published in the United States by Doubleday, an imprint of The Doubleday Broadway Publishing Group, a division of Random House, Inc., New York. www.doubleday.com

DOUBLEDAY and the portrayal of an anchor with a dolphin are registered trademarks of Random House, Inc.

Library of Congress Cataloging-in-Publication Data
Schwartz, Stephen, 1948–
   Is it good for the Jews? : the crisis of America's Israel lobby / by Stephen Schwartz.—1st ed.
      p.   cm.
   Includes index.
   1. Jews—United States—Politics and government—21st century.
2. Jews—United States—Politics and government—20th century.
3. American Israel Public Affairs Committee. 4. United States—Politics and government. 5. United States—Foreign relations—Israel. 6. Israel—Foreign relations—United States.   I. Title.
   E184.36.P64S39 2006
   305.892'4073—dc22   2006007732

ISBN-13: 978-0-385-51025-7
ISBN-10: 0-385-51025-X

PRINTED IN THE UNITED STATES OF AMERICA

10 9 8 7 6 5 4 3 2 1

First Edition

Dedicated to L.D.^{2}
for their inspiration;
to the Jewish genius of Larry David;
and to the "hidden imam"—
with "memories of grapes and pears"

CONTENTS

INTRODUCTION

A Schande *for the* Goyim

"A lobby is like a night flower," Steven J. Rosen, former policy direc-tor of the American Israel Public Affairs Committee (AIPAC), is reported to have written in an internal memorandum. "It flourishes in the dark and dies in the sun." Unfortunately, however, Washington is not a nocturnal town. Most business is transacted during the day, and Washingtonians rest at night. Café and bar life is limited even when compared to less important cities such as Frankfurt and Zurich, to say nothing of New York. That and its provincial love of gossip ensure that many significant actions taken in Washington, certainly by institutions and individuals as powerful as AIPAC and Rosen, will inevitably be made public.

The white marble and limestone of official Washington give it the feeling of a holy city, the center of a great empire. There is an implied chastity in the Capitol, the White House, and the Lincoln Memorial, as well as the museums and colleges and religious sites. In its own way there is no city more American, or at least more intellectually self-conscious of its American identity. Even the Pentagon has a uniquely American quality: the first thing a visitor sees on getting past the security checks is a vast shopping mall, offering everything from sports shoes and aspirin to hot lasagna and military badges. This is because, first, there are few businesses in the area around the building, and second, employees, especially senior and middle staff, are expected to remain in the building throughout their workday. For those important enough, meals may be served at their desks.

I had first come to Washington from California in my mid-thirties, during the Reagan era. My stays were brief, however, and I did not make the capital a home until sixteen years later, at the beginning of George W. Bush's first term. In the meantime I had gone from San Francisco, where I had lived forty-eight years, to the city of Sarajevo, Bosnia-Herzegovina, and an investigation of Muslim radicalism that would produce my book *The Two Faces of Islam*. But I had also been covering Jewish affairs since 1992 for the *Forward*, formerly a Yiddish daily, reinvented as a national Jewish weekly in English. At the end of 2000 I took a job as Washington bureau chief for the *Forward*.

Like any other sojourner from the hinterlands, in 2000 no less than in 1984, I was dazzled by the imperial gravitas of the Hill and its monumental institutions. But, as with any normal person, it all eventually grew familiar. There came a time when visiting the Pentagon for me was interesting mainly because you could buy terrific ice cream so near the offices I went to. Otherwise it was about as exciting as the police headquarters and bottom-rung courts in the municipal Hall of Justice I had covered as a reporter in San Francisco.

Nevertheless, I always had the sense that federal employment in Washington was a special calling; one had, after all, taken an oath before the flag and been sworn in as a U.S. government official. One owed the country something for that privilege. My vision was less that of James Stewart in *Mr. Smith Goes to Washington* than that of William Holden as a naively liberal newspaperman in the 1950 film *Born Yesterday*.

As summer 2004 drew to a close I traveled from Washington to another beautiful, inspiring, and historic city of white stone, distinguished in the annals of democracy: Dubrovnik in Croatia. In 1776, the illustrious commercial republic on the Adriatic coast, then called Ragusa, had been the first state in the world to acknowledge American independence. I went there to deliver a research paper on local Jewish history. The weather was perfect, and the houses, churches, and palaces of marble and limestone in white Dubrovnik shone in the sun like the most prominent buildings in Washington.

There, walking with a lovely American woman and her little dog, I first received word of the AIPAC-Pentagon spy scandal. It was written up in the *International Herald Tribune* at the end of August. The FBI was investigating a minor Defense Department official, Lawrence Anthony Franklin, age fifty-eight, for handing over secret information to Israel through AIPAC. Young, ebullient AIPAC spokesperson Josh Block hotly denied the accusations. In a situation potentially much worse than the 1985 case of Jonathan J. Pollard, a spy for Israel detected in the civilian ranks of U.S. naval intelligence, "America's Pro-Israel Lobby," as AIPAC prefers to be called, would be accused of espionage, having been caught with its hands in the world's most alluring cookie jar: the Pentagon.

Foreign-policy influence in Washington is always, finally, about the Defense Department and its universe of contracts. This was illustrated when AIPAC lost the 1981 battle over the sale of AWACS planes to the Saudi monarchy and was reinforced when U.S.-Israeli military cooperation resumed with the lifting of U.S. sanctions imposed after Israel's 1982 incursion into Lebanon. Vendors and lobbyists, representing every industrial, political, and state interest, from Saudi front men recycling their cash and technology offers in cahoots with shady enterprises in Sudan to run-of-the-mill promoters of American corporate giants and think tanks, always buzzed around the building.

Soon Franklin's fellow targets in the investigation were named. They were AIPAC policy director Steve Rosen and an Iran expert for the organization, Keith Weissman. Rosen and Weissman would be accused of transferring secret information given to them by Franklin, to Israeli embassy political officer Naor Gilon and another Israeli diplomat, Rafi Barak.

I was not particularly close to Rosen, but everybody who covered Jewish Washington as a reporter had met and observed the AIPAC chief commissar, who was in his early sixties, with short gray hair. He resembled the New York banker Felix Rohatyn, but unlike the urbane Manhattanite, his character was crude. AIPAC had once pressured the *Washington Jewish Week* to kill a story about a birthday party for Rosen at the organization's headquarters, where a stripper performed.

On Middle East policy and its related issues, Rosen was almost comically hard nosed, but he had the eyes of a shark and conveyed an air of something close to physical intimidation. It was said that his family had been Stalinist Communists, and Rosen himself was tarred with that association, which was generally employed to suggest that he had never lost the ruthlessness characteristic of the Muscovite milieu.

A lunch with Rosen was like meeting with a Balkan secret police official. One sat across the table and waited out the interrogation. I quickly learned from him that AIPAC, the American Jewish Committee (AJC), and the Anti-Defamation League (ADL)—the trifecta of the American Jewish lobbies—hated each other. But the only issues on which the groups seemed to disagree involved turf, personal rivalry, and cultural heritage. AJC came from a German Jewish background, ADL had originated in the period when millions of East European Jews immigrated to this country, and AIPAC prided itself on its homegrown American style. Each represented one of the great eras of Jewish life in America. While the Gentile world, both sophisticated and stupid, views "the Jewish lobby" as a single, homogeneous, and even monolithic body, it is anything but. It lacks the power, no less than the unity of will and vision, that many people ascribe to it. There is no single aim, tradition, or process by which Jewish interests are represented in the United States or through which U.S.-Israeli relations are clarified. Nor is it clear that Israel needs an elaborate American lobby as much as AIPAC needs Israel. Israelis often express contempt for irreligiosity, ultraliberalism, and unreliability among American Jews, and they have the example of American Jewish inefficacy in preventing the Holocaust to remind them that American Jews are involved in something that might best be called "Jewishness lite." American Jews seem to cleave to Israel as much to overcome long-enduring feelings of guilt over their passivity during the Holocaust as for love of Zion.

I knew Larry Franklin much better, since we had met and spoken a few times. Graying and rumpled, with a bushy mustache, Larry was not a typical Beltway policy wonk, although he has a doctorate in Asian affairs, speaks Farsi, and was an Iran desk officer in the Defense Department's office of Near East and South Asia. Larry is an extremely ordinary Gentile from Philadelphia who started out as a cabdriver and considers himself a street-smart, working-class guy. He made his way up through the armed forces and the Defense Intelligence Agency (DIA) to the Pentagon, where he was a colonel in the Air Force Reserve. He held a Top Secret clearance with access to "Sensitive Compartmented Information" (SCI). SCI includes information of which the unauthorized disclosure could "cause irreparable injury to the United States or be used to advantage by a foreign nation."

Larry lived with his large family in the West Virginia panhandle community of Kearneysville, which with the expansion of the Washington metro area has become a commuter town. His duties at the Pentagon in 2003 included liaison with the leading Iraqi Shia Muslim clerics in the United States, who, as it happened, were also my close friends. I helped introduce some of them to Larry as the Iraq war approached. They became known as "Shia-cons," a Shia parallel with the neoconservatives or "neocons," for their enthusiastic backing of the war against Saddam. Larry, who clearly supported the war in Iraq, if only because it was his job to do so, attended "Shia-con" parleys, held through a grab-bag organization called the Universal Muslim Association of America (UMAA), newly minted to represent Shia interests. He spent hours picking the brains of the Shia clerics about the situation in Iraq, to discern who would support U.S. policy and how factions in the U.S. community lined up with those in Iraq itself. Presumably, the information was handed over to his superiors. Later, I spoke to Larry repeatedly about ordinary Pentagon affairs. There was nothing charismatic or commanding about him. He was a very minor figure in something that would become a major drama.

Weissman I knew only secondhand. He was academic in background, with Middle East expertise. He had a reputation as an informal, even slightly slovenly person, but cold, and interested only in specific agenda items involving Israel's relations with the eastern Mediterranean countries. He seemed indifferent to anything other than his working tasks and would not volunteer information to those he lobbied, unlike the expansive and manipulative Rosen.

The AIPAC scandal could not have come at a worse time. In 2004, powerful Jews stood accused of subverting the American Republic and, for their selfish goals, driving the country toward war. Descendants of Abraham, Isaac, and Jacob, adherents of the Hebrew faith and devotees of Old Testament law, they were and are publicly alleged to hold a special loyalty to their own kind, above their American citizenship. While their own coddled offspring would stay far from gunfire and bombs, the Jews and their pawns, it is said, send the children of poor Gentiles to die at the hands of a powerful enemy—whom the Jews, rather than ordinary Americans, have caused to hate America. The so-called tyrants whom Americans are expected to die overthrowing have done America no harm. Indeed, the representatives of the supposed enemy have repeated many times that no conflict between them and America would take place if America were to cease following the counsels and suffering the control of Jewry.

World-famous celebrities, populist politicians, elitist intellectuals, hard-core radical leftists, and disaffected public servants unite to accuse the President of the United States of dishonesty in service to Jewish interests by inventing pretexts to extend American military power overseas. The president is charged by many opinion makers with having broken the law to help the Jewish war-lovers carry out their nefarious scheme. The Jews have fostered a war in the name of democracy when mean economic interest is what really stands behind the carnage, the destruction of families, the shocking atrocities, the hatred loosed against America by a horrified world. Furthermore, it is said with increasing openness by some, Jews embody values alien to America and have contaminated the country through their control of journalism and popular entertainment. America and its traditional beliefs are perceived as fatally vulnerable to foreign cultural and political infiltration.

The scenario should be familiar to any American, or, for that matter, anybody paying attention anywhere in the world in the year 2006. It is the argument offered in millions of words of news commentary and on the Internet, in almost every language and to followers of every religion, to explain the decision of George W. Bush to intervene in Iraq and topple Saddam Hussein.

The neoconservatives are the main group identified with the Jews in supposedly undermining American constitutional power to launch an armed conflict. They allegedly act in the interest of Israel rather than the United States. The rest of the litany is almost too familiar to enumerate: an unjustified war in Iraq against a ruler who posed no threat, as well as an Arab and Islamic adversary that, it is said, would harbor no grudge against America—rather, would love America— were it not for American support of Israel. But the neoconservatives, one is told, pay no attention to the logic of history or cultures: they are guided by the mysterious writings of a certain Leo Strauss, an obscure philosopher who mainly taught at the University of Chicago and who is charged with forging a cynical power ideology that inspires the "neocons" to lie for whatever purpose they (in their elite wisdom) consider worthy.

Global stars of music, film, and the literary class have transformed these primitive claims into artifacts of popular culture: a decrepit Mick Jagger sang about a "Sweet Neo Con" in an apparent jab at President Bush and his ally, British prime minister Tony Blair. Leftist actor Tim Robbins produced a vile play, *Embedded*, with a forged quotation attributed to Strauss, according to which the neoconservatives harbor the aim of "controlling the unintelligent majority." The apparent argument was that Straussians had manipulated America into war in Iraq in the belief that blood would unite Americans behind Bush. The play was staged, appropriately enough, in New York at the Public Theater, the brainchild of avant-garde Jewish theater impresario and ex-Communist Joseph Papp.

In the underside of the culture, Strauss and the neoconservatives have become topics for a series of hysterical, defamatory, shoddy screeds—thirty years after the philosopher died. Contentions by the authors of such works, including the Canadian academic Shadia B. Drury, are so bizarre that one is hard-pressed to respond to them appropriately. Drury's book *Leo Strauss and the American Right*, published in 1999, declared, "Relying on the conflict between America's puritanical spirit and her liberal regime, the neoconservative strategy consists in driving a wedge between American democracy and American liberalism." Thus, as I understand it, for Drury the neoconservative commitment to democracy is really authoritarian manipulation. These conceptions almost exactly reproduce the claims made in the spurious "Protocols of the Elders of Zion," in which Jews are portrayed as using the masses to suppress the masses.

Electoral rabble-rousers such as Virginia's Democratic congressman Jim Moran have stated, "If it were not for the strong support of the Jewish community for this war with Iraq, we would not be doing this." The disgraceful Moran was seconded by South Carolina Democratic senator Ernest C. Hollings, who wrote, "With Iraq no threat, why invade a sovereign country? The answer: President Bush's policy to secure Israel." Hollings went on to insist on the floor of the Senate that the Iraq war was begun "to secure our friend, Israel . . . everybody knows it." Georgia Democratic congresswoman Cynthia McKinney was particularly egregious, declaring, "What is . . . disturbing to me is that many . . . pro-Israeli lawmakers sit on the House International Relations Committee despite the obvious conflict of interest that their emotional attachments to Israel cause. . . . The Israeli occupation of all territories must end, including Congress." Even former Senator Gary Hart declaimed, "I don't think there is going to be peace between Israel and the Palestinians so long as we're in Iraq."

Bashing the Iraq intervention as a product of the neoconservatives and their Jewish associations is also a well-established habit among elite media commentators. Columnist Robert Novak, a longtime critic of Israel who opposed the first Gulf War, wrote at the end of 2002, "War with Iraq may not be inevitable but is highly probable.

That it looks like [Israeli leader Ariel] Sharon's war disturbs Americans." Eric Alterman of *The Nation* similarly opined, "[T]he idea of a new war to remove Saddam was partially conceived at the behest of Likud politician Benjamin Netanyahu." He wrote dismissively of "Jewish hard liners" and added, "What's more, many of these same Jews joined . . . in what may have been a ruse designed to embroil America in a broad military conflagration that would help smite Israel's enemies." Meanwhile, *Doonesbury* comic writer Garry Trudeau, whose strip has not been funny for decades, falsely accused a midlevel Washington policy figure and strong supporter of Israel, Richard Perle, of responsibility for the invasion of Iraq.

Western leftists generally have descended into depths of paranoid shrillness not seen since the aftermath of the Kennedy assassination. They repeatedly (and incoherently) charge that Bush and Blair are tools of "big oil" and "Jewish neocons." In both countries, legal proceedings are demanded against the political leaders who "lied their countries into war." A former Central Intelligence Agency expert on Osama bin Laden, Michael Scheuer, offered a backhanded "compliment" to Israel on its "ability to control debate in the United States." This followed a stream of abuse by Scheuer to the effect that Israel's lobbying of Congress amounted to "a clandestine activity, a covert activity." Scheuer added, "I just find the whole debate in the United States unbearably restricted with the inability to factually discuss what goes on between our two countries." Karen Kwiatkowski, a former U.S. Air Force colonel and very, very minor Pentagon official, likewise railed against "high clearances granted to publicly and at times, rabidly, pro-Likud past and present political appointees" among her superiors in the Defense Department.

The neocons, it has been argued, swindled America into combat in Iraq thanks to the machinations of Jewish reporter Judith Miller of the Jewish-owned *New York Times* and by stereotyping of a Muslim enemy in films and on television. Finally, it is asserted by opponents of the Iraq war, foes of the alliance with Israel, and critics of Jewish influence that America must come first. *America first!*

In March 2006, a new Jew-baiting front was opened up in the

American discourse when two academics, John J. Mearsheimer of the University of Chicago and Stephen M. Walt, then–academic dean of Harvard's prestigious Kennedy School of Government, issued an anti-Semitic manifesto entitled "The Israel Lobby and American Foreign Policy." Decorated with its Harvard seal of approval, this so-called faculty research working paper was no more a respectable academic product than were the "studies" by ultranationalist professors in Germany in the nineteenth century or in Eastern Europe in the 1920s and 1930s, railing against the Jews.

The professors argued that the Jewish lobby controls—that is, dominates, not merely influences—the American outlook on the Middle East. Their paper was based not on any sort of empirical investigation of political events but on misconstrued media coverage, ridiculous suppositions, and fantasy. In their minds, and in their text, Larry Franklin was transformed into "a key Pentagon official," a description with only one aim: to exaggerate his power and thus further attack the Jews at AIPAC. In the view of Mearsheimer and Walt, all the Jews of a pro-Israel persuasion, including neoconservatives and AIPAC leaders, are members of the same body. This "lobby" even comprises, aside from AIPAC and the Jewish neocons, anyone who shares the views of the neocons, including the Gentile John Bolton and the Arab Shia Fouad Ajami.

Mearsheimer and Walt also regurgitated the shoddiest second-hand clichés about the Muslim world in pursuit of their anti-Jewish crusade. According to them "There is no question, for example, that many al-Qaeda leaders, including bin Laden, are motivated by Israel's presence in Jerusalem and the plight of the Palestinians." Only distant commentators with no knowledge whatever of Islamist radicalism could make such an absurd claim. When the Saudi-financed al-Qaeda allied with the Islamic Movement of Uzbekistan (IMU) to fight in Tajikistan and Afghanistan, where the IMU was wiped out, who among the jihadists thought the combat in Central Asia had anything to do with Jerusalem? Who among the Saudi extremists who have infiltrated the Chechen struggle in Russia believes that war in the Caucasus has anything to do with Palestine? When Saudi-backed radicals kill in Saudi Arabia itself, the Philippines, and Indonesia, who imagines these actions have anything to do with Israel?

The Mearsheimer-Walt travesty was almost immediately endorsed with great glee by the most corrosively anti-Israel entities in America: the Council on American-Islamic Relations (CAIR), a Saudi-financed front for the terrorist Hamas movement, plus the U.S. office of the Palestine Liberation Organization (PLO), and former Ku Klux Klan promoter David Duke. As it happens, the paper came out within three months of the delivery of a $20 million gift to Harvard from Saudi prince Alwaleed bin Talal bin Abd al-Aziz al-Sa'ud.

The most prominent victim of this defamatory campaign has been former deputy defense secretary Paul D. Wolfowitz, now president of the World Bank. The *New York Review of Books* contributed to this "debate" by printing a David Levine caricature of Wolfowitz with the unmistakable leer of a literal wolf; the cartoon would not have been out of place in the Nazi *Der Stürmer*.

Remarkably, the American Jewish leadership did not defend Wolfowitz or the younger Washington neoconservatives associated with him, such as William Kristol, editor of the *Weekly Standard*. Wolfowitz and the neocons were frightening to the American Jewish leadership, problem cases creating quicksands in which blame would fall on the Jews for events in which they had played almost no role.

But while the most prominent Jewish leaders in AJC, ADL, and AIPAC acted as if they had never heard of Wolfowitz or the other neoconservatives, Wolfowitz risked becoming an American equivalent of Captain Alfred Dreyfus, the victim of infamous Jew-baiters in France. The specter of an American Dreyfus had haunted American Jews for a century. Now it had come shockingly close to reality. Yet a silence like velvet cloaked that particular topic.

If these allegations have become commonplace in America and the world today, they should also be familiar. There is nothing new in this witches' brew of magical thinking, slander, rumor, superstition, prejudice, *lumpen* intellectuality, and demagogy.

Indeed, the anti-Jewish, antineoconservative, "antiwar" hysteria of the twenty-first century weirdly revives the atmosphere in the United States at the end of the 1930s, with the approach of the Second World War, but in a metastasized, malignant, and more menacing form. Sixty-five years ago it was the Germans who had, according to isolationists, been provoked by the Jews into attacking the Western democracies. Hitler, like bin Laden, had repeatedly offered peace to the West if the democracies would accede to his demand to simply be left alone. Just as it is said today that Saddam posed no threat to the United States, so was it shouted far and wide that the depredations of Hitler, Mussolini, and the Japanese imperialists were no affair of ours and that the Axis powers had no interest in a war with us. And just as it is repeated that bin Laden and Saddam are natural enemies rather than accomplices, so antiwar propagandists of the late 1930s insisted that Hitler and Mussolini were rivals rather than allies.

Then and now, the Jews were portrayed as rapacious for conflict, destruction, and chaos, whether supposedly following the "Protocols of the Elders of Zion," the Talmud, or the polemics of Karl Marx. Like President Bush today, President Franklin D. Roosevelt was said to have violated the law and employed other devious means to satisfy Jewish bloodlust when he provided naval vessels to the embattled British before U.S. entry into the Second World War.

Historical shadows stand behind people such as Mick Jagger as well as Moran, Hollings, McKinney, and Hart when they rain filth on the Jews and Israel. In the 1930s, the hero aviator Charles A. Lindbergh Jr. lashed out, in a speech in Des Moines on September 11, 1941, at "the British, the Jewish and the Roosevelt administration" for "pressing" the United States to war with Germany. (Perhaps conspiratorialists can find significance in the coincidence of dates.)

Virginia's Moran had his counterpart then, in the form of Jacob Thorkelson, a Montana Republican who castigated his critics as those "no doubt of the variety which prefers the Protocols of the Learned Elders of Zion to the Constitution of the United States." Lindbergh and Thorkelson were united in support of an isolationist movement that called itself "America First." Meanwhile, in the American literary and artistic elite of the 1930s, distaste for the Jews was almost a given: T. S. Eliot, E. E. Cummings, and Ezra Pound were all notorious for it, and open admirers of Nazism included such individuals as the architect Philip C. Johnson. It is notable, however, that at the time of Lindbergh, Thorkelson, and Pound, few in American journalism would have retailed the sinister commodities today offered by Robert Novak and others like him. This is a point to which we will return: namely, that the crude anti-Jewish prejudice that was largely disreputable to Americans in the era of Hitler was mainstreamed in the United States a half century later, after the commencement of the Iraq war in 2003, with the rise of conspiracy agitation against the neocons.

But there is another difference between the present moment and the beginning of the Second World War. Then, agitators against the Jews were beaten (literally) in the streets of American cities, whereas today the hue and cry against the neoconservatives is barely discussed in the suites of the Jewish domestic and Israel lobbies and is elsewhere a phenomenon nobody wishes to confront.

Thus, the Jewish lobbies—AJC and ADL, as well as AIPAC—responded with further indifference to efforts to sweep the neoconservatives out of public life and into jail, as in the case of I. Lewis "Scooter" Libby, former chief of staff to vice president Dick Cheney. (Though it is not often mentioned in press reports, Libby is Jewish.) The silence of the lobbies was a product of timidity rather than guilt when it came to the neocons, because the lobbies had well and truly kept their distance from the latter. But the lobbies also reacted with complete paralysis when AIPAC's top operative, Steve Rosen, was arrested and charged with breaches of U.S. governmental security.

The AIPAC scandal was what older Jews called "a *schande* for the *goyim*," that is, a public embarrassment to the Jews that calls attention to a level of power and influence that many Jews recognize exists but which few wish to see exposed to the broader public. Such disclosure is typically considered "bad for the Jews." Yet far worse for the Jews is the abject failure of will visible among the leaders of the Jewish organizations.

Regarding the neocons, who were not and are not products of the American Jewish community leadership, the latter have failed their first major test of the twenty-first century. When the neocons embarked on a major attempt to positively transform the Middle East in the direction of capitalism and democracy, the Jewish leadership refused to become significantly involved. This abstention, as I will argue at length, is largely due to the seemingly unbreakable bond between Jews and the Democrats. But the AIPAC controversy was different; there the Israel lobby exposed its incompetence more than its pusillanimity and the burden of its political obligations. The AIPAC scandal could sink the flagship vessel of American Jewish power.

Rosen and Weissman were indicted on charges of conspiracy and overt acts involving transmission of classified information to unauthorized recipients. Rosen faced twenty years' imprisonment and Weissman ten years.

The two had been informed by the FBI of its interest in them from the beginning of August 2004. Questioned by the feds about his relations with Franklin, Rosen lied and denied they existed. The Israeli daily *Haaretz* reported that the FBI was determined to complete a serious investigation of AIPAC, encompassing the overall operations of the lobby and not merely the Franklin case.

But understanding what happened to Franklin was not simple. Franklin pled guilty and received a 12½-year sentence, contingent on his testimony against Rosen and Weissman. Judge T. S. Ellis III, who pronounced sentence, referred to the Franklin matter as "a very odd case." Franklin testified that while employed in the Pentagon, with access at the highest level of decision making, he had become concerned about events involving Iran and had decided to try contacting the National Security Council via AIPAC. Considering that Franklin's then boss, Donald Rumsfeld, sits on the NSC and is the cabinet's most strident critic of Iran, the story makes no sense. That someone in the security establishment—FBI or CIA, most likely—with an animus toward AIPAC, the neoconservatives, and all other Jews and friends of Jews would seize on a contact between Franklin and Rosen to entrap AIPAC does make sense.

With the speed of an avalanche, the twenty-year career of Steve Rosen, as the private Jewish official with more power on the Hill than any other in Washington history, began collapsing. And AIPAC's castle could crash to the ground with him.

It would be bad enough for Steve Rosen, once known (and feared) universally in Washington, to land behind bars. But the outcome of the Rosen case could also result in AIPAC being ordered to register as a lobby for a foreign government. This would seriously undermine its fund-raising abilities and inexorably reduce it to a body with no more clout than a chamber of commerce for a former Soviet republic. In addition to which, of course, the long-asserted canard of American Jewish "dual loyalty" to the United States and Israel could gain widespread credibility.

I intended originally to make this book no more than an accurate account of events I witnessed, about which absurd misrepresentations had been made throughout the land and across the globe. But in its writing I developed a thesis: that the question of *who* decides what is good for the Jews is, in the end, more important and compelling than a mere statement of opinion as to *what* is good for the Jews. The good of the American Jewish community has more often been furthered by courageous, nonconforming individuals or small groups than by elaborate defense and lobbying organizations and impressive political alliances.

The disastrous AIPAC affair came at the end of a long road marked by one abdication after another by America's top Jewish leadership. Refusal to fight pro-Nazi elements in the streets of New York in the late 1930s, surrender to the political blandishments of a corrupt Democratic Party, obliviousness about the Holocaust, evasion of problems involving Jewish-black relations, disdain for the original neoconservatives, incapacity to recognize the horrific danger posed by Saudi Wahhabism (the cult that inspires al-Qaeda), time wasted on exaggerated fears about Christian fundamentalists, anxiety over Jewish and Israeli associations with American policy in the aftermath of September 11, 2001, refusal to defend the younger neoconservatives during the Iraq intervention, diffidence about the Iraq war itself—all led inevitably to lethargy, and AIPAC found itself in serious trouble.

Above all, lost in the imaginary New Deal theme park of Democratic rhetoric, eternally feeling as if they had just got off the boat from Europe and were still huddled on the Lower East Side, the mainstream Jewish leadership simply could not grasp that the initiative in American policies relevant to Jews had been seized by the neoconservative "third force," representing neither the traditional domestic Jewish defense groups such as AJC and ADL nor the aggressive pro-Israel lobby AIPAC. They were especially disturbed that the neocons had forged a new political alliance with the Republicans. The Jewish leadership that, throughout its universal history, has achieved the most— the American Jews—now finds itself on the edge of an abyss. But the warning signs were always there, for those who were willing to do something other than keep their heads down and their actions discreet.

The moment has come for a consequential response to the tidal wave of Jew-baiting lies that has swept across America since the Iraq intervention began.

That is the matter this book will address.

CHAPTER 1

ASSAULT ON "JEW YORK"

Jewish Self-Defense Before the Lobby

He was seventeen, sensitive, with brooding eyes, and wept easily; little more than five feet tall, slender and dark, but handsome. He felt alone, angry, and confused, and outrage overwhelmed him.

He was a Jew. And he had a gun.

Herschel Feibel Grynszpan was born in Hannover, Germany, but held Polish nationality. In 1938, he had undergone three years of chaos. The Nazis were in power, and he was not allowed to become an apprentice or otherwise gain employment. He wanted to go to Palestine but found no way to get there, even after a year spent studying Hebrew. A visa to the Promised Land was refused him. Finally he went to Belgium, then crossed the border to France without authorization.

He was a refugee, an illegal immigrant, non-Christian, unemployed, a troubled youth.

He had an uncle and aunt, Abraham and Clara Grynszpan, in Paris. Abraham Grynszpan was a tailor; the family spoke Yiddish better than French. France was unfriendly to Jews fleeing Germany. Herschel could not obtain legal permission to stay, and eventually the French authorities ordered him deported and began, unsuccessfully, to hunt him down. He hid in an attic. He wrote to American president Franklin D. Roosevelt appealing for help for himself and his family.

Then, late in 1938, came the expulsion of his father, Zindel, along with his mother, sister, and brother, who, having stayed behind in Germany, were dragged from their Hannover home and sent to Poland. The Poles, in a typical fit of anti-Semitism, had threatened to revoke the passports of Polish citizens—mainly Jews—residing in Germany. The Nazis retorted by deporting some 15,000 Jews, including the Grynszpans. The Jewish victims were refused entry into their alleged Polish homeland, and massed in misery at the border.

In Paris, the agitated Herschel argued with his aunt and uncle. He had received a note from the German-Polish frontier describing the conditions his family suffered. He had fantasies of joining the French Foreign Legion, but he had probably been refused a visa to Palestine because of bad health, and it was unlikely he would succeed as a soldier of France. He threatened suicide, then slammed the door of his uncle's house and was not seen for a night and a day. He had gone to stay in a hotel on the Left Bank, under the name Alter Heini.

On November 7, 1938, Grynszpan went to the German embassy on the rue de Lille and asked to see ambassador Johannes von Welczek. An undersecretary, Ernst vom Rath, was sent to the anteroom to find out what the visitor wanted. Grynszpan pulled his gun out and shot at vom Rath repeatedly. Two bullets struck the Nazi diplomat, who later died.

Grynszpan was seized by other embassy personnel, but surrendered and laid down his gun. He was turned over to the French police.

He told the press, "Being a Jew is not a crime. I am not a dog. I have a right to live and the Jewish people have the right to live on this earth. Wherever I have gone I have been hunted like a beast."

By a terrible coincidence, the shooting came on the twentieth anniversary of imperial Germany's capitulation to the Allies and the proclamation of the Berlin monarchy's end—which the Nazis and other German anti-Semites blamed on the Jews, who allegedly "stabbed the nation in the back." Nazi leaders ordered that the controlled press in Germany focus on Grynszpan's act. The Nazis claimed that Grynszpan represented a powerful conspiracy of all the world's Jews against Germany. Newspapers and radio broadcasts in Berlin and every other German city denounced him as a tool of the British "war party," and printed his picture alongside that of Winston Churchill.

On the night of November 9, the Nazis used his reckless protest as a pretext for retaliation. The date would forever be known as "Kristallnacht"—the "night of broken glass." Violence began in the city of Kassel and spread throughout the country, to nearly every town. The windows of almost 10,000 Jewish stores were smashed and their inventory stolen; packs of adults and children followed after and repeated the pillage until the shops were empty. Nazi "wrecking crews" rushed to blow up and set fire to synagogues, destroying as many as 2,000. Firemen put out the flames in the shops but only prevented the fires in houses of worship from spreading to neighboring structures. Some non-Jewish enterprises were devastated as the gangs careened through the cities. American-owned stores, one displaying the Stars and Stripes in its window, were demolished. Foreign diplomats and tourists who tried to observe or photograph the disorder were harassed and arrested. An incident of surrealistic madness featured a piano moved to the sidewalk, where the vandals, in jolly German style, entertained the mob by playing popular tunes.

Some in the crowds that watched the attacks were displeased with the violence; some even helped Jews escape. Indeed, foreign newspapers reported that poor and working people were not involved in the crimes. A man in Berlin, in a laborer's outfit, shouted, "Arson is arson!" when he saw a synagogue burning. Uniformed Nazi storm troopers clearly incited the participants, who were then protected by police.

Assaults on Jewish property continued, beginning early the next day, November 10. The *New York Times* described "a wave of destruction, looting, and incendiarism unparalleled in Germany" since the seventeenth century. Insurance companies soon announced they would not compensate Jewish clients for the damages. All over Germany Jews were arrested—in some cases after searches of non-Jewish homes where it was suspected they were sheltered. Thousands were detained in Vienna, recently occupied in the German annexation of Austria; there some committed suicide. Other Jews were badly beaten; almost a hundred were murdered.

Governments and media in the democratic nations denounced German lawlessness. The United States called its ambassador to Berlin home for emergency consultations on the crisis. On November 15, at his 500th press conference, President Franklin D. Roosevelt expressed himself in restrained but pointed language: "The news of the past few days from Germany has deeply shocked public opinion in the United States. Such news from any part of the world would inevitably produce a similar profound reaction among American people in every part of the nation. I myself could scarcely believe that such things could occur in a twentieth century civilization." He went on to announce that the United States would, in case of war, prepare a single "continental" defense "from Canada to Tierra del Fuego."

The Nazi press replied by denouncing Roosevelt for "imperialism" and war preparations to benefit the armaments industry. The Nazis also complained that America had mistreated its black citizens, as if that equaled or outweighed attacks on German Jews. Germany had begun a campaign in favor of the Palestinian Arabs, and the Nazi papers warned that if Britain's House of Commons condemned Germany, the latter would respond by publicizing British anti-Arab incidents. Joseph Goebbels, the Nazi propaganda minister, sneered that Kristallnacht was obviously spontaneous, because if he and his colleagues had organized it, ten times as many Germans would have joined in and "the results would have been more radical."

Goebbels concluded by threatening that Nazi treatment of Jews in Germany would depend on the "good behavior" of Jews outside the country. Air Marshal Hermann Goering, the number-two Nazi after Adolf Hitler, announced a fine of $400 million levied on the German Jews for the assassination in Paris. New legal restrictions on Jews, including curfews and confiscation of radios, soon followed.

Understandably, a Jewish representative inside Germany, whose name has not survived, condemned Grynszpan. Unforgivably, many other Jews around the world saw him as a figure of horror—he had, it was said, justified Nazi cruelties. The World Jewish Congress, never as important as its pretentious title might have indicated, "deplored" Grynszpan's act before protesting against Nazi "reprisals . . . after the crime" (i.e., of Grynszpan). A French Jewish newspaper, *L'Univers Israélite*, published a statement addressed to the German diplomat vom Rath's mother, expressing its "great sorrow" at her son's death and blaming Kristallnacht on "rabble" rather than the German leaders.

As for the leading American Jewish communal organizations, the American Jewish Committee (AJC) and Anti-Defamation League (ADL), they produced no press releases or other emergency statements defending Grynszpan. The American Communist Party, then including a significant Jewish component, treated the events in Germany ambiguously. The *Daily Worker*, New York's Stalinist sheet, featured a column by Mike Gold, who had become famous with his 1930 novel, *Jews Without Money*, renowned in its time but forgotten today except by sentimental leftist academics. Gold described Grynszpan as "mad with grief and shame." Shame about what? one might ask.

The Communist paper elsewhere referred to Grynszpan as "grief-crazed" and referred in one brief reportage to Goebbels as a member of "the extreme anti-Semitic wing of Nazism"—as if such distinctions meant anything. The American Communists were anxious to draw attention away from their ratio of Jews, and once the brutalities of Kristallnacht began, they loudly warned that the Nazis were about to turn on Catholics in the same fashion. But Stalin had already begun sending discreet messages to Hitler indicating his interest in a pact, which would be consummated in August 1939.

The *New York Times*, Jewish-owned but sunk in a cowardly attitude of constraint about asserting any Jewish interest, treated Grynszpan with barely concealed contempt. The *Times* referred to his having studied Hebrew but with "no intention of becoming a rabbi," and later headlined the young man's description of the shooting as carried out in "a trance."

The *Times*, it must be said, had not always been so craven; decades before, it had served with outstanding valor in exposing atrocities against the Jewish masses in the Russian empire. But the horrors of tsarism had only temporarily broken through a basic fear of identification with Jewish ambition. That reluctance had transformed the *Times* into a deplorable exemplar of what, in Europe, was known as the *shtadlan* mentality. In the *shtadlan* pattern—deeply rooted in the history and culture of the Old World ghettoes—"court Jews" influenced Gentile rulers by deferential influence behind the scenes at the highest level, for whatever ends the Jewish leaders deemed to be good for the community. In the Christian kingdoms, this attitude had a history of alternating achievement with disaster.

Jews could attain great influence in Christian Europe, but narrow access to power and lack of autonomy made whatever security the Jews gained a fragile matter. Jews flourished in Christian Spain and Portugal but were expelled; they were tolerated in Italy, where they could print their holy books, but then saw the Talmud burned by order of the Roman Curia; they had exalted financial relations with the rulers of England, France, and the German lands, which did not prevent their eventual banishment. They flooded into Poland, where enlightened, Renaissance-era kings favored them, but this stirred the resentment of the impoverished Christians; frightful outbreaks of violence culminated in the Cossack massacres of 1648, in which hundreds of thousands of Jews were killed.

With the coming of the Christian Reformation to the Netherlands, Amsterdam and other Dutch cities welcomed the Jews and provided a unique example as places where the *shtadlan* strategy was consistently successful. The Dutch Protestants honored the religious tradition and admired the piety of the Jews and were willing to let them live, pray, and work among them largely unmolested. But until the Napoleonic era and the emancipation of Jews by Bonaparte's armies, Holland was a magnificent exception in Western Europe. Although Jews were permitted to reside in England after the mid-seventeenth century, they did so under numerous legal handicaps and in fear, as they did in the German dominions.

In a situation that would seem ironic to twenty-first-century readers, Jews in the Ottoman Empire and other Muslim lands enjoyed a
better civil condition, including the unimpeded right to print their
holy books. They paid a tax known as *cizye,* which exempted them
from service in Muslim armies but also guaranteed their security.
When the Jews were forced out of Spain, they were welcomed in
Morocco and Turkey. But the Muslim states in which Jews formed
colonies never produced a *shtadlan* tradition. Rather, their rabbinical
jurists, alongside Christian clerics and courts, participated in a rational system of community administration. The *hahambashi* or chief
rabbi of the Ottoman lands, for example, was a high court official and
valued adviser of the Turkish sultans. In contrast, *shtadlan* representatives in the Christian states were episodically appointed and occasionally effective, but their status was always uncertain. Above all,
shtadlan Jews in Christendom avoided public exposure, which they
feared would inevitably excite anti-Jewish prejudice. *Shtadlan* habits
were therefore essentially those of meekness and subordination.

Grynszpan, after his impetuous act, was an unfortunate victim of
such attitudes. As the years went by, the Stalinists who described him
as driven insane were habitually echoed by others. No less a figure
than Hannah Arendt, author and former lover of the philosopher
(and temporary Nazi) Martin Heidegger, described Grynszpan as "a
psychopath, unable to finish school, who for years had knocked about
Paris and Brussels, being expelled from both places."

Yes, Grynszpan had been unable to finish school under the Nazis
and had "knocked around" Paris and Brussels—although Arendt
made him sound like a Bohemian literary vagabond rather than a
Jewish refugee. And yes, he had been ordered expelled from Paris. One
wonders where she thought he could have gone. Certainly, he would
not have found a place in the exalted company of Heidegger.

Today Jews remain ambivalent about Grynszpan; he is still seen
by most as a warped and tormented figure whose only significance is
that he helped bring about the tragedy of European Jewry—as if the
Holocaust would not have occurred if Grynszpan had not murdered
the Nazi diplomat vom Rath. Of course, if the intention of the Nazis

to exterminate all the Jews in the world had been understood at the time, he might have been seen as a hero.

Then again, maybe not. For the treatment of Grynszpan by history, including by Jewish chroniclers, raises the issue of Jewish self-defense and the morality to which it must be held. Jews had previously employed violent direct action to protect their communities in Russia at the beginning of the twentieth century. They would do so again after the foundation of the independent state of Israel. Yet such acts have almost always been greeted with disquiet by Jews and non-Jews alike. Under what circumstances is it permissible for Jews to commit acts of assassination, terror, and even military conquest in the name of self-defense? This would become the great question of the twentieth century for the Jews, and a major challenge for the world—and so it persists.

Of the few people, Jewish or Gentile, who would stand up for Grynszpan, one was an American reporter and columnist, Dorothy Thompson. She was married to the Nobel Prize–winning author Sinclair Lewis, and she was the first American journalist to be expelled from Germany by the Nazis, in 1934. Thompson, then a special writer for the *Washington Post,* delivered an eloquent speech on the *General Electric Hour,* one of the most popular radio shows in the United States. She declared, "I want to talk about that boy. I feel as though I knew him." She reminded her listeners of the indignities visited on Jews in Germany, including the humiliation of Jewish schoolchildren, whose "criminal" features were pointed out to their peers by teachers, and she spoke about famous intellectuals who were forced to clean the streets.

Thompson acknowledged that nearly every American newspaper had editorialized against Kristallnacht, their words echoed by prominent politicians including former New York Democratic governor Al Smith and Thomas E. Dewey, then a candidate for the same post on the Republican ticket. But she went on to demand, "Is there not a higher justice in the case of Herschel Grynszpan, 17 years old?" Noting that he would be tried in France and might be executed by guillotine, she asked, "Must the nation whose Zola defended Dreyfus ... cut off the head of one more Jew? Who is on trial in this case? I say we are all on trial. I say the Christian world is on trial. . . . Therefore, we who are not Jewish must speak, speak our sorrow and indignation and disgust. . . . If you are not Jewish and you feel as I do I ask you to wire or write me in care of this station."

The next day Thompson announced she had received 3,000 telegrams of support, with "uncounted thousands of letters, many enclosing money." She called on "Christians only" to donate, so that the Nazis could not exploit the campaign to carry out further acts of revenge. How could she know the worst was yet to come?

Another protest was raised from Mexico City by a man of Jewish birth who had disclaimed his religious heritage: the Russian revolutionary Leon Trotsky, who also knew the experience of forced exile and cruel treatment—including banishment and murder—of his relatives. His son Lev Sedov, age thirty-one, had been killed in Paris by Stalin's agents less than a year before, in February 1938.

Trotsky wrote, "The policy of the fascist gangsters directly and sometimes deliberately provokes terrorist acts. What is most astonishing is that so far there has been only one Grynszpan. Undoubtedly the number of such acts will increase. . . . We Marxists consider the tactic of individual terror inexpedient in the tasks of the liberating struggle of the proletariat as well as oppressed nationalities. . . . But we understand only too clearly the inevitability of such convulsive acts of despair and vengeance. All our emotions, all our sympathies are with the self-sacrificing avengers even though they have been unable to discover the correct road. Our sympathy becomes intensified because Grynszpan is not a political militant but an inexperienced youth, almost a boy, whose only counselor was a feeling of indignation."

Trotsky observed, "People come cheap who are capable only of fulminating against injustice and bestiality. But those who, like Grynszpan, are able to act as well as conceive, sacrificing their own lives if need be, are the precious leaven of mankind." He concluded by repeating that individual terrorism could not be substituted for a mass movement, and insisted, "Our open moral solidarity with Grynszpan gives us an added right to say to all the other would-be Grynszpans, to all those capable of self-sacrifice in the struggle against despotism and bestiality: *Seek another road!*" Trotsky's "critical support" for Grynszpan reflected the Russian revolutionary's experiences under a dying tsarist despotism, where anti-state terrorism was frequently taken up by Russian and Polish liberal Gentiles. Muslim warriors were also glorious in their resistance to Russian imperialism, and those who denounced such tactics were often viewed as cowards and traitors to the cause of freedom. But such resistance inspired the activist combat of American Jews against fascist agitators in the 1930s, and guided those influenced by Trotsky in the defense of Jews later in twentieth- and twenty-first-century America.

At the end of November 1938, a Communist-front rally of 20,000 people at Madison Square Garden heard Thompson and more than a dozen other speakers. They mainly condemned the treatment of Jews in Germany, although in the typical fashion of such events, speeches also demanded support for the Spanish Republic (then fighting a civil war against the rightist forces of General Francisco Franco), the end of British rule in Northern Ireland, and fair treatment of African Americans. Thompson repeated her call for Grynszpan's defense, but otherwise the seventeen-year-old appeared to have been, perhaps conveniently, ignored.

And what of the desperate youth himself?

His ultimate fate is unknown even today. Grynszpan never saw trial. He was held in the French prison of Fresnes until the arrival of German troops in Paris in June 1940, when he was sent south by the Parisian authorities, to a jail in Bourges. On the way he experienced a brief period of freedom when the train he was riding in was attacked by German aircraft. From Bourges, he was kidnapped by the Nazis and transferred to Germany, where he disappeared in the night and fog of the Holocaust. He vanished without trace, although rumors later proliferated describing his survival somewhere in France.

The specter of Grynszpan briefly haunted the world; like a blazing silhouette, he had in an instant illuminated the deepest contradictions and challenges facing his people and all of oppressed humanity. The slight young man's pistol shots in the German embassy in Paris had led to the obvious question—is it good for the Jews? This query is often uttered by Jews themselves in a spirit of self-conscious irony, but it is neither a matter of humor nor an expression of crass self-interest. The descendants of Abraham, Isaac, and Jacob bear a unique burden. They were chosen among the peoples of the world to receive and preserve divine law, and were then scattered across the globe. They are small in numbers, never having enjoyed, in two millennia, the immense power of Christian and Muslim rulers, whose religious revelations were in their fundamentals the same as those given to the Jews.

The Jews dedicated themselves to the common welfare of themselves and their Gentile neighbors throughout those many centuries. Usually surviving in closed or excluded communities, they had too often been at risk, if only because they were few. Was it good for them to struggle for universal justice, by which the demands of their sacred history might be honored, even if they remained crushed by their apparently inevitable fate as outsiders to the affairs of the rest of the world? Or should the Jewish people accept their place apart, looking only to their own needs, while surrounded by others? Should they declare that they, like the multitude of Gentile nations, had a particular interest to guard and nurture? And who would decide what was good for the Jews, and how it could be realized?

When Napoleon emancipated the Jews under his rule, they had responded with extraordinary gratitude, even love. As a result, however, Jews were challenged practically with the question: Should they abandon altogether their history as a "stiff-necked" people and assimilate to the point of becoming undistinguishable from their Christian neighbors? The rise of the socialist movement, with its vision of a unified humanity, seemed to demand the dissolution of Jewishness into a common identity. In Germany, England, America, Hungary, and Croatia, a Reform Jewish tradition became dominant, with the same goal, but without renouncing religion: it would let Jews ignore dietary laws, marry whomever they wished, and change their names, without, in some sense, losing their Jewish identity.

But none of these alternatives answered the main question: could Jews defend themselves? Could they take up the sword when threatened?

Only in America would this question never need to be directly posed. Only in America would Jews experience, miraculously, a continuing and permanent liberty and security. "Only in America" also became a Jewish meme, employed to describe the almost dreamlike quality of Jewish life here. Why, then, would a *shtadlan* outlook be appropriate in these states?

Finally, there was only one answer: if nothing else, Jews, like all humans, have the right to defend themselves. Grynszpan had said it in a few words: "I am not a dog." But the need for self-defense had contradictory effects. It produced armed Jewish fighters against the tyranny of the Russian tsar—but also the creation of *shtadlan*-style "defense" organizations in the United States, beginning in 1906 with the American Jewish Committee. Later, it impelled the heroism of the Warsaw Ghetto fighters of 1943—but, as the Warsaw uprising was drowned in blood and fire, Jews witnessed indecision about the "problem of Jewish refugees" by Democratic politicians in America and similar leaders elsewhere to whom Jews had pledged their political support. Ultimately, Jewish self-defense was embodied in the state of Israel and a lobby in America dedicated to Israel's survival. Yet when a new terror racked the world at the beginning of the twenty-first century, neither the *shtadlan* organizations, the Democrats, nor America's pro-Israel lobby was prepared for the challenge.

In 1938, the sadistic spectacle in Germany could, it seemed, be repeated everywhere. Even Trotsky, a passionate internationalist or, better put, a Jewish universalist who considered religious Judaism a reactionary impediment to the progress of the Jewish people, began to sympathize with Zionism after witnessing the atrocities in Germany. It seemed impossible to deny that a separate Jewish state might be the only solution.

American Jews were never threatened with such an outburst of medieval horrors. Yet neither were they able to feel perfectly at ease. Though it is largely forgotten today, the Great Depression produced its own homegrown fascist movements that targeted Jews as the cause of American social and economic ills. Indeed, as the fascist tide swept over Europe in the thirties, New York seemed, in the minds of many Jews and Gentiles alike, liable to be the next major global city to see multitudes of thugs, shielded by the armed bodies of the state, brutalize a vulnerable people.

The most infamous exponent of this fascist discontent was a Catholic priest with an innovative and popular radio show, Father Charles E. Coughlin, of Royal Oak, Michigan. Coughlin was originally a champion of Franklin Roosevelt and the New Deal. But by the middle 1930s, in imitation of Hitler, Coughlin had combined fascist radicalism and anticapitalism with an old vocabulary of fear, warning of a new world war to promote Jewish "money power." Coughlin and his admirers had fused with the followers of other Depression-era merchants of panic, including Francis Townsend and Huey P. Long— the latter assassinated in 1935. Coughlin's followers called for "social justice" in a nation to be cleansed of Jewish influence through a "reorganization" like that of the Nazis. He described Kristallnacht as revenge for Jewish mistreatment of Christians. He and his cohort were also fervent isolationists who stridently demanded that America stay out of foreign entanglements.

Coughlin's aim was obvious: to guarantee Hitler and his fellow bandits, Mussolini and the Japanese imperialists, a free hand. As the Second World War came closer, Coughlin gained financing from Berlin. He mobilized a paramilitary cadre, the Christian Front. It mainly recruited working-class Irish Americans, who loathed the possibility that the United States might go to war to defend Britain against Germany. Coughlinites, as the fascist rabble became known, grew increasingly militant, their campaign augmented by a more explicitly ethnic movement, the German-American Bund, formed as a legion of uniformed storm troopers.

In 1939, in emulation of Franco's forces then fighting in Spain, Coughlin commanded the Christian Front to confront Jews and Communism in the streets of America. The Christian Front swarmed over Manhattan, which had one of the largest Jewish populations in the world. Thus it was that New York, the city in which a unique political culture produced so much intellectual vitality, also generated a horrifying "New York fascism." Irish Americans and others hostile to Britain or sympathetic to Germany roamed the world's greatest metropolis, terrorizing Jewish and Gentile residents who dared voice a differing opinion. Coughlin's Christian Front beat up Jewish-looking passersby in the streets and conducted raucous demonstrations in the five boroughs. The huge Irish contingent in the New York police department aggravated the problem by their open sympathy for the fascists.

There were then no American Jewish or Zionist lobbies with such power as exists today. American Jews were gaining in political influence but still weak in social weight, with a leadership grossly hesitant to appear too assertive, as the Grynszpan case showed. Instead, Jewish and other Stalinist Communists responded to the Coughlinites and the Bund with pamphlets, speeches, and attempts, occasionally successful, to draw the ruined and bereft followers of fascist demagogy into the Communist orbit. Reputedly, Jewish gangsters Meyer Lansky and Davey Berman (the pair who helped Bugsy Siegel create the casino statelet of Las Vegas) first led their *shtarkers*—Yiddish for "tough guys"—to break up pro-Nazi meetings. But the fascist offensive against "Jew York," as the Coughlinites habitually referred to the city, was finally defeated by Jewish and other socialists and anarchists, using militant tactics of self-defense learned in the labor movement. They were led into action by Trotskyists, followers of the man in Mexican exile. A tiny and despised revolutionary minority, they counted no more than a few thousand in the whole world. But they wielded outsized influence in the longer run of history, as some of them went on to become or inspire prominent neoconservatives.

In July 1939, journalist James Wechsler alleged that the Christian Front had spent the previous six months organizing an open anti-

Jewish movement in New York, facing no obstacles from the police and enjoying the indifference of the press. Wechsler enumerated specific incidents of violence and called for suppression of brawls begun by the Coughlinites while selling their thin printed organ, *Social Justice*.

But the most famous incident in the battle for New York was provoked by the German-American Bund. In February 1939, the Bund flooded New York with multicolored images showing an angular, ugly "Aryan" male pressing a spear into a snake marked with the Communist hammer and sickle. The lance-and-serpent image was a well-known fascist symbol dating from the 1920s and was incorporated, remarkably enough, into the insignia of the Alfa Romeo automobile company in Italy, where a socialist revolution had been defeated by the ruthless Mussolini. The Bund posters advertised a "Mass Demonstration for True Americanism" to be held at Madison Square Garden on February 20, 1939.

The Bund had assembled in the Garden before, but the February 1939 rally was notable because the Bund hung a sixty-foot-high poster of George Washington alongside colossal fascist banners, and festooned the Garden with their slogans: "WAKE UP AMERICA! SMASH JEWISH COMMUNISM! STOP JEWISH DOMINATION OF CHRISTIAN AMERICA!" The rally caused a national outcry after *Life* magazine reproduced a sequence from a newsreel, such as was then screened with feature movies. It showed a young Jewish workman, Isador Greenbaum, rushing the stage and being beaten and hauled away by Bund goons. *Life* noted, "Newsreel shots of this violent scene were withdrawn from theatres after two days when managers complained they incited audiences to riot." According to the *New York Times*, around 20,000 American Nazis filled the Garden, protected from 100,000 antifascist demonstrators by a detachment of 1,700 police—the largest in New York history. The *Times* stated that while young Greenbaum had been tackled by Bund troopers, he had been removed from the Garden by police officers with his trousers torn off and booked for disorderly conduct. In the next sentence, the *Times* noted that "Mention of President Roosevelt and other critics of

Nazi Germany drew resounding boos." The *Times* also discreetly reported that Nazi speakers pronounced the chief executive's name "Rosenfeld," expressing their outlandish claim that he was actually Jewish. It was left to a Trotskyist newspaper, the *Socialist Appeal*, to publicize the disturbing news that the longest and loudest Nazi ovation had been given to the New York police (which had beaten up the young Jew, Greenbaum), for protecting the meeting.

The assembled Nazis asserted that Jews obeyed an ulterior tribal loyalty, apart from their American citizenship; the pro-German traitors and brutes therefore added a word to the Pledge of Allegiance, bellowing, "I pledge *undivided* allegiance to the flag." Bund führer Fritz Kuhn denounced Jews, who he claimed harmed America. Kuhn shrieked: "History is not written in ink but in blood!"

Blood was in the air and in the gutters near Madison Square Garden that night. The many thousands of furious protesters gathered outside were mainly Jewish union workers, joined by war veterans, Italian and Spanish anarchists, African Americans from Harlem, and plain white Gentiles who hated Hitler—including not a few left-wing German Americans. The large and enraged anti-Nazi force skirmished with police for hours along Eighth Avenue. Amazingly, only a dozen or so people were injured. The Nazis in the Garden were tense and skittish, as menacing sounds were audible from outside while within the walls the ravings of Jew-baiting agitators blared on. Bomb threats against the meeting had been conveyed to New York Mayor Fiorello LaGuardia, whose own mother was Jewish but who had vowed to protect the Nazis' free speech rights. Rumors of a tear gas attack on their suddenly vulnerable ranks spread through the Nazi audience. When a photographer's flashbulb was dropped and burst, the speaker stopped and the entire crowd turned fearfully in the direction of the noise. The rally ended, and the Nazis scurried out of the Garden under police guard. But they could not escape the storm of blows, kicks, spit, and insults from their massed enemies.

The *Times* duly noted that "the Socialist Workers Party, an organization pledged to the principles of Leon Trotsky . . . [was] the only organization calling for a public demonstration at the meeting." In fact, the Trotskyists had managed an extraordinary feat of mobilization. The Socialist Workers were joined in their organizing work by members of the Young People's Socialist League, the former youth arm of the Socialist Party, known as the YPSL, or "Yipsels." The Yipsels were under Trotskyist influence. As recounted by a Trotskyist writer, B. J. Widick, "some husky Yipsel comrades" lifted Trotskyist speakers to their shoulders to address the demonstrators; the orators included the Jewish Max Shachtman and the Gentile James Burnham, both of whom will appear again in this chronicle.

The Madison Square Garden confrontation had repercussions around the world. In Berlin, the Nazi press now printed headlines complaining of "Jewish Terror in New York." The *New York Times*, for its part, was satisfied to affirm that "there is no occasion to worry about what happened in and around Madison Square Garden on Monday evening." The *Times* concluded, "We are not, to state the case mildly, afraid of the Bund." At least, there was nothing to fear in the *shtadlan* paradise of the *Times* newsroom.

The Trotskyist-led action against the Bund was repeated with even greater effect in August 1939, when Coughlin's riffraff threatened a march on Union Square, a favored meeting place of Manhattan leftists. By then the Coughlinites were under constant fire from hostile New Yorkers, and fascist street speeches and rallies frequently led to bloody fistfights and even stabbings. A thousand antifascists had marched to stop a Coughlinite meeting in the Bronx; police once again covered a retreat from the scene by the Christian Fronters. In the Union Square confrontation, the Socialist Workers Party issued 300,000 leaflets warning working-class New York, "After weeks of anti-Semitic propaganda, 'Buy Christian' campaigns, and anti-labor attacks, these Fascist mobsters on August 19 will try to carry out their threat to invade Union Square. . . . This fascist parade is no 'manifestation of Christianity.' . . . Don't wait for the concentration camps—act now!" On that occasion, 4,000 police were sent to Union Square, with a backup of 3,500 more—nearly four times as many as had been deemed necessary to preserve order at Madison Square Garden; but the Coughlinites backed down and canceled their march.

Yet with the outbreak of the Second World War, only weeks later on September 3, 1939, the isolationism of Coughlin and his acolytes suddenly became a substantial movement in America. A more genteel form of Anglophobia, and/or Germanophilia, was mainly represented by prominent enemies of Britain such as Joseph Kennedy, chieftain of the Boston Irish political clan. This unfortunate trend also drew in many former Progressives from the American Midwest and Far West, who had opposed American involvement in the First World War; they now became compromised by the importation of Nazi-style Jew-baiting to America.

In the stratospheric environment of the rich, as well as among credulous bumpkins from the grain belt, isolationism was defined as "American" while, by a spurious dialectic, "internationalism" was labeled "Jewish." But if Joe Kennedy used terms more polite than hate-mongers such as Coughlin, scheming Jewish financiers were nonetheless blamed by both for seeking war with Germany out of an unbridled craving for revenge against Hitler. Hitler's uncontrollable seizures of Jew-baiting rhetoric, culminating in events such as Kristallnacht, had shocked the world. Never before had the leader of a powerful state appeared to regularly succumb to epileptic fits while speaking in public before newsreel cameras. But while American Jewish workers and radicals fought domestic Nazis, the American Jewish business and community leadership limited itself to verbal protests—convinced, in the *shtadlan* way, that raising the profile of American Jews in dealing with Germany would provoke rather than defeat anti-Semitism.

Some Republican politicians joined the isolationist chorus without leaping into the sewer of anti-Semitism: they merely discounted the threat of Hitler to civilization. Ohio's senator Robert Taft asserted that Republicans like him did not believe that "Hitler presents such a threat to the trade or safety of the United States as requires the sacrifice of several million American boys on the battlefields of the world." Writing shortly before the Japanese attack on Pearl Harbor in 1941,

Taft argued that the "war party" was composed of "the business community of the cities, the newspaper and magazine writers, the radio and movie commentators, the Communists and the university intelligentsia." References to urban commerce, journalism, and movies were euphemisms for the Jews. But Taft had the decency not to befoul himself in the manner of Charles A. Lindbergh Jr., the outstanding symbol of Midwestern ex-Progressivism. The first pilot to fly solo from America to Europe, Lindbergh had become famous by an act that embodied American expansiveness. But he had lately become an apostle of American withdrawal from the world. Thus he became the standard-bearer of the America First Committee.

Lindbergh was the son of an antiwar politician from Minnesota. After the abduction and death of his child in 1932 and the trial of kidnapper Bruno Hauptmann in 1935, the young Lindbergh and his wife, Anne Morrow, daughter of a U.S. ambassador to Mexico, decamped to Europe. There he became entranced with the technical élan of the new German state. In 1938, Lindbergh was decorated by Goering with the Service Cross of the Order of the German Eagle (automaker Henry Ford, an original sponsor of Hitler, was awarded the Grand Cross of the same order). Lindbergh repaid this honor by libeling the British and the Jews, along with Roosevelt, as conspirators trying to force America into war with Germany.

In August 1939, Stalin and Hitler agreed on a nonaggression pact—until June 1941, when Stalin was disappointed to find that Hitler was a less-than-faithful ally. For two years, American Communists and their "liberal" fellow travelers maintained a working alliance with the Nazi sympathizers and gullible isolationists of America First. The worst aspect of this betrayal by Stalin was visible in the small faction of New York Jews that defended the party's directives. In May 1941, only weeks before Hitler brusquely ended his alliance with Stalin, *The Communist,* the official ideological organ of the Communist Party of the USA, included some remarkable gems from this group.

Paul (Pesach) Novick was a writer for a New York Yiddish Communist daily, the *Freiheit,* which trailed a poor second among Jewish radical readers to the Socialist daily *Forward (Forverts).* Novick wrote in *The Communist,* "It is not true that 'every Jew' is praying 'for the victory of the British Empire (against Hitler),' or that Jews generally are engaged in that pursuit. It is most emphatically not the case. . . . The Zionist leaders seek to draw the Jewish people into the imperialist war. . . . Contrary to the wishes and interests of the Jewish people in the United States as well as Palestine, Zionist leadership is trumpeting for war. . . . Zionism represents a dangerous instrument for dragging the Jewish people into the war and thereby for aiding the forces working to drag America into the war."

Novick, obviously Jewish himself, thus echoed the slanders of Hitler and Lindbergh: the Jews wanted war. At the same time, Senator Taft, a Republican, seemed to echo Communist rhetoric when he called for opposition to "risking the lives of five million American boys in an imperialistic war for the domination of Europe . . . and the supposed 'manifest destiny' of America." But Democratic Senator Burton K. Wheeler, a former Progressive from Montana, was most strident in joining Lindbergh under the banner of America First. The Montanan's antiwar fanaticism had led him to virulent apologetics for Nazi crimes in Europe.

Hitler, having brought about the division of the Czechs and Slovaks in 1939 and partitioned Poland with Stalin, soon sent his armies sweeping through Denmark, Holland, Belgium, and France. In 1941, Wheeler denounced Roosevelt's "lend-lease" policy of providing warships to Britain by declaring that it would "plow under" (kill) every fourth American boy. The Almanac Singers, a Communist cabaret folk music group that included banjoist Pete Seeger, immediately took up the phrase, yelling that "Plow under! Plow under! Every fourth American boy!" was the pro-war program of the Roosevelt administration.

While the Stalinist Seeger picked his banjo, active fascists were practicing with firearms. In January 1940, New York was electrified by the arrest of eighteen members of the Christian Front in a conspiracy to overthrow the United States government. J. Edgar Hoover, chief of the

Federal Bureau of Investigation, revealed that the Christian Front had formed a "Sports Club" for weapons training, and infiltrated a local unit of the National Guard. The accused, armed with rifles and bombs, allegedly planned attacks on numerous Jewish and leftist targets, including the offices of the Jewish *Forward* and the Communist *Daily Worker*. Although the ranks of the defendants were small and underresourced, New Yorkers reacted with considerable alarm.

The führer of the group was allegedly a certain William G. Bishop, although it intended to install Major General George Van Horn Moseley, a former U.S. military officer, as the dictator of the United States. Bishop claimed to have fought for Franco in Spain and, before that, to have served alongside T. E. Lawrence in Arabia. He also boasted of blowing up an oil tanker in New York harbor, and gave conflicting answers as to his place of birth.

Exposure of the seditious intrigue led to a demand that Mayor LaGuardia investigate infiltration of the New York police department by the Christian Front. A preliminary count, based on a questionnaire, suggested that as many as 1,000 out of the 19,000 members of the force were sympathizers of the fascist gangs. New York, and particularly Jewish New York, the latter accounting for some 2 million people, remained under attack. When the Christian Front went on trial in Brooklyn, a witness described how a photograph of Roosevelt was used for target practice by the plotters. Soon it was reported that thirty members of the Newark police department were also members of the Christian Front, and consequently, that city's Jewish mayor, Meyer Ellenstein, assumed control of law enforcement.

Ellenstein, the only Jew in the city's history to serve in that post, is forgotten today except as a historical figure evoked in the works of the Jewish novelist Philip Roth. A Newark native, Roth recalled through the glass of metafiction the impact of Lindberghite isolationism on his hometown in his 2004 novel *The Plot Against America*, a dark, alternative account of the United States after 1940, in which Roosevelt is defeated for a third term by Lindbergh. In Roth's counterfactual narrative, Lindbergh's platform brands the Jews as warmongering aliens who manipulate popular passions through their "large ownership and influence in our motion pictures, our press, our radio, and our government."

Roth's Lindbergh takes Senator Wheeler as his running mate. Lindbergh and Wheeler win election, while Hitler consolidates his triumphant march across Western Europe. Lindy meets Adolf in Iceland, and the two agree on peace with Germany. The aviator then travels to Honolulu to sign a "Hawaii Understanding," which recognizes the Japanese conquest of French Indochina and the Dutch East Indies. Lindbergh also names the feral Jew-baiter Henry Ford as secretary of the interior.

Perhaps Roth intended—though probably he did not—that his book should shame all those who during the U.S. intervention in Iraq assailed as warmongering Jews the neoconservatives who supposedly drove Bush administration policy in Baghdad. Parallels between Lindberghite isolationism and present-day neocon-baiting are striking. Few Americans sixty-five years later realize how close America once came to a descent into fascist turmoil. Most Jews, and many Gentiles, genuinely believed then that the country was at risk of a terrorist onslaught, if not an outright fascist coup. And once it was over, most preferred to forget it.

With the Christian Front trial, New Yorkers remained terrified through 1940 and early 1941 that Axis agents were actively conniving to seize the city. In May 1940 it was reported that 2,300 people had tried to join the Christian Front in Brooklyn, including 500 police. New York, rather than Washington, was believed to be the bigger target not only because of its economic importance but because of its Jewishness. Testifying at the Christian Front trial in June 1940, newspaper reporter Gertrude Wilbert recalled that a Front member exclaimed, "You exterminate rats; therefore you should exterminate Jews."

On June 21, 1940, anxiety turned to shock when bombs went off at the German commercial office on the eighteenth floor of 17 Battery Place, just below the German consulate, and various offices at 35 East Twelfth Street, headquarters of the American Communist Party. Ten people were injured. No perpetrators were ever identified, but since the Nazis and Communists had formed their united front against

American intervention in Europe, it is not impossible that the wave of bombings was the work of Italian or Spanish anarchists, notably embittered by Communist cooperation with Hitler.

Four days later, ten defendants in the Christian Front trial were acquitted in a Brooklyn court, with a hung jury gained by four more, including the main figure in the proceeding, William Bishop. Leaving the courthouse, the accused were cheered by a crowd of some 500, with cries of "hurray for our side." Father Coughlin, who had previously sought to dissociate himself from the Brooklyn plot with the preposterous charge that the conspirators were Communists, took to the radio to celebrate the acquittals and predict that the Christian Front and its crusade against the Jews would soon triumph. On July 4, 1940, a victory rally was held by the Christian Front in Brooklyn, with 2,000 in attendance and speeches by four men, including two prominent Catholics: Rev. Edward Brophy, a priest from the borough of Queens, and Patrick Scanlon, editor of a Catholic newspaper, the *Brooklyn Tablet*. Brophy restated the common themes of anti-Jewish agitators: America was founded as a Christian nation, and Communists had taken over the press and public schools.

The same Independence Day saw another bombing. This time explosives were placed at the British Pavilion of the New York World's Fair, with two police killed and five more injured after they removed the device from the structure. The pavilion had received telephone threats for several days. New York police immediately arrested twenty-one men at pro-Nazi street meetings at Columbus Circle in Manhattan, a favored location for political rallies.

Investigators speculated inconclusively about the latest bombing. Perhaps it was related to those at the German commercial office and Communist headquarters. It might have been the work of the Irish Republican Army (IRA), which had formed an alliance with Germany and launched a terrorist campaign in 1939 in Britain (nationalist southern Ireland remained neutral during the war). The next day, the mysterious William Bishop, who the FBI had determined was born in Austria, was ordered deported. Only six weeks before, he had been identified by J. Edgar Hoover as the architect of an attempted fascist putsch in New York. The head of the German-American Bund, Fritz Kuhn, had meanwhile been sent to a New York state prison shortly after the Christian Front case broke, for theft of Bund funds.

It is difficult for non-Jews to grasp how profoundly, when Nazis rallied and bombs went off in Manhattan, Jews looked for protection to President Roosevelt. So powerful was Jewish identification in that time of anguish with this Hudson Valley aristocrat of *patroon* Dutch descent that even today, Jews reflexively vote Democratic the way freed slaves and their descendants voted for the Republican Party of Lincoln, long after they ceased to gain any benefit from that loyalty.

Franklin Roosevelt had placed more Jews in major federal appointments than the total named by all the presidents before him. But as we shall see, submission to Roosevelt and the New Deal had its disadvantages, since the Democratic Party, then as now, remains dominated by machine politics. A Brooklyn Democratic ward boss, Hymie Schorenstein, is alleged in 1940 to have described the relationship of Roosevelt to other Democrats as follows: "Did you ever go down to the wharf to see the Staten Island Ferry come in? . . . When the ferryboat comes into the wharf, automatically it pulls all the garbage in, too. The name of your ferryboat is Franklin D. Roosevelt."

Jews were destined to represent one among many constituencies in Roosevelt's New Deal coalition. But the New York Jews were overwhelmingly Socialists and therefore universalists, who would not equate a share of a spoiled political pie with the disappearance of interreligious and interethnic rivalries, a transcendence in which they so profoundly believed.

Love of FDR is the bedrock of Philip Roth's fictional evocation of the period when America First propagandized against "Jewish warmakers." *The Plot Against America* is also faithful to history in portraying Jews such as Roth's father, Herman, as passive in the face of the fascist threat and unlikely to fight back by physical means. In Roth's what-if account, the Coughlinites and other America Firsters are beaten by a resurgent Roosevelt. But the actual defeat of the American fascists did not take place in Newark or any other suburb, and it did not involve mild-mannered Jews who, like Herman Roth, preferred ballots to bullets as guarantors of their rights.

The war against the American fascists was won in the streets of New York by radical Jews, most of whom despised the party-line Communists no less than they did the fascists. Along with their Gentile allies, Jewish union workers led by a few Trotskyists had embraced the historic antifascist slogan: "An eye for an eye, blood for blood, fire for fire, steel for steel!"

For their part, the established American Jewish leadership, then already in place for three decades—the real-life embodiment of the petit bourgeois Herman Roths—stood apart from the fray. At the climactic moment of the Nazi rally in Madison Square Garden, the American Jewish Committee, created for "Jewish defense," publicly defended the free-speech rights of the Bund and opposed any interference with it. The Anti-Defamation League of B'nai B'rith had been set up in response to the lynching of Leo Frank, a Jewish businessman, but it contributed nothing more to the fight against the New York Nazis than an investigation of violent Jew-baiters.

One Yiddish paper, *The Day (Der Tog)*, warned its readers, "Jews of New York! Do not let your sorrows guide you! Avoid Madison Square Garden this evening! Don't come near the hall! Don't give the Nazis the chance to get the publicity they desire so much!" Fortunately, the paper's advice went unheeded. Yet the whole matter was, even worse, resolutely ignored by the small, activist Zionist movement in America. The Zionists declined to support direct action against the local Nazis on the argument that Zionism was a Jewish emigration movement concerned only with politics in Palestine.

Young people led the struggle at the end of the 1930s to protect New York, and the world, from the Nazis, as the young did during the mass protest movements of the 1960s, against less feral enemies. Think of Grynszpan trembling with emotion as he laid down his gun in the German embassy, Isador Greenbaum beaten on the floor of Madison Square Garden, Yipsels carrying antifascist leaflets everywhere New York's workers gathered.

A portrait of this battle from the other side of the barricades appears in a forgotten short work published in 1939 by the classic American novelist James T. Farrell, entitled *Tommy Gallagher's Crusade*. Farrell depicted the fear and prejudice of New York's Irish Catholic working class, who grappled to climb higher in society and, maddened by their frustrated ambitions, poured into the ranks of the Christian Front. The book's protagonist, the unemployed and perhaps unemployable Tommy, still living with his exasperated parents, joins a group of hooligans who peddle fascist gutter sheets in New York City, hollering anti-Jewish slogans. They are typically met with verbal expressions of disgust but further exercise their hormones by isolating and setting upon individuals of Hebraic appearance.

Tommy and his band pursue their provocations more or less unopposed until they run into a small Trotskyist meeting. There Tommy hears, "When the Fascists rear their heads here, only the revolutionary working class can smash them. . . . Comrades, this is the lesson of revolutionary defeats suffered in Europe, and this is the lesson we must learn in America before it is too late . . . be prepared to smash the Fascist gangs." Yelling anti-Jewish insults, the Irish boys move against the radicals and are surprised to be met with angry shouts and solid blows. "Tommy moved to polish off a little Jew in front of him. Just as he took a step forward with fists cocked, he was smashed in the left eye. He seemed to see streaks of irregular light. He felt a sharp pain in his left eye. He had a sick thudding headache. His whole body seemed to grow weak and powerless. He bent forward, holding his eye. He was pounded on the face until he dropped. He moaned." The fascists are driven off in a hail of taunts and bricks.

Anti-Communist socialists also fought totalitarianism within the ranks of liberal organizations. In February 1940, 3,000 American young people met in Washington for a four-day citizenship institute hosted by the American Youth Congress (AYC), a left-leaning group with political backing from the Roosevelt administration. With the Stalin-Hitler pact in full effect, AYC had been swayed to an antiwar posture. A young lady named Robin Meyers, who attended the gathering as a Yipsel, introduced a resolution declaring it inappropriate for any individual to serve as an AYC officer or staff member or for any group to be admitted as an affiliate if that person or organization "supports totalitarian dictatorship in any country.... Within this category we include organizations in the United States supporting the totalitarian governments of the Soviet Union, and of the fascist and Nazi countries (such as the Communist Party and the German American Bund)." The text also condemned native "anti-democratic" organizations.

Meyers was shouted down, and the AYC's national chairman, an ordained Methodist minister and Stalinist front man named Jack McMichael, ruled the resolution out of order. This was nothing surprising at the time. More remarkable, if not astonishing, to present-day readers was that Meyers' proposal was based on a similar resolution successfully passed by the leadership of the American Civil Liberties Union. The ACLU even issued a statement explaining that the action was impelled by the extent of Communist "peace" propaganda in the service of the Moscow pact with Hitler.

The Communists, of course, became superinterventionists after Hitler invaded Russia. The anti-Jewish rhetoric of America First became disreputable and embarrassing with U.S. entry into the Second World War. Although Coughlin was silenced by the Catholic hierarchy and never regained his public prominence, and Lindbergh was permanently stained by his isolationist blandishments, Americans proved quick to forget Joe Kennedy's pro-Nazi sympathies. Similarly, Chester Bowles, a leading Democratic functionary, and Gerald Ford, a Republican president, were both supporters of America First—biographical items that would later be assiduously ignored by the media and the general public.

Americans growing up in the aftermath of the Second World War, and later, may be excused for their ignorance of the shocking events in New York between 1939 and 1941. Even more distant for them is the misadventure of Henry Ford, the quintessential American inventor, industrialist, and Jew-hater. Ford, although respected as a capitalist, was dismissed as a crank for his anti-Semitism, just as America First was repudiated as a treasonous conspiracy.

But ignorance of history is dangerous; in the philosopher Santayana's words, "those who cannot remember the past are condemned to repeat it." The neoconservatives were assailed by critics of the Iraq war in the same anti-Jewish terms peddled by Ford, Coughlin, and Lindbergh. And the garbage was recycled, with an idiom even cruder than before, in the pages of the *New York Times,* the *Washington Post,* the *Christian Science Monitor,* and other mainstream media organs. There, such hallucinations were granted respectability and a veneer of wisdom. And until 2006 and the appearance of the Mearsheimer-Walt anti-Jewish pamphlet at Harvard, much of the Jewish leadership said little or nothing about it, just as their forebears said nothing about Grynszpan and cautioned against fighting the Nazis at Madison Square Garden. Judeophobia and *shtadlan* heedlessness to its danger had metastasized.

The bombings in New York near the middle of the twentieth century also anticipated events at its end, as anxiety over terrorism combines today with anti-Jewish paranoia about Iraq. But one of the differences between the two periods is more important: in 1940 the Jews' interests and those of the Roosevelt administration were clearly identical, and few Jews doubted the president's careful but determined anti-Hitler policy. With Roosevelt a staunch enemy of "terror"—the term the New Deal president typically used to refer to the atrocities of Nazism, Italian fascism, Japanese imperialism, and Soviet totalitarianism—Jews of all classes and political backgrounds felt compelled to support him.

In 2006, by contrast, liberal Jews—the apparent majority—are too repulsed by president George W. Bush and his policies to recognize his virtues. In addition, the domestic Jewish and Israel lobbies are politically dependent on Bush's Democratic enemies, thanks in great part to a Jewish nostalgia for the New Deal—a yearning for the past that has become utterly detached from reality.

The lobbies were lesser powers in 1939–41, and perhaps could not be blamed for their weakness in defending their fellow Jews. Today they have no such excuse. Yet the permanence of their aversion to risk exposes the ever-fragile nature of Jewish power. *Shtadlan* fear that a high profile will lead to persecution still deprives the Jewish lobbies of any clear vision of what is actually good for the Jews.

The confluence of the anti-Nazi and Depression-era social reform struggles would lead Jews through the New Deal coalition to the Democratic Party in a political exodus that revived a celebratory sense of arrival in a Promised Land on American shores. But the twentieth-century trajectory of the Jews in their relation with the Democrats would much more resemble the forty-year desert wandering of the Jews after their liberation from Egypt. Various individuals would seem to resemble Moses, but Moses was at first rejected, soon after the escape from Pharaonic bondage. These and other precedents would be repeated between the 1930s and the dramatic events beginning on September 11, 2001.

CHAPTER 2

✡JEWS AND DEMOCRATS
Origins of a Dysfunctional Marriage

While their union brethren fought the fascists in the streets, the New Deal elevated Jews to positions of governmental responsibility—and visibility—in unprecedented numbers. Major American Jewish personalities—few of them leaders of Jewish civic groups and more of them individuals known for accomplishment in their professions— were placed by Franklin Roosevelt in appointments of substantial distinction.

This marked the most important political journey of the American Jews in the twentieth century, the watershed event in a series of migrations back and forth between conservatism, radicalism, and liberalism, between Republicans, Socialists and Democrats. Roosevelt, recognizing the value of their affection for him, brought much of the American Jewish world to a political wedding with his party.

There was no real honeymoon, but the marriage has lasted seven decades. And though it has now become dysfunctional, the relation-

ship in its time appeared to be a real achievement for American
Jews. Before the New Deal, elite Jews from the political mainstream,
who had gained great public respect from Gentiles as well as Jews,
often still saw their coreligionists as a poor and undesirable relation
within the American family, who could approach the heights of power
only by the back door, through *shtadlan* representatives. They were
contemptuous of working-class immigrants from Eastern Europe
and their children (who came to constitute the majority of American
Jews), and were afraid of radical action. This was a consequence
of collective reticence as much as of worry about American anti-
Semitism. In truth, there was then more anti-Semitism in the Gentile
elite, as symbolized by restricted Jewish entry to universities, than in
the streets, so Jews naturally felt at risk even when they gained public
success. But as anti-Semitism appeared in a more dangerous form in
the late 1930s, the official Jewish leadership cleaved to *shtadlan* lobbying and disdained the alternative—to fight boldly for recognition of
their rights.

It is one of the many paradoxes of American Jewish life that Roosevelt's sympathy for Jews gave new legitimacy to the traditional
shtadlan approach to political power. The Jews should not risk security for influence, but they should not risk the loss of influence by
fighting too hard for security. Their basic principle was that it was not
good for the Jews to ask for too much. This compromising attitude
was expressed in other rules: be satisfied with crumbs; do not expect
a major gain to produce greater advantages. Such contradictory
impulses aggravated the passivity of the *shtadlan* leaders even when
they won victories for their people.

The Jewish romance with Roosevelt seemed to resolve the choice
between security and influence in a way no less glorious than the bib-
lical narrative of Queen Esther of Persia, who saved the Jews from the
evil politician Haman. On the holiday of Purim, which celebrates the
rescue of the Persian Jews, Hebrew males are expected to drink so
much wine that they forget they are Jews. One could compare the
American Jewish intoxication with Roosevelt to a very long Purim
party, in that the Democrats' embrace made many forget, until the

Holocaust, that they had any particular Jewish interest. But that habit did not begin with the New Deal.

Through their history, American Jews have pursued their interests in different ways, expressing the distinctive attitudes of successive major waves of Jewish immigration. First came small numbers of Sephardic Jews in the seventeenth and eighteenth centuries, who wanted nothing more than to live peacefully and without great notice among their neighbors. They attained their goal; nobody interfered with them, and their ways were almost indistinguishable from those of other Americans. They assimilated so well that they are essentially unrepresented in official American Jewish life today. These were followed by the Germans, who were profoundly committed to America and felt a cultural kinship with the country's Protestants. They had begun as European liberals—revolutionaries in deed but not in doctrine—and believed they had found in the United States the place where all their ideals were realized. Then the great flood of impoverished Russian and Polish Jews swept over America's shores. They were much more radical and sought to remake American politics according to their socialist beliefs. They largely succeeded in that endeavor.

The vision of the East European Jewish immigrants was destined to clash with the bourgeois and dependent attitudes that had overtaken the German Jews in America. The Germans had come as reformers but in gratitude for America's blessings became deeply conservative. They differed from the older *shtadlan* mold in Jewish affairs only by becoming well enough accepted, regardless of social discrimination, that Jewish advocacy long seemed unnecessary; but, unlike the Sephardim, they did not vanish into the American landscape. At the beginning of the twentieth century, as the numbers of East European immigrants rose dramatically, the German Jews were aligned with the Progressive wing of the Republican Party, which embodied the most enlightened values of the Gentile business class. The East Europeans, following Socialist leaders, would rebel against the Germans and eventually lead the Jews, after a period of hesitation that was never truly resolved, into the New Deal coalition.

The entry into Franklin Roosevelt's administration was celebrated in the manner of Purim, but to emphasize, it assumed a gravity in the Jewish consciousness comparable to an even greater event in Jewish history: the escape from Egypt led by Moses. Yet Moses himself never saw the Promised Land. Did the Jews find a just reward in Democratic ranks? By 2006, some of the Socialists' political descendants would attempt to reverse the exodus, bringing the Jews back to the Republican Party. Between the parting of the waters by the New Deal and the newly dangerous years at the beginning of the twenty-first century, international and domestic events exposed the Jewish-Democratic alliance as a worship of the golden calf of fraudulent "liberalism."

Previously the Democrats, a party of corruption in both the southern states and the northern cities, had little to offer American Jews. Many German Jewish immigrants were adherents of the antislavery movement, a cause the Democrats repudiated and on which the Republicans were founded. Since the German Jews mainly settled in the northern states, Jewry in that section of the country revered Lincoln as they would later adore Franklin Roosevelt. The prestige of the Republicans had increased since the 1870s, when the administration of President Ulysses S. Grant named Benjamin F. Peixotto, a Sephardic Jew from San Francisco, as America's first consul in Bucharest. This came about just as vicious Romanian attacks on Jews began to draw the world's attention. The relationship reached its peak in 1906, when President Theodore Roosevelt appointed a Jew named Oscar Solomon Straus his secretary of commerce and labor—a key post for the president's reputation, which was that of a reforming Progressive Republican.

Oscar Straus—a member of the family that purchased the R. H. Macy department store—had graduated from Columbia College, earning a law degree from the same school in 1873. He proudly recalled that his father, Lazarus Straus, although owning a Bavarian estate, had participated in the German revolution of 1848. Crossing the Atlantic in 1854, the Strauses first found a home in Georgia. Oscar's elder brother, Isidor Straus, moved to New York to begin a commercial career in 1865. The firm of L. Straus and Sons sold crockery and glassware. Isidor Straus was elected to Congress for the Democrats but served only one term before returning to the business world. (He died in 1912 in the sinking of the *Titanic*.) New York Jewish allegiance to the Democrats was, then, a consequence of the party's dominance in the metropolis, where the entrenched Tammany machine resisted any challenge.

Oscar also began his political activity with the New York Democrats. He was named American minister to the Ottoman Empire in 1887 by President Grover Cleveland and served there for two years. Despite Turkey's being a Muslim domain, the appointment to that country was considered a natural "Jewish post" in that the empire then included as many as 300,000 Sephardic Jews. Indeed, over the succeeding decades, Turkey has remained the most frequent assignment for Jewish ambassadors from the United States.

Straus moved away from Cleveland's Democrats in 1896, after the party named William Jennings Bryan as its presidential candidate. A spellbinding populist widely viewed as an extreme demagogue, Bryan was no Jew-baiter. But for Jews, such populist proclivities were considered potentially dangerous. Bryan and others drew support from the midwestern and southern states, where fear of the "money power" was growing. Farmers believed that agricultural markets were dominated by speculation, including Jewish speculation. Jews would remain suspicious of populism and of southerners in general. Indeed, decades after southern anti-Semitism had largely disappeared, urban Jewish prejudice against southerners and populists endured. It continues today, even though the most pro-Jewish president in American history, in terms of federal appointments, was Bill Clinton, a southern populist. Jewish anxieties over the southern cultural type were not assuaged by Clinton and feed Jewish reluctance to support the Republican Party in what now is called its "red-state," if not "redneck," base among southern and midwestern Protestants. Many of these red-staters are Christian fundamentalists who also happen to be extremely pro-Israel, as we shall see.

Oscar Straus was named a second time as American representative to Turkey by Republican President William McKinley in 1900, and after the latter's assassination, he became a leading adviser to Theodore Roosevelt, McKinley's successor. He was appointed by Roosevelt to the International Court of Justice at The Hague in 1902, followed by his selection for the commerce and labor cabinet post, which he occupied until 1909. While many Jews already supported the Republicans, Straus reinforced the party's Progressive element, increasing its appeal in big cities where political corruption had become a critical issue.*

The *Washington Post* listed Straus' qualifications in descending order as "philanthropist, publicist, merchant, and the first Hebrew to accept a cabinet portfolio from a President of the United States." The *Post* warmly quoted the new secretary's declaration that he would "resign from every business connection, and devote my entire energies to my work as Secretary of Commerce and Labor. It is the work for which I have waited fifty-six years, and it is nearest to my heart." In the turbulent atmosphere a century ago, employers and unions were bitter foes, and such issues as child labor stood at the forefront of American attention. Straus's passionate commitment to his political duties was taken as evidence of an advanced social consciousness among Jews of his class. Straus himself described the typical American Jew as characterized by spirituality, "intensely patriotic," and "yield[ing] neither his traditions nor his ideals."

Interviewed by the capital's newspaper of record, Straus did not disappoint those who expected him to pursue the Progressive agenda. "If I had been given the choice of any place in the President's Cabinet, I should have chosen the one I am to have," he averred. "In it is embraced the work of a sociological and economic nature in which I am interested more than any other." He soon reaffirmed this pledge

---

* In 1912, Theodore Roosevelt ran for president again, this time as a third-party Progressive or "Bull Moose" Republican, and managed to outpoll the regular Republican candidate, William Howard Taft; both were defeated by Democrat Woodrow Wilson. Oscar Straus appeared on the Progressive ticket in a losing bid for governor of New York. He later became a distinguished internationalist, joining Wilson in promoting, albeit unsuccessfully, American membership in the League of Nations.

by declaring, "One of the most prominent labor leaders of the country said to me . . . 'When you occupy your position we feel that we can come before you, because we have met often before, and you understand us and we understand you.'" The *Post* went on to gush over Straus' choice of "one of the most beautiful houses built in Washington in recent years," the Venetian Palace at Sixteenth Street N.W. and Euclid Avenue.

The *New York Times* was even more enthusiastic. It described a Republican mass meeting in New York City where "[f]or several minutes shouts for the 'next Cabinet officer,' the waving of American flags, and continued handclapping and cheering saluted Oscar S. Straus when he passed along the aisle to his place on the stage." There, Straus denounced the New York gubernatorial campaign by newspaper publisher William Randolph Hearst, whom he accused of "pander[ing] to evil prejudice and passion . . . [to] deceive you into thinking him the devoted friend of the masses. I deny that he is a friend to the masses." According to Straus (and the *Times*), Hearst was an inciter of class hatred who obstructed the legitimate goals of the labor movement. The Jewish Progressives were stern enemies of those they deemed to be rabble-rousers. Hearst lost the election.

Straus became so great an example to his coreligionists that Jews in Russia appealed for his help. The *Jewish Chronicle* of London proclaimed that his appointment "reflects honor not only upon the people who are proud to claim Mr. Straus as one of themselves, but upon Mr. Roosevelt and the great Republic over which he presides." The British periodical, then considered one of the most authoritative Jewish voices in the world, recalled Roosevelt's comment in response to the 1903 massacre of Jews in Chisinau, a city in Moldova: "If a man is a good American, that is all we ask, without thinking of his creed or his birthplace." Roosevelt was praised for his rebuke to "bigoted anti-Jewish governments in other lands." Straus was soon appointed to an international commission of the Zionist movement.

But Straus was also a surprisingly popular figure with American Gentiles; indeed, this was perhaps the most remarkable aspect of his political career. He was a hero to working-class and midwestern America, where his Jewishness was either invisible or ignored. Such public enthusiasm demonstrates that anti-Jewish prejudice was not yet a substantial American phenomenon and belies the general belief among Jews today that red-state America was always latently anti-Semitic. In reality, significant anti-Jewish feeling only took hold later in the twentieth century, in alarm over East European immigration. Social discrimination before then, as experienced by the Sephardim and German Jews, was inconsistent, even at its worst, though it became notable in some places with the emergence of German Jewish wealth in America during the last quarter of the nineteenth century.

Oscar Straus epitomized the Germanic culture that, at the time of his cabinet appointment, had dominated the American Jewish community for half a century. The discretion, high-mindedness, and persistent enterprise of the Germans reinforced the public image of American Jews as a valuable addition to the national fabric. They were widely viewed as apostles of the common good, through their support for civic improvements, general opposition to slavery, and, after the Civil War, advocacy for the new labor movement. Accordingly, German Jewish opinion in America was marked in its enthusiasm for the Progressive Republicans, who advocated, in a more moderate and rational manner than populists like Bryan, new regulatory restraints on commercial practices and other policies intended to enhance both economic and political accountability and popular sovereignty.*

Meanwhile, for urban American Gentiles who sought fairness, equal treatment, and clean administration in public affairs, German-American Jews were perceived as natural allies. (In 1912, for example, Victor Rosewater, a Jew from Omaha, served as chairman of the Republican National Committee, although his name seldom appears

---

* The Progressives were also exemplified by California governor Hiram Johnson, a Republican elected to the statehouse in 1910, who would serve as Roosevelt's running mate two years later. Johnson introduced such political innovations to California as the ballot initiative and referendum, the recall of elected officials, and direct primary elections.

in historical reference works.) In short, Progressive politics, then as now, was considered good for the Jews; and Jewish participation was believed to be a positive asset by the reformers themselves. Yet history is never linear; as previously noted, many of the Progressives with whom the Jews allied in Theodore Roosevelt's time would oppose the First World War and, by 1939, would follow Charles A. Lindbergh Jr., Burton K. Wheeler, and other ex-Progressives into the Jew-baiting isolationist movement. The ex-Progressives did not remember how they had once gained help from Jewish reformers, and the Jews forgot the days when Progressivism was their political model.

In America, German Jews such as Straus were more politically advanced than many of their Gentile neighbors; the German Jews had been progressive minded and liberal before either term was common in America. But on Jewish issues, to the degree such existed in America in the nineteenth century, the German Jews were steadfastly cautious and unobtrusive in the *shtadlan* manner.

The proletarian Jews who rushed to America from tormented Russia knew nothing of a *shtadlan* tradition. Under the tsars they long had no option but to submit to tyranny, abuse, and unspeakable misery. Their lives were filled with violent death at the hands of Christians, rape of Jewish women by Christians, murder of children by Christians, burning of whole towns, frame-up trials, compulsory military service (in which Jewish soldiers were often killed on the cruel whim of Christian officers), impoverishment, and disease. Their only way upward in Russia was through extremely hard work, exceptionally good luck, and, of course, conversion to Christianity. Jews were largely restricted to a geographical zone in the western part of the empire, the Jewish Pale of Settlement, and had no representatives who could approach the throne of the tsar. There were no "court Jews" at the court of the Romanovs, any more than there were Catholic deputies; Russian Orthodox Christianity, embodied in the throne, was officially, arrogantly, and stubbornly anti-Jewish and anti-Catholic— and remains so today.

The only means to achieve Jewish ends in the tsar's vast domain were to bend the knee, pray for mercy, or flee, until a revolutionary

convulsion began in 1903. Then Jews took up arms to defend themselves, but they were defeated and once again had to seek escape; when
a refuge was found in America, so many came so fast they soon threatened to sweep the German Jews aside as Jewish advocates. Few of
them ever acquired a real *shtadlan* outlook; they went from socialist
radicalism to New Deal liberalism to Zionism and finally, for at least
some of them, to neoconservatism—without spending that much
time arguing over whether what they did was good for the Jews. For
the victims of tsarist oppression, just being in America was good for
the Jews, and they would exercise their new freedom by testing (and
occasionally risking) their lives, not by staying in the background and
subserviently asking for Gentile favors. What was good for them as
refugees and radicals was considered to be good for the Jews, not vice
versa. This attitude was passed on to the American generation that
followed them.

Straus himself was a transitional figure between the two emigra-
tions. He was a German Jew in background, but it would be unfair to
equate him with *shtadlan* habits. He was closer in his Progressivism to
the temperament of the original German Jewish liberals who had
come to America after the European revolutions of 1848 and who saw
Jewish interests as indivisible from wider American interests. One
could not imagine *shtadlan* advocates, concerned with a narrow definition of what was good for the Jews, openly embracing the labor
movement as Straus did. A similar figure who preceded Straus was the
founder of the American Federation of Labor, the cigarmakers' union
leader Samuel Gompers, born in England of Dutch Jewish ancestry.
Gompers had built up the American union movement without wor-
rying about being Jew-baited or whether union organizing (which
often involved violent conflict) was good for the Jews as a distinct
community. Straus' appointment by Roosevelt was a challenge to
the American descendants of the German Jews to break out of the
shtadlan mold. Roosevelt may also have been partly motivated by a
desire to rub in the face of the tsarist Russians the equality enjoyed by
Jews in America, and this liberty, to men like Straus, made the *shtadlan* approach unnecessary.

And yet the *shtadlan* attitude persisted. The same year Straus was named to Roosevelt's cabinet the first domestic Jewish lobby was born, in the form of the American Jewish Committee. AJC was founded in reaction to the frightful pogroms in Russia. The spasms of savagery in the tsarist empire from 1903 on, incited by a fearsome antecedent of the Nazis, the Black Hundreds (officially titled the Russian People's Union), could in 1906 no longer be treated as episodic affairs. Russian riots took hundreds of innocent lives, stimulated protest meetings all over America and the world, and inspired countless grieving poems. American Jewish businesses pledged shares of their receipts to the relief of the victims. Much solidarity was also forthcoming from Gentiles. Actors in a Chinese theater on New York's Lower East Side put on plays and collected funds for the Jews under tsardom, and the evening was described in touching phrases by the *New York Times:* "It was remarked again and again by the Jews and the entertaining Chinamen that it must be the first affair of its kind that had ever occurred in the world. . . . [A congressman's representative], Mr. Rosenthal, said, 'Let us extend a hand of welcome and hope that the Chinese may stand upon the broad platform of Americanism with us.'"

The tsarist terror reached its climax in 1905. Bright red headlines across the planet announced one horrific bloodletting after another from Warsaw to Siberia. The world stood agape at the spectacle. In response to all this, sixty prominent German Jews, led by a New York lawyer, Louis Marshall, created the American Jewish Committee. When AJC was launched in February 1906, its mission was to "watch closely over legislative and diplomatic matters of interest to American Jews and to convey to the President, State Department, and Congress, requests, information, and if need be, political threats," according to the historian Judith S. Goldstein. But while it was conceived as a Jewish defense agency, AJC was also a perfect exemplar of the *shtadlan* attitude. It was formed to defend Russian Jews, not American Jews, by seeking action against Russia by American diplomats and issuing indignant statements rather than organizing mass demonstrations or adopting other aggressive tactics. AJC, like Straus, was a product of the German Jewish business class, and its formation was intended to prove that German Jews and their descendants in America had not abandoned the Jews of Russia. It perceived no major Jewish grievance in America that might require its intervention. The AJC saw a specific Jewish interest but few problems in America; Straus saw occasional problems and little in the way of a separate American Jewish cause. In this he remained a classic German Jew, without surrendering to *shtadlan* tendencies.

AJC pioneer Louis Marshall, although he became a leading Zionist, is now nearly forgotten. Born in 1856 in Syracuse, New York, to poorly educated German Jewish immigrants, his upbringing left him with a lifelong sympathy for the disadvantaged and especially for Jews left behind in Europe, facing exclusion and poverty. He graduated from Columbia Law School in 1877 and moved to New York City in 1894, where he became an officer of Temple Emanu-El, the leading Reform Jewish congregation in the United States, rising to its presidency. But he felt a close bond with Conservative Jews, arguing that there was only "one Judaism."

Following the creation of AJC in 1906, Marshall led a successful movement for cancellation of an 1832 commercial treaty between the United States and Russia. The issue was simple: Russia refused to let native-born or naturalized American Jews, even with United States passports, travel without hindrance on tsarist territory. The treaty was abrogated in 1911 by President William Howard Taft, thanks to Marshall's patient work with members of Congress as well as the White House. At the height of debate over the treaty, Marshall testified before the House of Representatives and revealed that Catholic priests and Protestant ministers, as well as Jews, had been victims of tsarist discrimination.

The campaign against the Russian trade treaty was a harbinger of Jewish lobbying against Communist Russia sixty years later, although by then tsarism, like Marshall, had fallen off the historical horizon. It was also an outstanding proof in favor of *shtadlan* methods. But then too, the injustice it was intended to redress was in Russia, not in the United States. It is questionable whether, if such issues had existed in America,

a *shtadlan* strategy would have prevailed over the tactics of socialist agitation, which had more in common with rough-and-ready American
solutions to injustice—an aspect of reality that created a bond between
East European Jewish socialist labor leaders and Gentile unionists. Both
immigrants and native-born American labor organizers knew that negotiation, petitions, and appeals to government were often of limited util-
ity. For example, Oscar Straus was appointed secretary of commerce and
labor at a moment when leaders of the American Federation of Labor
announced that they would defy court injunctions against strikes or
picketing. The law, according to the labor leaders, was abused by the corporate powers, and while in their enthusiasm for Theodore Roosevelt
and Oscar Straus the unionists were open to government help, in that
generation, at least, they would not depend on it.

In 1912, fresh from victory over the Russians, Louis Marshall
became AJC president. In the Russian treaty effort and subsequent
controversies, including a major campaign against the Jew-baiting of
Henry Ford, Marshall remained typical of the *shtadlan* legacy: he
would act at the political and social summits, speaking directly to the
Gentile elite. The divide between the German Jews, whether represented by Straus or by Marshall, and the Eastern European socialists
who succeeded them was never healed. American Jews remained split
along class and quasi-ethnic lines until the Great Depression of the
1930s, and in many respects they are still so split.

AJC has continued to harbor this same internal contradiction
throughout its history. Established because of the suffering of the proletarian East European Jews, it maintained the upper-class *shtadlan*
mentality in its dealings with the American Gentile authorities. Its
subservience made it little more than a research agency for many
decades. The year 1913 saw the foundation of the Anti-Defamation
League, the second domestic Jewish lobby, in reaction to the lynching
of Leo Frank in Atlanta. The active force in ADL's creation was
another forgotten pioneer, Chicago lawyer Sigmund Livingston
(1872–1946), also of German background.

Following after the German Jews, with their Democratic, Republican, and Progressive Republican political involvements, the Jewish

Socialists, who founded such periodicals as the daily *Forward* and the *New Leader*, were the most successful leftist movement in American history, gaining permanent respect for their ideals and achieving their essential goals—labor rights and social equality. Like the German Jews when they first came to America, and like Oscar Straus, they advanced a common American agenda in which Jewish needs would be recognized along with all others', rather than conceiving of their own interests as distinctly and irreducibly Jewish.

Was this, finally, good or bad for the Jews? From the viewpoint of Jewish religious tradition, which emphasizes the special burden of divine law, it may have been better for Jews to remain a people apart. But in the American environment it seemed increasingly unjustified. The huge immigration from Russia was the foundation for the shift to the Democrats and a lasting, if complicated, change in the mentality dominating American Jewish life. The German Jews had stressed patient upward progress, enlightenment, and respectable public service, but later generations would call more emphatically for social and economic justice, rather than simple opportunity and acceptance.

The Socialists gained overwhelming moral and political leadership of New York's teeming Jewish masses. But they also encountered new enemies, who were not necessarily Gentiles. In the 1920s and 1930s, the Jewish Socialists in the New York labor movement administered a major defeat to the Communists, who emerged in America after the Bolshevik Revolution in 1917. Having attracted some Jewish supporters, the Communists attempted to capture the powerful New York garment unions. The Communists were famous for their contemptuous ditties aimed at the Jewish Socialists, such as this song:

> *The Cloakmakers' union, it's a no-good union,*
> *It's a company union by the bosses.*
> *The A.F.L. fakers and the Socialist jakers*
> *Are makin' by the workers double crosses.*

Jewish workers proved largely impervious to Communist influence. The *Forward,* their beloved Yiddish paper, then had a daily cir-

culation above 200,000 and was the social arbiter for successive immigrant generations; it pounded the Communists mercilessly. *Forward*
readers were typically secular Jews but viewed their Yiddish intellectual traditions as sacred. They fought for the liberation and development of Jewishness in a new society on a par with non-Jewish
culture—a struggle they maintained in Poland after the Bolshevik
Revolution in Russia. They were disgusted by Soviet efforts to label
affirmation of Jewish identity as a reactionary vestige of capitalism.
The traditions of their organization in the tsarist empire, the General
Jewish Workers' Union, were carried forward by the Jewish Labor
Committee (JLC) in New York, which remains a significant, if less
prominent, element of the domestic Jewish leadership. The Depression of the 1930s forced the Jewish Socialists, the trendsetters in Jewish New York, onto their difficult road to the Democratic Party.

Along with the rest of the country, many Jewish business owners,
ruined by the economic downturn, abandoned hope in the Republicans. Franklin Roosevelt, elected president in 1932, assembled a group
of advisers that included several prominent Jews, notably Felix Frankfurter and Henry Morgenthau, Jr. Roosevelt's close friend Herbert
Lehman, partner in the Lehman Brothers investment firm, had been
elected his lieutenant governor in 1928 and succeeded him as governor of New York when Roosevelt rose to the presidency. The Roosevelt
administration rapidly assumed a more Jewish cast than any presidency before it; one estimate holds that 15 percent of Franklin Roosevelt's presidential appointees were Jewish, at a time when Jews
accounted for no more than 3 percent of the U.S. population.

The Viennese-born Frankfurter, a Harvard professor of law and
prominent liberal, had been an adviser to President Woodrow Wilson
and now became a leading recruiter of Jewish legal talent for Roosevelt. Benjamin V. Cohen, a Frankfurter protégé and a disciple of
another famous Jewish liberal and Zionist, Justice Louis Brandeis,
joined the Roosevelt "brain trust" and drafted much of the most significant New Deal legislation, including that establishing the Securi-
ties and Exchange Commission (SEC) and Federal Communications
Commission (FCC).

Cohen additionally wrote the draft legislation that became the Wagner Act, which provided federal protection for union organizing. Morgenthau was named secretary of the treasury, while labor economist Isador Lubin also helped guide Roosevelt's vision for the revival of American prosperity. Roosevelt rewarded Frankfurter in 1939 by appointing him to the Supreme Court. The very term "New Deal" is credited to Samuel Rosenman, a Jewish adviser to the president. New York governor Lehman would establish a "Little New Deal" involving social assistance, public housing, and other such programs in his state. In addition to securing labor and economic reform, Jews were active in major relief programs, especially the Works Progress Administration's writers' and artists' projects. Thanks to the New Deal, major unions acquired greater public power, including the Socialist- and anarchist-led International Ladies' Garment Workers (ILGWU) and the Amalgamated Clothing Workers (ACW). This was certainly good for the Jewish industrial workers of New York; given the Jewish enthusiasm for unions, it was also good for the American Jews and American workers in general.

Sidney Hillman (1887–1946) was the head of the ACW, a major element in a newly founded labor federation, the Congress of Industrial Organizations (CIO). Hillman became especially close to Roosevelt. Born in tsarist-ruled Lithuania, and a youthful participant in the General Jewish Workers' Union, he remained a left-wing labor leader and socialist, becoming a sympathizer of Moscow.

But Hillman was averse to confrontation. He was closer to the Oscar Straus and Louis Marshall styles of Jewish advocacy—working through the political system or pursuing *shtadlan* strategies—than his militant rival, David Dubinsky (1892–1982), the tougher, tested leader of the ILGWU. Dubinsky was also a veteran of the General Jewish Workers' Union under the tsars and a longtime Socialist who shared Hillman's enthusiasm for the industrial model of union organization. But Dubinsky was a fierce anti-Communist who would shun Hillman's Sovietophilia. He was a major figure in creating the Jewish Labor Committee (JLC) in 1933 as a common front for the Jewish Socialists of a militant variety, the garment unions, and a few grumpy

Zionists. The JLC's first major goal was to publicize anti-Nazism. At its beginning, reflecting its socialist orientation, the JLC specifically rejected Zionism, at the same time as it declared that it would remain independent of the AJC and its *shtadlan* peers. The Polish-born militants of the General Jewish Workers' Union held out for universal socialist liberation rather than a Jewish national project.

In his first term, Franklin Roosevelt and his elite Jewish supporters contended with a major obstacle in winning over the Jewish masses: Although he was the state's former governor and won New York state in the presidential election, during the 1920s New York working-class Jews obstinately refused to vote for the local Democrats. As long as a grossly corrupt, mainly Irish machine controlled the Democratic Party, few Jews would vote for anybody except the Socialists or the "good-government" Republicans, even with the liberal Jewish Democrat Lehman as governor. In the 1932 presidential election, 200,000 New Yorkers had cast ballots for the Socialist presidential candidate, Norman Thomas. The same number was tallied for the Socialists in the 1935 New York municipal vote. To some degree, this attitude represented expectations at the time that revolution, not government, would solve the Depression crisis. It also reflected skepticism about the New Deal coalition's inclusion of bigoted southern Democrats. As Edward J. Flynn, Democratic boss of the Bronx, bluntly declared, New York Jews "would not join the Democratic Party." Frances Perkins, Roosevelt's secretary of labor, explained that Jewish unionists "couldn't bring themselves to vote for Roosevelt under the Democratic [symbol] because they were *bona fide* Socialists, or more than that, and they had always regarded Tammany as their enemy." For similar reasons, New Deal mayor LaGuardia had been elected on a "Republican-Fusion" ticket.

The New Deal needed voters, not mere good wishes. To resolve this problem, Sidney Hillman stepped forward in 1936, backed by his competitor Dubinsky, who resigned from Socialist ranks in that year to endorse Roosevelt. Dubinsky had concluded that the Socialist Party, riven with ideological disputes, and incapable of electing a significant number of its candidates, had become an obstacle to the goals it shared with Roosevelt's New Dealers. That New York Jewish workers had remained loyal to the Socialists for the first four years of the New Deal was impressive but appeared self-defeating to Hillman and Dubinsky, since it continued to deprive them of a stronger link with the White House. With Roosevelt's approval, Hillman and Dubinsky proposed to establish a new electoral framework that was, in reality, a halfway house to Democratic ranks. It was eventually dubbed the American Labor Party (ALP) and operated only in New York.

Along with Hillman and Dubinsky, the creators of the ALP included the editors of the *Forward;* Dubinsky's lieutenant in organizing the Italian garment workers, Luigi Antonini—also a charismatic leader and firm anti-Communist; and two Jewish leaders of the hat and cap makers' union, Alex Rose and Max Zaritsky. Antonini became the new party's state chairman. Statewide assistance came from railroad unions, which had few Jewish members but were firmly pro-Roosevelt, and national endorsements were furnished by the philosopher John Dewey and other intellectuals. Financing was provided by Dubinsky and the ILGWU.

Dubinsky was the stronger figure in the Moses-and-Aaron relationship he had with Hillman. But Hillman was more successful in gaining access to President Roosevelt's circle. Dubinsky would not back off confronting the Communists in New York; he would not support accommodation with the Soviets internationally, and he freely contributed his union's support to the anarchist and anti-Stalinist forces in the Spanish Civil War of 1936–39. None of these personality features would appeal to the core of the New Dealers, who sought to neutralize the Communists by co-opting them into government. In 1933 Roosevelt had ended a U.S. diplomatic blockade of the Soviet Union by recognizing the Stalinist state. Communists took positions in the New Deal once that tactic was approved by Moscow in 1934–35. But the Roosevelt administration wanted as little to do with revolutionary Spain as possible. Roosevelt himself would never feel as comfortable with Dubinsky as with Hillman.

In his principled and consistent anti-Communism, Dubinsky could be described as a proto-neoconservative, although his hatred of the Muscovites was much more motivated by his view that they had betrayed the radical workers who followed them. Dubinsky had left the Socialist organization, but he remained extremely militant in his street unionism—another way in which he contrasted with Hillman, who favored compromise whenever possible. Dubinsky's union conducted tough organizing efforts and even sent its agents into the southern states, where textile workers, a logical constituency for association with the garment workers, were brutally suppressed (Hillman officially headed the textile campaign).

Some New York unionists stayed loyal to the Socialists and out of the ALP—the most distinguished being the African American advocate A. Philip Randolph—but they, too, eventually became Democrats. In the 1936 presidential election, the ALP's vote in New York reached 275,000, twice that of the established Socialists and the Communists. The ALP endorsed Mayor LaGuardia, who remained a Republican stalwart. Socialist fragmentation continued, as a Social Democratic Federation (SDF) also was formed in 1936 by disgusted veterans of the party, led by the Jewish Louis Waldman, after the main organization again nominated Norman Thomas as an opponent of Roosevelt. The SDF was as aggressively anti-Communist as Dubinsky. Communists were officially prohibited from joining the ALP but infiltrated it, mainly thanks to the sympathies of Hillman.

By 1944, the Communists had produced such factional conflict in the American Labor Party that a split occurred, with the emergence of the Liberal Party, backed by Dubinsky and the SDF. The ALP became a shameless Stalinist front group and went out of business in 1954, but the Liberal Party slate continued in New York. Its spirit had been enunciated at its beginning by Dubinsky when he excoriated Hillman for cozying up to the Communists. Recalling Communist attempts to take over the garment workers' movement in the 1920s, Dubinsky shouted "We will never be a party to a united front [with the Communists]!"

Roosevelt, unfortunately, was friendlier to Hillman and his inclusive approach—even after the Stalin-Hitler Pact—than he was to Dubinsky. The Roosevelt-Hillman association led to numerous anti-Jewish gibes at the president, labeled by the adherents of Father Coughlin as Roosevelt's puppet master. Thus the New Deal was damned by some as "the Jew Deal." After 1944, Roosevelt's name was even more venomously coupled with that of Hillman. It was widely alleged that Roosevelt, responding to a proposal that he replace Vice President Henry Wallace, a strident leftist on the Democratic national ticket, had told his White House staff to "clear it with Sidney." Foes of Hillman's CIO had come up with a satirical version of the refrain made famous by the Seven Dwarfs in Walt Disney's animated feature *Snow White:*

> *Hi ho, hi ho, we join the CIO,*
> *We pay our dues to the goddamn Jews, hi ho, hi ho.*

Still, the majority of Americans demonstrated their enthusiasm for and confidence in the president and his appointees by granting Roosevelt majorities in the three elections after 1932. Moreover, the contribution of liberal Jews to America's recovery and the growth of the labor movement inspired widespread admiration for the Jewish aspect of the New Deal. As a result, the public profile of the "established" Jewish organizations, the AJC and ADL, diminished even further.

Hillman's *shtadlan* manner was viewed by Gentile bigots as good for the Jews, since it gave him access to the White House. But Hillman was inconsistent in his service to the Jewish people. Nothing illustrated the difference between Hillman's "left *shtadlan*ism" and Dubinsky's combative attitude than their differing positions when, in 1943, the terrible news reached New York that Stalin had done to death the two outstanding leaders of the Jewish Socialist movement in Poland, Henryk Erlich and Victor Alter. Erlich and Alter had been heroes to Jewish Socialists—not least among readers of the *Forward* and the vast membership of the New York garment unions—for many years. They had been comrades of men such as Hillman and Dubinsky, joining the Russian revolutionary movement during the pogroms and other disorders of 1903–1907.

The lives of Erlich and Alter were representative of an entire generation of young Jews who stayed in Eastern Europe, leaving neither for America nor Palestine, as well as young Gentiles who turned to socialism with equal devotion. Like the Jewish Socialists in America, Erlich and Alter were universalists who favored Jewish equality in a transformed society. Erlich's eyes were "filled with yearning," according to Emanuel Nowogrudsky, a Jewish Socialist close to Dubinsky. Erlich was born into a pious family of Hasidic Jews—extreme separationists who preserved a Yiddish culture that kept them apart from their Christian neighbors—but "was also a son of the Polish soil; the aspirations to freedom of the Polish people were very dear to his heart," Nowogrudsky wrote. "The fight for a new, just, and righteous order would lead to the realization of the sublime visions delineated by the Jewish prophets and their disciples."

It would be hard to imagine a more eloquent statement of the Jewish Socialist ideal than these few words by Nowogrudsky, whose name has vanished from standard Jewish histories. Erlich became the outstanding polemical journalist among the Jewish Socialists in Poland, lashing the enemies of working people as if his pen were a whip, more often in Polish than in Yiddish. In 1937, he recalled the agony of the pogroms and failed revolution in the Russia and Poland of 1905–1906: "While the Jewish bourgeois elements sang words of blessing for the bloody tsar; while the religious Jews preached humility . . . and the Zionists promised the tsarist ministers, people dripping with workers' blood and Jewish blood, to remove the Jews from Russia—Jewish workers, under red banners, fought for freedom in the front ranks of revolution; self-defense groups, with guns in hand, bravely defended the Jewish masses."

Alter also came from the Hasidic environment. He joined the revolutionary movement in 1905, at fifteen. Like Erlich, he was an internationalist, uninterested in a narrow Jewish agenda. His history as a Socialist leader began with his membership in a committee coordinating a massive strike, demanding Polish-language school instruction in "Russian Poland." He was imprisoned, then released as a minor and handed a "wolf ticket" (*vulchii bilyet*)—an order barring him

from returning to any school on the soil of the tsarist empire. He
became a clandestine activist in the Jewish Socialist organization and
turned a house owned by his family into an arsenal of guns and explosives. One day a fire and explosion shook the building, and the head
of the Warsaw police led a group of officers to the scene. On the way
the police chief's car was attacked with a bomb by a group of armed
Socialists who happened to be Polish Catholics, rather than Jews. They
had been waiting for such an opportunity. Alter escaped and fled to
Western Europe.

Erlich and Alter became distinguished for their courage in one
battle after another—against the tsarist regime and its anti-Semitic
brutes, against the Bolsheviks, against Jew-baiters in independent
Poland after the First World War, against the Nazis. Along with many
more extraordinary exploits, both served on the Warsaw city council
after Poland gained its independence. Until the Holocaust, the great
metropolis of Warsaw was the European equivalent of New York as a
capital of Yiddish culture. Its most notable address is still the inter-
section of Jerusalem Boulevard and New World Street, which seems a
poetic evocation of both the past and future of the multitudes who
passed through it.

Erlich and Alter, like Dubinsky and others, did not believe socialism existed in Stalin's Russia. They had faith that worldwide collec-
tivism, by unifying humanity, would end anti-Jewish hatred. Once
again, was the socialist attitude good for the Jews? Clearly, any trust
in the Stalin regime was not.

Erlich and Alter had been arrested by the Russians in 1939, in the
Soviet occupation zone established after Poland was divided between
Hitler and Stalin. Unfortunately, notwithstanding their experience as
veteran opponents of Stalinism, they apparently believed the Soviets
would defend Jews against Hitler. In this, they seem either insanely
naive or disastrously idealistic; incapable of guile, they could not
imagine its depth in others. They were executed in 1941, according to
an insolent announcement made in 1943 by Soviet foreign minister
Maxim Litvinov, after four years of protests and inquiries by Jewish
and other labor and Socialist leaders around the world. Albert Ein-

stein, the most famous Jew in the world, along with William Green, president of the American Federation of Labor (and a dedicated anti-Communist), and several more prominent liberals, had demanded clarification of the case. They were supported from behind the scenes by Eleanor Roosevelt. Litvinov replied in a letter to Bill Green that Erlich and Alter had been sentenced to death for allegedly promoting a truce with the Nazis. Their real offense, in Soviet eyes, was that they defended their Polish Christian compatriots against Russian imperialism and supported Trotskyists and other Bolsheivik victims of Stalin. Alter was shot; many years later it was learned, with the opening of files in post-Soviet Russia, that Erlich had committed suicide.

Jews all over the world were passionately loyal to Erlich and Alter; declarations of solidarity poured into New York from Yiddish-speaking groups as far away as Argentina and Australia. A Socialist, M. Kusher, wrote in the *Australian Jewish Forum,* "The hand trembles; it is almost impossible to write down the words; Henryk Erlich and Victor Alter, the two most respected and beloved Jewish labor leaders in Poland, have been executed by the Soviet government. . . . It is not an evil dream, not a mere nightmare, but a grim reality."

America was fighting Hitler, and Russia was its chief ally in continental Europe. But the Jewish socialists in New York refused to excuse Stalin's crimes. If Americans and Jews needed Russia, were not the Russians called upon to respect the rights and feelings of their helpers in the antifascist war? Roosevelt had provided the devastated Soviet armies with immense military resources; was the answer to be a terrorist act, a blow to the face of every non-Stalinist liberal and leftist? How did the Russian Communist rulers who ordered the liquidation of Erlich and Alter differ from the tsarist Cossacks and Black Hundreds who preceded them in tormenting the Jews? How did they differ from the Nazis?

Protest in New York against the deaths of Erlich and Alter began with the AFL's Green but was mainly driven by the indomitable Dubinsky, whom the Stalinists now routinely described as an advocate of surrender to Hitler. Notwithstanding the good wishes of Eleanor Roosevelt and a pat on the back from Hillman, the Democrats were uninvolved in the outcry over Moscow's injustice. The surviving "official" Socialists took responsibility for a memorial meeting addressed by Mayor LaGuardia, still a New Dealer but also still a Republican. The mayor's speech included an extraordinary statement: "When we started out as liberals we started out to defend the rights of anyone, whether we liked them or not. Now we are becoming sort of specialized liberalists—defend anyone that is with you, never criticize those who are with you, and oppose the other guy. That is not the liberalism that I have dedicated my life to."

LaGuardia foresaw how liberal Democratic politics in America, through the end of the twentieth century, would become known for its immoral posture of "no enemies on the left." The events surrounding the dreadful deaths of Erlich and Alter repeated the pattern seen in the battle for New York in 1939–41: when Jews were in trouble, militant unionists and Socialists fought back. They gained support from LaGuardia, as well other Republicans such as Wendell Willkie, an internationalist who had run against Roosevelt for the presidency in 1940. A full-page advertisement in the *New York Times*, signed by Green, Dubinsky, the editors of the *Forward*, Norman Thomas, and a few others from their circle, described Erlich and Alter as "symbols of the vast army of martyrs who have gone to their graves on orders from the Kremlin murder machine." Hillman's signature was absent. But the anti-Communist response to the deaths of Erlich and Alter was yet another early harbinger of neoconservatism.

In short, the role of a "Jewish lobby" was filled, until the end of the Second World War, much less by the communal advocacy organizations than by Socialist agitators, labor leaders, and New Deal appointees. The AJC and its peers in the ADL seemed quite happy with this situation, insofar as the main burden of deciding what was good for the Jews was lifted from their shoulders. Thanks to the New Deal coalition, it seemed, the discreet *shtadlan* tradition, embodied since its founding by the AJC, now merged with the radical activism of the Jewish labor movement. The "Jewish agenda" that was the off-

spring of this match included a civil rights and ethnic equality element, represented by the *shtadlan* groups, and a labor and social
welfare component, embodied in the unions; this was a microcosm
of the New Deal promise. Though in its time and for several
decades this agenda put American Jews on the right side of history,
the agenda is now seventy years old, an age when retirement is
appropriate.

The New York atmosphere of Jewish radicalism, opposition to the
Stalinists, and recruitment to the New Deal also added another new
feature to the American landscape: a group of New York Jewish intellectuals who were to become known for "arguing the world." Some of
the New York group began as acolytes of Stalin and were affiliated
with a Communist party-line literary magazine, *Partisan Review,*
founded in 1934 by Philip Rahv and William Phillips. But Rahv and
Phillips soon broke with Stalinist orthodoxy, passionately opposing
the Moscow purge trials of the late 1930s, the NKVD's murderous
international campaign against Trotsky and his followers, and the
Soviet role in the Spanish Civil War, which undermined the Spanish
Republicans who opposed Franco and condemned their cause to
defeat.

The "Trotskyism" of *The Partisan Review* circle attracted some
authentic supporters of the exiled Bolshevik. One was James Burnham, the Gentile philosophy teacher and Trotskyist street speaker who
had urged the antifascists on in the battle against the Bund at Madison Square Garden in 1939. They were also distinguished by their ability to draw in other talented individuals whose Trotskyism was less
developed. These included the Marx scholar Sidney Hook, the critics
Mary McCarthy (who became Rahv's lover) and Dwight Macdonald,
the young writers Saul Bellow and Delmore Schwartz, the art critics
Meyer Schapiro, Harold Rosenberg, and Clement Greenberg, and the
social thinker Nathan Glazer. Not all were Jewish—note, in particular, Burnham, McCarthy, and Macdonald. But most were.

Trotskyism itself effectively ended as a movement in 1940 with the
assassination of its namesake by a Stalinist agent in Mexico. Even
before that, a long period of reflection had begun for the New York

intellectuals, in which the great majority moved to the political center and many to the right. The Stalin-Hitler pact and a Soviet invasion of Finland caused many anti-Stalinists to question whether the Moscow government could be described, or defended, as embodying any positive principles of the historic socialist movement. American Trotskyism then split, and Burnham and Shachtman, star orators in the Bund affray at Madison Square Garden, formed an independent group that attacked Soviet Russia as totalitarian and rapaciously imperialistic. The new anti-Soviet trend (which soon lost Burnham) became known as "Shachtmanism." Tiny in numbers, with a major Jewish contingent, its larger political significance was hidden to most Americans for decades, as it followed a parallel course with the anti-Soviet Social Democratic Federation. But Shachtmanism later reemerged as a vital force when the New York Jewish left again suffered a crisis in the 1960s, and it helped in the birthing of neoconservatism.*

Irving Kristol, who departed from Trotskyism around the time of the Burnham-Shachtman defection, would become the most important individual in the creation of the neoconservative movement, through a periodical he launched with Daniel Bell called the *Public Interest* (from which Bell, who had been a Social Democrat, later defected). Kristol and others traced their intellectual development back to their experience as victims of discrimination by the rulers of American collegiate leftism in the 1930s, the Communist Party, at the City College of New York. There they had been relegated to "alcove two," an inferior location along one wall of the basement of Shepard Hall, where they ate lunch, played Ping-Pong, or sat reading, by the Muscovite sympathizers who held forth in "alcove one." The alcoves were often disturbed by loud debate and even by physical fights. American Stalinist propaganda, employed in a constant screeching barrage of insults against the Social Democrats and Trotskyists, had a strong Jew-

---

* As decades passed, the critic Irving Howe, alone among the leading New York intellectuals, remained loyal to a vision of socialist revolution, even to the point of defending the Sandinista dictatorship in Nicaragua in the 1980s against the encroachments of the Reagan administration.

baiting tone that seemed to echo Hitler's psychopathic speeches. In the American Communist press, Trotsky and other anti-Stalinists were portrayed as flashy, ambitious, pseudo-intellectual, corrupt, deceptive, dual in their loyalty, prone to manipulating both sides of a conflict, and defeatist. These clichés were familiar as Jewish stereotypes in the hate literature of the tsarist secret police, and were as much or more applicable to Gentile Stalinists, of whom there was no shortage in the 1930s, than to their Jewish opponents. The same idioms would resurface in the baiting of the neocons decades later.

The anti-Stalinists had their revenge, however, more than once. In 1939 they, not the Communists, had beaten the Bund; and the names of those who met in "alcove two" would in time help transform American public life, while the only inhabitant of "alcove one" to leave any permanent memory was a chemistry student named Julius Rosenberg, executed with his wife, Ethel, in 1953 for his part in handing over American nuclear secrets to the Russians.

Above all, the "alcove one" leftists were driven by worship of state planning and social engineering, and displayed a kind of forced optimism about the future, even as they embraced a hideous negation of human sympathy in the form of the Stalin regime. The "Trotskyists" in "alcove two" appear to have been much more sensitive to human weaknesses and pessimistic about history, which may be why they defended a more humanistic version of socialism. In time, the fanatical enthusiasm of the Stalinists would spread among American liberals and leftists, while the intelligent skepticism of the Trotskyists came to be the main characteristic of the neoconservatives.

The Stalinists had begun as ferocious critics of the New Deal as a "fascist scheme," but they constructed their own alliance with the Roosevelt administration. In competition with the Social Democrats and Dubinsky, and utilizing their influence in Hillman's CIO, they infiltrated such crucial agencies as the newly created National Labor Relations Board (NLRB), which became a colonial possession of the Soviet secret intelligence services through the appointment to its staff of two Soviet spies, Nathan Witt and Charles Kramer.

The Trotskyists, like many Jewish socialists, were suspicious of the New Deal. Instead they held out for a socialist revolution as the answer to the problems of America and the world. They were also greatly aggrieved when unions in which they were active—including the Teamsters and the Sailors' Union of the Pacific, on the West Coast—were victimized by the Stalinist-controlled NLRB, which denied them jurisdiction in favor of Communist-run unions. Trotsky himself had written, in a text found in his desk after his killer struck, "In the United States the Department of Labor with its leftist bureaucracy has as its task the subordination of the trade union movement." He was right. The Labor Department had strayed far from the high ideals embodied in the stewardship of Oscar Straus.

Still, neither the Stalinists nor the Trotskyists among Jews questioned whether the high Jewish profile in the New Deal was anything but good. Both factions had definitively abandoned anything resembling *shtadlan* hesitation about their role in Gentile society. They differed in that the Stalinists saw their turn to the Democrats, and (except for the period of the Stalin-Hitler pact) dependence on the Roosevelt administration, as a proper means to protect Jewish communal interests while pursuing the rest of their goals. In contrast, the Trotskyists believed, as shown in the battle of New York, that support for a union-based antifascist effort, on American soil as well as in Europe, was the best policy in defending the Jews. The former attitude, of course, allowed Soviet agents to infiltrate and influence the U.S. government, while the latter might open the door to proletarian revolution. This was the Stalin-Trotsky conflict reduced to essentials.

Once consummated, however, the Jewish alliance with the Democrats became a nearly unchallengeable institutional fact. By 1938, it was clear that Dubinsky and his cronies had successfully broken the Jewish union workers out of the straitjacket of sectarian socialism and lifted them to the heights of political influence, beating the *shtadlan* advocates at their own game. But the Democratic Party also tended to cut the Jews off from their roots in street agitation, their raw militancy and their spontaneity, the very qualities that had gained them the sense of unity and voting power that made them valuable to Roosevelt.

Thus as always for Jews, success was plagued with difficulties. Where the *shtadlan* representatives of the past were often contemptible in their timidity, as when they refused to do more than call for diplomatic pressure over the Russian massacres of 1903–1906, or when they appealed to Jewish workers not to go to Madison Square Garden to fight the Nazis in 1939, the Jewish-Democratic alignment created a different syndrome of passivity, not unlike a drug addiction. In either case, what seemed good for the Jews carried with it a new form of bondage.

After the Japanese attack on Pearl Harbor, public concern about the anti-Jewish activities of the Coughlinites and America Firsters remained pronounced, even though the advocates of fascism and isolationism were almost universally scorned. The claustrophobic environment in New York and elsewhere, where spies were believed to lurk behind every door, is portrayed in Alfred Hitchcock's 1942 thriller *Saboteur*. (Though heavy with complicated pro-Communist clichés inserted by its screenwriters, it remains one of the British director's great works.) In 1943, a journalistic account of the fascist movement in New York, by an investigator who called himself John Roy Carlson, was published with the title *Under Cover* and became a bestseller. Carlson, an Armenian, had posed as an Italian to infiltrate the anti-Jewish movement, and the revelations of the boldness and extent of its activities amazed ordinary Americans.

Carlson described the pro-Nazi ravings of the America Firsters, as well as such exotic political fauna as the African American fascists who shook up Harlem with pro-Japanese activities. The leader of the so-called Black Muslims, Elijah Poole, who called himself Elijah Muhammad, was imprisoned during the war for interfering with the draft, and Malcolm Little, later famous as Malcolm X, also evaded service. *Under Cover* went into several printings and remains to this day a source of great irritation to those who, like Pat Buchanan, seek to revive the America First movement.*

After 1945, the country suddenly confronted the problem of Judeophobia through the most powerful educational weapon then in existence: Hollywood films. The 1947 picture *Gentlemen's Agreement*, directed by Elia Kazan, starred Gregory Peck as a Gentile who poses as a Jew to expose discrimination. *Gentlemen's Agreement* won three Oscars (best picture, best director, and best supporting actress for Celeste Holm). It received five more Oscar nominations, including one for Peck as best actor and one for Moss Hart's screenplay. *Gentlemen's Agreement* was made, let it be noted, against the objection of Jewish studio heads in Hollywood, who did not want attention drawn to the "Jewish problem." Although today it is taken for granted by far too many people that Hollywood Jews have always aggressively pursued an ethnic agenda, in the heyday of the studio system Hollywood Jews played no role in the communal leadership except to echo the insistence by the *shtadlan* types on extreme politeness in Jewish advocacy.

The year 1947 also saw the release of the noirish mystery *Crossfire*, about the murder of a Jew by a brutal, bigoted soldier. Produced by a group of Hollywood Communists that included producer Adrian Scott and director Edward Dmytryk, it was based on a novel, *The Brick Foxhole*, by another Hollywood Red, Richard Brooks. Brooks's book originated in an event he himself had witnessed: the slaying of a homosexual by a group of servicemen during the war. But homosexuality as a subject was still off-limits in Hollywood. *Crossfire*, starring Robert Young, Robert Mitchum, and Robert Ryan, received five Oscar nominations but won none, perhaps because it was darker than *Gentlemen's Agreement*; yet it represented a major step forward in the treat-

---

* In one of history's more amazing ironies, thirty years after he became famous for his investigation of Jew-baiting in New York, Carlson was kidnapped in Lebanon by the Popular Front for the Liberation of Palestine, which seized his personal papers and handed them over to the Soviet KGB. But Carlson was always a resourceful individual, and he escaped from a Palestinian refugee camp in Tripoli, making his way to the U.S. embassy in Beirut.

ment of Jewish issues in American popular culture, and remains a film classic.

Having proven their fidelity to the common good by supporting Roosevelt, thousands of American Jews also demonstrated their willingness to sacrifice their lives in the U.S. armed forces. While established Jewish organizations such as the AJC and ADL published position papers, ordinary Jews—union adherents, creative intellectuals, and war veterans—had earned what seemed an unchallengeable position of public respect. Old social barriers, such as the exclusion of Jewish professors from major universities, began to fall.

But in the longer view of history, American Jews could be reproached for dancing on their ancestors'—and European relatives'—graves. In the Nazi extermination camps and occupation zones of Eastern Europe, an inconceivable crime had taken place, in the face of which the majority of American Jews, and their friends in the non-Jewish elite, had shown themselves to be helpless. Contrary to the lies of the Coughlinites and America First, America did not join in the Second World War for the benefit of the Jews, just as today America has not intervened in Iraq to assist Israel. Although Roosevelt had recourse to vast military resources, they were not used to save the Jews under German rule. The survivors of the Nazi death camps were liberated by Allied troops, but the New Deal was of no help to the victims of Auschwitz, and where Jews organized armed resistance, as in the Warsaw Ghetto uprising or the partisan groups in the forests of Poland and Lithuania, they were guided by Socialists and other radicals against their own *shtadlan* representatives, who stood forever condemned as Nazi collaborators.

The horror of the Holocaust was barely realized on this side of the Atlantic until it was over. The lesson, when it came, should have been more shocking and sobering than it was. While American Jews had improved their own lot, realizing the long-stated promise of America, their peers elsewhere could be wiped out in the millions almost without notice. So what was good for the Jews? As in the late nineteenth century when American Jews petitioned President Grant to help the oppressed Jews of Romania, and as in the crisis a century ago when the drama of the Russian Jews stirred the whole world, American Jews were called to account for the fate of Jewry worldwide. But the succor forthcoming in the Romanian case, and a half century later in response to the Russian pogroms, was lacking when it was most needed. What had changed in Jewish and global history? How was the world different in 1943 from its situation in 1870 and 1903? This question has yet to be adequately posed, much less answered.

Some critics of Israel and Zionism, both (apparently) well- and (obviously) ill-intentioned—and including some Jewish commentators—have accused Jews of exploiting the Holocaust to justify Israel's policies, good or bad. But I spent the entire 1990s writing on the horror of Serbian fascism in ex-Yugoslavia and made a pilgrimage to Warsaw, that monument to Jewish and Catholic martyrs and angels in struggles against totalitarianism, and I cannot blithely engage with such a question. From America it may seem immoral to "exploit" the Holocaust. In cities like Sarajevo and in the towns of Kosovo, before the twentieth century ended, thousands of non-Christians—Balkan Muslims in this case—were once again murdered for nothing other than their names, their faith, and the small fact that both Jews and Muslims can be identified by circumcision. In the presence of "Christian" Europe's forgetfulness about the Holocaust, it seems it may not have been sufficiently "exploited" to teach a permanent lesson, even though "*Shoah* business" has in too many cases produced clichés and kitsch.

In 1948, the state of Israel was born, and the American Jewish leadership and Zionist movement were transformed into the lobbies we now know. Each step they made was undertaken, for a generation more, in the enveloping embrace of the Democratic Party. Roosevelt's successor, Harry Truman, recognized Israel, and the political coalition with the Democrats further solidified as activist socialism diminished in fact and in Jewish memory. The unions, for another generation, remained a powerful force in American life, realizing goals the Jews had treasured. The New Deal's creation, the American welfare state, expanded. And finally, civil rights movements in both the United States, involving African Americans, and in Russia, affecting Jews, bound American Jews tighter to the Democrats. It was a long period of tranquillity in the marriage, only occasionally broken by storms. But within the alliance, potential remained for grave dissension.

CHAPTER 3

HOPE'S ORPHAN

Israel and Its American Friends

The uniquely Satanic evil of the Holocaust had been carried out by the Nazis with little direct interference from the democratic powers.

Some pro-German governments, including that of Spain under Franco, did more to save Jews than such paragons of Western, liberal values as Switzerland. But the established American Jewish leadership also acted insufficiently to prevent the genocide. It protested Nazi atrocities and supported a commercial boycott against Germany, but both actions were inconsistent. In the middle of the war, once Polish Catholic and Socialist representatives confirmed the extent of the atrocities committed under German occupation, some American Jews began pressing Churchill and Roosevelt to bomb the German death camps. The failure of the Allied commanders to take stronger action has led many later commentators to condemn the democratic leaders. Yet the real failure was that of the leading American Jewish representatives for their *shtadlan* docility.

Shortly after the fiftieth anniversary of the liberation of Auschwitz in January 2005, former New York mayor Ed Koch erupted: "There is no question that many lives would have been saved if the Allies had bombed the railways leading to Auschwitz." Koch said of Roosevelt, "I am sure he is in purgatory, for his sin of abandoning the Jews," and elaborated, "There was a lot of anti-Semitism in America in those years, but that is no excuse for Roosevelt's inaction, which was vile." Koch even claimed, preposterously, that Roosevelt "undoubtedly shared in the social anti-Semitism of that era." Nor did Koch spare the American Jewish leadership. "Jewish leaders did not do enough," he said. "They should have stormed the gates of the White House to demand action. But they were afraid of anti-Semitism—afraid they would 'make things worse.'" No words could better describe the *shtadlan* attitude.

Koch was wrong about Roosevelt. FDR would not have filled so many high posts with Jews if he held to the biases the former New York mayor ascribed to him. It is also ridiculous to think that Eleanor Roosevelt would have shared the infamous "suburban prejudice," as Ezra Pound, in an expression of apparent contrition at the end of his life, referred to the classic Jew-baiting impulse he himself had embodied.

But Koch was right about the Jewish leadership. American Jewish institutions proved incapable of anticipating, let alone mitigating, the full extent of Nazi brutality.

The shocking facts of the Holocaust—still, in a real sense, inconceivable and incomprehensible to many non-Jews today—were made public by news photographers entering the death camps with Allied liberators. American Jewish leaders seemed as stunned as the rest of the world. But there was little immediate open debate among the American Jewish elite about the factors that had allowed Hitler to operate with a sense of near impunity. Passivity in the face of fascist aggression and the evil examples of Stalin's terror had so encouraged Hitler that no crime could be excluded, from mass murder and deliberate starvation of whole regions to hideous medical experiments that make the most outlandish Hollywood horror movies seem dull by comparison. And a failure of will by the American Jewish leadership, the most successful group of Jews in modern history, had contributed to the Nazi danger.

In this perilous environment, Franklin Roosevelt had in reality offered rare, articulate, and vehement warnings. In his 1937 "Quarantine the Aggressors" speech he proclaimed, "The present reign of terror and international lawlessness . . . has now reached a stage where the very foundations of civilization are seriously threatened. . . . Without a declaration of war and without warning or justification of any kind civilians, including vast numbers of women and children, are being ruthlessly murdered." Roosevelt further lashed "those ignorings of humane instincts which today are creating a state of international anarchy, international instability from which there is no escape through mere isolation or neutrality." In a militant tone that anticipated that of President George W. Bush almost seventy years afterward, Roosevelt pointed an accusing finger at the perpetrators of global terror and scored the acolytes of "realist" indifference to events far from the United States. And like Bush, Roosevelt was rewarded by considerable ingratitude, at least in retrospect.

The revelation of the Holocaust further discredited anti-Semitism (including the genteel, upper-class variety common among white Anglo-Saxon Protestants, or WASPs), knocking down the last social obstacles to Jews in America. In addition to attaining greater influence in business, law, and academia, Jews now came to the fore of postwar American literature. The new generation of American Jewish authors, led by Saul Bellow, Bernard Malamud, and Philip Roth, and including such lesser figures in tone, quality, and seriousness as Norman Mailer, Lawrence Ferlinghetti (with Sephardic forebears from the Caribbean), and Allen Ginsberg, outshone anybody in the Gentile literary establishment, as well as their predecessors among Jewish radicals. In Hollywood, Elia Kazan embodied a new burst of Jewish talent in reinventing American film with pictures such as *A Streetcar Named Desire* and *On the Waterfront*, in which he far surpassed the liberal pieties of his film on anti-Semitism, *Gentlemen's Agreement*.*

In the wider world, the argument for a secure Jewish national home in Palestine had become unanswerable. The disaster that had befallen their people compelled numerous prominent American Jews, especially among labor figures, to finally embrace Zionism, which they had previously opposed in the name of socialist international-ism. At the beginning of the Zionist movement, socialist and rabbini-cal figures had equally condemned it. The socialists saw Zionists as rivals in the modernization of Jewish life, while religious anti-Zionists viewed them as enemies of tradition, which called on the Jews to wait patiently for the coming of Messiah. But after 1945, colo-nization of the Holy Land appeared to be the only means to prevent the tragedy of Jewish liquidation from being repeated. In 1947, David Dubinsky announced a change in his attitude to the Zionist move-ment: "I have never been a Zionist . . . but there are large and impor-tant elements within our [union] who are devoted to that cause," he said. From then on, Dubinsky's union was among the most important advocates of the Zionist cause in the United States.

The same reality forced American Jewish leaders to take greater account of developments in Washington. Israel could not immediately support itself on its own, and with the obliteration of the majority of European Jews and the captivity of the gigantic Russian Jewish pop-ulace behind what Winston Churchill memorably called the Iron Cur-tain, greater responsibilities for nurturing the Jewish homeland, as well as world Jewry in general, fell to the Americans. As *New York Times* reporter Ira Freeman observed, "With the fulcrum of Zionism

---

* Until then, the mainstream of American writing had been a restricted club, many of whose most popular and idolized figures—including Ernest Hem-ingway and E. E. Cummings—were (no less than Pound and Eliot) Jew-baiters of the first magnitude. The California anarchist poet Kenneth Rexroth referred specifically to Cummings when he wrote, "Anti-Semitism is unknown in America except among lunatics." Rexroth offered this judgment of Cummings a decade after the Second World War: "Everybody pretends not to notice that among his comical cut-ups are some of the most scurrilous bits of anti-Semitic doggerel in any language, including German."

shifted dramatically to the new state of Israel, the power arm of the international movement to settle the Jews in Palestine now definitely is in the United States." The moment had arrived for American Jews to think in worldwide terms—a novelty for most Jews, notwithstanding the paranoid fantasies of those who claimed that all Hebrews acted according to a common international plan and interest. Would that it were true!

The new global role for American Jews would also require a new style of Jewish leadership; more than that, it would require a move away from the parochial atmosphere of New York and a focus on Washington, the center of the new American supremacy. Though not specifically Jewish in its identity or aims, a CIO political action committee (PAC) had been established by Sidney Hillman and would become the model—first for labor and liberals, then for the country as a whole—of how to formulate a specific agenda and press it in Washington. But AJC and ADL, the domestic Jewish lobbies, did not initiate major activities in Washington. To this day both groups remain headquartered in New York, with nothing more than branch operations in the capital. The process by which a small group of Zionist supporters was transformed into AIPAC, the King Kong of Washington lobbies, would take at least thirty-five years.

It is sometimes forgotten in present times of conservative political dominance in the United States and appreciation of Israel as a major American ally that, for years, Israel was considered an anticolonialist and even socialist country, governed by a leftist Labor Party. American Jews assumed a leading role in building up the Jewish state, but even here, the main burden of financial and political assistance to Israel remained, for most of the decade after the Second World War, with the labor movement. Once the new state proclaimed its independence in May 1948, its first president, longtime Zionist leader Chaim Weizmann, received a $1 million loan from Dubinsky's ILGWU. By the end of the year the sum had been paid back and a second loan of $500,000 was made, along with $370,000 in outright donations from the ILGWU. Dubinsky was later joined by Jacob Potofsky, successor to Hillman as head of the Amalgamated Clothing

Workers, in establishing a framework for the sale of $6 million in bonds to finance Israeli housing.

Pro-Israel activism by the garment unions also attracted support within the Gentile majority of organized labor. Most union leaders were extremely grateful for Jewish sacrifices in the long struggle for labor rights in the United States. American unions helped build up the Israeli labor federation, Histadrut, and by extension the socialist sector of the Israeli economy. U.S. labor and pension fund investment in Israel grew colossally. The results of this long association included a legacy of pro-Zionist attitudes in the AFL-CIO that, by the first decade of the twenty-first century, set some elements of the union movement apart from most of the American left. Indeed, it became common to hear labor and civil rights figures such as the late Bayard Rustin criticized for their staunch defense of Israel. But Israel also became a valued asset in the portfolios of many other American and European institutional investors, including banks, insurance companies, and universities, and its bonds would come to be backed with U.S. government loan guarantees.

In the drama of American support for the founding of Israel, the leading protagonist turned out to be President Harry S. Truman. Remarkably, Truman acted on his own, without significant pressure by a domestic Jewish or Zionist lobby, neither of which yet had a presence in the capital. However, he had been "lobbied," after a fashion, to favor partition of Palestine between its Jewish and Arab inhabitants. Eddie Jacobson, his partner in the early 1920s in the haberdashery of Truman & Jacobson, in Kansas City, Missouri, convinced Truman to meet with Weizmann. Against the counsels of the State Department and other advisers, Truman extended recognition to the Jewish state the day its independence was proclaimed.

During the Second World War, Truman had come out for the postwar resettlement of displaced European Jews in Palestine. His friendship with Jacobson, who prodded him on this topic, counted for more than a little. Truman's deeper motives may be open to question: he may have considered an influx of Jewish refugees to the United States undesirable. Disclosures from his personal archives show that he was not above the sort of primitive anti-Jewish prejudice one might expect from a midwestern politician of his era.

In 2003, publication of a Truman diary of the postwar years revealed him calling Jews "very, very selfish." Truman wrote in 1947, "They [the Jews] care not how many Estonians, Latvians, Finns, Poles, Yugoslavs or Greeks get murdered or mistreated as D[isplaced] P[ersons] as long as the Jews get special treatment. . . . Yet when they have power, physical, financial or political, neither Hitler nor Stalin has anything on them for cruelty or mistreatment to the underdog." Truman's prejudices were perhaps mitigated by his equal-opportunity contempt for those in possession of newfound power: "Put an underdog on top and it makes no difference whether his name is Russian, Jewish, Negro, Management, Labor, Mormon, Baptist, he goes haywire. . . . I've found very, very few who remember their past condition when prosperity comes."

Nevertheless, Truman stuck by his pro-Israel decision. Opposition by leading pro-Arab figures in the State Department was widely publicized. No sooner had the war ended in August 1945 than Loy Henderson, director of the Near East Agency at State, wrote to his boss, Secretary James Byrnes, arguing that support for Jewish aims in Palestine would deprive the United States of any moral or diplomatic standing it had in the Middle East. Meanwhile, a small but strident segment of the American political elite began to evince an open pro-Arab slant.

The view that backing Israel must inevitably turn Arabs against the United States was also espoused by General George C. Marshall, who succeeded Byrnes as secretary of state. In the opposition of State to America's presumptive friendship with Israel, an enduring pattern would emerge. State would always put the interests of "the Arabs"— defined as the corrupt misrulers of the Arab and Muslim states—first. The once pro-Nazi King Ibn Sa'ud of Saudi Arabia, with his offspring, would stand in the forefront of America's Muslim friends, according to the Arabists at State. A bandit tribe, the Sa'uds were patrons of Wahhabism, the fundamentalist sect of Sunni Islam elevated to the role of a fascist state ideology, which would later spawn al-Qaeda's ruthless war against the West.

In embracing Saudi Arabia as an element in postwar strategy, the West, and chiefly the United States and Britain, utterly failed to comprehend the nature of Saudi Islam, with control of the holy cities of Mecca and Medina, as a radicalizing element in the vast Sunni majority among the world's Muslims. Western governments, academia, and media could not begin to understand the nature and internal developments in the global Muslim community, or *ummah*. Westerners, even the most brilliant, such as the historian Bernard Lewis, did not recognize the importance and character of the Saudi Wahhabi sect, which they typically described as "austere" apparently without recognizing that it was also murderous in its pursuit of Islamic "purification." Every Muslim in the world knew this, having learned of the trail of massacres by which the House of Sa'ud gained control of the holy cities. After 2001, Lewis himself was compelled to admit that he had "overlooked" the Wahhabi problem. But ignorance of Wahhabism was encouraged by the closure of the Saudi kingdom to Western journalists and social scientists. Simplistic in their view of Islamic history, unable to gauge the realities of life under the Wahhabi system, Westerners, including Jews, found it only too easy to concentrate their attentions exclusively on countries that appeared more immediately troublesome, such as Egypt, Iran, and Iraq. Notwithstanding the claims of demagogues, United States involvement with the Saudi kingdom, rather than with Israel, has been the great unmentionable topic in American public life.

This obliviousness was aggravated by the protection extended to the Saudis by major Western oil companies, chiefly the Standard Oil successors such as ExxonMobil, as it is now known. Breakup of the Standard Oil trust had been a major goal of Theodore Roosevelt, Oscar Straus, and their Progressive colleagues. But Standard Oil, the most rapacious corporation in the history of capitalism, and its supposedly divided successors found ways to evade the strictures imposed on them by the Progressives. The continuation of Standard's domination of global petroleum could be considered a colossal failure of the antitrust doctrines of the Progressive and New Deal eras. It would not, however, be consistently treated by the United States authorities as a conspiracy to evade antitrust laws.

Indulgence of the Standard successors and their operations in the Saudi kingdom was supplemented by the flow of Saudi money into the West. The Saudis achieved an absolute and extraordinary corruption of academic Middle Eastern studies and the scholarly field of comparative religion—both of which until 2001 also completely ignored Wahhabism, but more intentionally than had Bernard Lewis. The bandit monarchy gained further political influence through think tanks and high-powered lobbying that would often make the Jewish and Israeli lobbies look like pathetic amateurs. This would become especially obvious during the crisis over the multibillion-dollar sale of AWACS advanced military technology to the Saudis in 1981.

The United States vacillated for decades between the positions represented by the pro-Israel Truman and the pro-Arab Marshall. The two poles could better be described as those of Zionism as a representation of European democracy in the Middle East and Arabism as a cult of colonialist patronage. The long-standing direction of American policy toward the Arab countries had already been indicated in 1945, when Ibn Sa'ud met Franklin Roosevelt aboard a U.S. warship, the USS *Quincy*, in the Great Bitter Lake on the Suez Canal. The American president tried unsuccessfully to gain Saudi approval for increased Jewish settlement in Palestine. However, the king accepted a U.S.-Saudi economic alliance, which would prove useful, to say the least, to the personal fortune of the Sa'uds.

American military and technical personnel would be admitted to the Saudi kingdom, but Saudi Arabia had become a business partner of the United States, much more than a military ally. For many more years, Britain retained nearly equal responsibility for Western security interests in the Arabian Peninsula and the Persian Gulf. The new arrangement had been predicated on Saudi Arabia's declaring war on the Nazis and Japan, which it did within a month of the Roosevelt–Ibn Sa'ud encounter—and which allowed the Saudi state to be included in the founding conference of the United Nations. The Arabist line at State, founded on trusting the Saudis, would be significantly broken only in the presidency of George W. Bush, with the department ripped from the "appeaser" grip of Colin Powell, who never met a Saudi prince he didn't like, and handed over to the sterner Condoleezza Rice.

Support for Israel in 1948 also came from the Soviet government and its worldwide Communist supporters. The Zionists fought vicious opposition by the British in Palestine, and the Russians opposed the British while also seeking to reinforce the false Stalinist image as the leading antifascist force and, therefore, friends of the Jews. Truman may have believed it politically wise to beat the Russians to recognition of Israel. Furthermore, that year Truman faced reelection, and he was certainly motivated by a desire to secure American Jewish votes. The president's advisers were reputedly concerned by the surprise springtime victory of Leo Isacson, a candidate for the American Labor Party, now Stalinist controlled and viewed by all observers as moribund, in the Bronx's 24th Congressional District.* But Soviet action to help the Zionists was not limited to propaganda. Legendary shipments of weaponry from the former Czechoslovakia, then under the Soviet thumb, rescued the newborn Jewish state after it was attacked by its Arab neighbors.

In America, Communist affection for Israel was purely sentimental and designed to keep the loyalty of the small Jewish Communist constituency. Throughout the 1950s, America's quintessential Stalinist, the banjoist Pete Seeger, appeared in the folk ensemble the Weavers, which included rousing Israeli songs in its repertoire. Thus even Jewish children who grew up in an atmosphere of extreme Leninist irreligion would at least be exposed to the Hebrew language in which such songs were performed—the primary artifact of their people's religion that had been revived as modern speech by the Zion-

---

* A former one-term state assemblyman, Isacson, the new ALP congressman, had campaigned as a strident advocate for the Jewish state in Palestine. Although he is neglected by Jewish political historians, the sad reality of Isacson's meager career—he remained in Congress for a single term—is that he was an untalented politician whose sole distinctions were his youth and his willingness to serve the Communists.

ists. Some offspring of pro-Communist Jews who favored Israel until the Soviet line inevitably changed also learned a few letters from the Hebrew alphabet by collecting Israeli postage stamps. It was their first exposure to the holy script of which the poet Karl Shapiro wrote,

> The letters of the Jews as strict as flames
> Or little terrible flowers lean
> Stubbornly upwards through the perfect ages.

For some, it would be their last.

The collective farm movement of Israeli *kibbutzniks* gave the Zionist cause a long-lasting legitimacy with Gentile as well as Jewish leftists. By the 1960s, however, the Moscow stance on Israel had switched to active support for the Arabs. Soon Pete Seeger and those like him would no more sing Israeli songs than they would have intoned Irving Berlin's "God Bless America" (composed as an anti-fascist anthem in the Coughlin and America First period).

Truman's position in 1948 was internationally controversial. America's main European ally, Britain, engaged in a reprehensible war against the Zionist refugees in Palestine. U.S. identification with Israel threatened the Anglo-American alliance, the basis of American global policy, although America emerged from the war clearly uncomfortable with any attempt to fully restore British imperial authority worldwide. Britain, for its part, repeatedly showed that its sympathies lay entirely with the Arabs.

For the American public of the time, Jewish and Gentile alike, the often tragic struggle by the European Jewish survivors of Nazism for entry into and control over the territory of Israel was riveting. The reality was obscene: having been nearly wiped out by the Nazis, the survivors of that ordeal faced yet another threat at the hands of Britain, the supposed enemy of Hitlerism. Jewish colonists formed diverse regular and guerrilla forces to combat the British, including the outright and unapologetic terrorists of the Irgun Zvai Leumi and the Stern Gang (the latter known by its Hebrew initials as LEHI).

American Jews, some of them gangsters like the *shtarkers* who once beat up Nazi sympathizers in New York, helped smuggle weapons as well as people into Palestine. Leaders of business, religious, and social institutions in the worldwide Jewish community were called on to sacrifice as much as they could, or forever be considered traitors. Though it is largely forgotten today, for many Jews and Gentiles the terror wreaked at that time by the Irgun and the Stern Gang represented thrilling blows against injustice and imperialism, with the morality of their actions almost never debated. Violence by the Jewish resistance included the 1946 Irgun bombing of British military headquarters in Jerusalem's luxurious King David Hotel and the Stern Gang's assassination of a United Nations representative, the Swedish aristocrat Count Folke Bernadotte in 1948.

These acts are frequently cited by Arab extremists as evidence that Jewish terrorism preceded Arab terrorism in the Holy Land. The argument is childish. There was Arab terrorism before there was Jewish terrorism; for example, 1929 saw Arab pogroms in Palestine, which were perversely defended by the Communists (who condemned Zionism then). But Congressman Isacson, speaking in 1948 for the Muscovite left, refused to criticize the Irgun; the epoch of Herschel Grynszpan, left nearly friendless after his daring attack on the German embassy in Paris, and of the Warsaw Ghetto fighters, unaided by everyone in the world except for the Gentile Socialists in occupied Poland, was over.

Still, if today Israel and its foundation loom large in the collective memory of American Jews and have come to influence all Americans in their understanding of the Middle East, in 1948 Israel was clearly a subsidiary issue for the United States—just as Washington, compared with New York, was still a secondary field of action for American Jewish leaders. Truman was mainly occupied with resisting Russian pressure in Europe. Indeed, throughout the 1950s and 1960s, American leadership focused its strategic attentions successively on Berlin, Korea, Hungary, Cuba, and Indochina, rather than on the Middle East. The only major exceptions were the 1953 U.S.-British intervention in Iran and the 1956 Suez crisis. Both the Iranian action, which overthrew a populist demagogue, Mohammad Mossadegh, and reestablished the authority of Shah Mohammad Reza Pahlavi, and the Suez affair, which will be discussed further on, were viewed as distractions from the main Western agenda in the Cold War. This pattern would continue for almost two decades, until the 1973 Arab-Israeli conflict.

Three years after Israel gained independence, the organization that would become AIPAC relocated to Washington. In 1951, when it set up its office in the capital, it was called the American Zionist Committee (AZC). The move was unobtrusive but undeniably momentous. Its aims were, at first, only somewhat more ambitious than those of the pro-Zionist labor unions and its methods a bit more practical than those of the *shtadlan* leaders. While Dubinsky's movement, as well as AJC and ADL, sought to mobilize Jews through speeches and collection of ordinary donations, loans, and bond purchases for Israel, AIPAC would concentrate on U.S. foreign aid and specific political commitments to the Jewish state.

The central figure in the establishment of AIPAC was a Canadian-born actor and journalist named I. L. "Si" Kenen. Like Louis Marshall, his predecessor in the birthing of AJC, and ADL's Sigmund Livingston, Kenen is largely forgotten today. He became a newspaper reporter in Cleveland, Ohio, where he was a founding member of the Newspaper Guild. In 1943 he moved to New York and formed the American Emergency Committee on Zionist Affairs, which became the AZC when it was transferred to Washington. It adopted its present title, AIPAC, in 1954. Most important among the original, fairly modest goals of AIPAC was that of any other Washington lobby—promoting its cause by information, to counteract anti-Zionist attitudes entrenched in the State Department. But the United States now also bestowed massive amounts of foreign aid on the world, and a share was available for Israel.

Several things about AIPAC were new. It was the first domestically based lobby seeking comprehensive help for a foreign state. But it was also the first major Jewish organization with no *shtadlan* legacy; it worked for Israel, but it represented an indigenous, North American Jewish outlook. It carried none of the baggage of the German or East European immigrants, while it shouldered the burden of harmonizing official United States and Israeli interests.

Communists had sought advantages for the Soviet empire, but mainly through espionage and infiltration, rather than legitimate lobbying. The Irish Republican Army's supporters, although deeply rooted in America and operating with impressive political protection, did not seek foreign aid for the Irish Republic. The Marshall Plan, which brought about the economic revival of Western Europe after 1945, was largely unconnected to domestic political considerations among the descendants of immigrants from the countries affected. Greeks, Turks, and the anti-Communist Chinese exiled to Taiwan advocated for American military action favorable to their countries of origin, with financial assistance to governments a subsidiary consideration. And efforts on behalf of the Saudis were, as indicated, handled by the oil companies. Further, Saudi Arabia never asked for economic help, although it later sought military and related infrastructural assistance. Support for Israel by the United States was considered from the beginning by many Gentile observers as a trade-off, closer to domestic political patronage in nature than the rest of the foreign-aid program. Israel was seen as a touchstone for gathering Jewish votes.

AIPAC's first real lobbying proposal was for $150 million in direct aid to Israel. As the fiscal year ended in mid-1954, Congress spent $165 million in the Middle East, with $74 million to Iran and the remaining $91 million divided evenly between Israel and Arab states. Israel by then had received $140 million in U.S. aid. Kenen retired at seventy in 1974, a year when cumulative U.S. aid to Israel passed the billion-dollar mark.

AIPAC under Si Kenen was a modest phenomenon, which is among the reasons Kenen himself is almost unknown today. It issued the *Near East Report*, intended to keep sympathetic journalists informed of the Israeli position in regional affairs, maintained a small staff, and through the Kenen years was, like him, barely noticed in

Washington. The foreign-aid process has always had a rather dull life of its own in the legislative process. The temper and orientation of a presidential administration may improve or diminish the share of American global largesse received by a particular nation or nongovernmental organization more than the humdrum style of congressional lobbying within the portals of the Capitol, as pursued in AIPAC's early years. This reality would be reflected in AIPAC's shift of attention toward the White House in the Reagan era, but in the 1950s, shoe leather still counted for more than fancy schmoozing in the world of the foreign lobbies. The friends of Israel were naturally friends of AIPAC and included some prominent Republicans as well as Democrats. But domestically, the main result of Truman's recognition of Israel was a greatly strengthened Jewish-Democratic marriage.

The strategic value as well as the vulnerability of the American relationship for Israel was illustrated at Suez in 1956, when conflict broke out between Israel, Britain, and France on one side and Egypt, then under nationalist leader Gamal Abdel Nasser, on the other. The clash represented, for Israel's activist supporters in America, their first real crisis. That year Nasser nationalized the Suez Canal, which had been a joint British-French enterprise. Britain and France, supported by Israel, resolved to regain control of the waterway by force of arms, and, implicitly, to overthrow Nasser, a veteran of the Egyptian forces fighting against the Jewish state in Israel's 1948 independence war.

Israel was less interested in the canal itself than in delivering a blow to Nasser, since Egyptian terrorists had long been engaged in clandestine raids across Israel's borders. Military action began at the end of October. President Dwight Eisenhower learned on the twenty-eighth of the month that Israel's mobilization of its army, which had already been reported in the world press, was accelerating. Eisenhower called on the Jewish state not to initiate combat, although nobody yet knew whether Israel might attack Jordan. Eisenhower soon learned that Israel was committed to a flanking action against Egypt, where Britain and France would also land their own troops.

Eisenhower had long indicated his distaste for the pro-Israel line pursued by his Democratic predecessor in the White House. A stony soldier less susceptible to emotion than Truman, Eisenhower would confess to Philip Klutznick, a president of B'nai B'rith, that he doubted whether he would have supported recognition of the Jewish state. "Now that it was done," he said, "we'll have to live with it." Regarding Suez, Eisenhower endorsed calls for UN sanctions against Israel, with a cutoff of official U.S. aid to be followed by interception of private aid and a blockade of oil supplies to Britain and France. The British currency went into a financial slide, revealing London's dependence on the United States and the impact of Eisenhower's anger. NATO was divided. But the president and his cabinet suddenly felt themselves isolated and besieged. Secretary of State John Foster Dulles worried with good reason that Israeli-Anglo-French action against Egypt would threaten American efforts to undermine Soviet imperialism in Europe. Dulles railed to Henry Cabot Lodge Jr., the U.S. ambassador to the UN, against "the terrific control the Jews have over the news media and the barrage [to] which the Jews have [subjected] Congress."

This estimate of the situation was absurd. Dulles' view may have been distorted by his fear of the Jewish-owned *Washington Post* and *New York Times*. But much of the American press was suspicious of Egypt at Suez, and Dulles' ascription of this to Jewish control was an expression of prejudice. The so-called barrage aimed at Congress was little more than an ordinary campaign of rabbinical sermons and letter writing by citizens with a right to express themselves. In reality, American Jewish "pressure" on Eisenhower over Suez was understated and deeply conflicted. The message was articulated by figures such as Rabbi Balfour Brickner of Temple Sinai in Washington, who preached that the United States had chosen incorrectly by favoring "neutralism" between Israel, representing Western democracy, and Egypt, which Brickner described as providing a "veil" behind which Russia was hiding. But Brickner also called for a "suspension of judgment on the morality of Israel's course." American Jewish leaders were uneasy about Israel siding with the old colonial powers. They could not bring themselves to justify Israel's involvement in the Anglo-French attack except as a defensive action, which convinced few Gentile Americans, or as a move to punish Russia by a proxy attack on Egypt.

Dulles, in the typical way of Judeophobes, saw hidden powers at work behind normal events when he lashed out at Jewish "control." Still, in a more general sense Dulles was right and Israel was wrong. The assault on Egypt came at the end of a year of extraordinary world turmoil, mainly focused on Russia, where the dead Stalin had been denounced by Communist boss Nikita Khrushchev. Khrushchev then launched a bloodbath in Hungary, which had attempted to assert its autonomy within the Soviet bloc. While this drama gripped the attention of the world, Israeli prime minister David Ben-Gurion and his colleagues had thrown themselves into a useless adventure at Suez that ended in a solid political victory for Nasser. Had Israel possessed a logical or compelling case for intervention, it would have been made by the Jewish labor leaders, at the time Israel's main American advocates.

Yet even on the basis of anti-Communism, the attack on Suez could not be justified by most American Jewish leaders, including Zionists—who had always defined themselves as enemies of the old imperialist powers and had committed themselves to worldwide decolonization. For example, in the middle of November 1956, Manhattan saw a rally of 5,000 for Histadrut, the Israeli union federation, called by the Labor Zionist Assembly and its union allies, Gentiles included. With tortured logic, speakers at the event warned that Russian support for Egypt could lead to a Soviet nuclear attack on Israel and a third world war. Fear of a nuclear exchange was ubiquitous, but many ordinary people around the world saw both sides at fault in the Suez clash.

Israel was lucky in that Americans generally viewed the Suez shambles as set afoot by the British and French, with the Jewish state as a marginal element. The Anglo-French attempt to recover Suez was mostly seen, then and now, as an exercise in gross stupidity, like the French war in Algeria. Whatever one's opinion of the politics of the Arab world, Suez and the concurrent bloody French response to Algerian nationalism did not represent intelligent options for the resolution of regional problems. Indeed, the Suez fiasco had two much wider and extremely negative consequences.

First, Suez diverted attention from the extraordinary shock of Khrushchev's "secret speech" as well as from Russian atrocities in the suppression of the Hungarian Revolution. Khrushchev's speech excoriating Stalin devastated international Communism, especially its intellectuals, while the horrors of Hungary had enraged ordinary people everywhere, including in such Red strongholds as Italy, where the Communists suddenly became extremely unpopular.

Then, however, in a remarkable example of history's revenge on gamblers, Suez revitalized the European radical left and even restored the anti-imperialist status of the Russians (as supporters of Egypt) at exactly the moment when the spectacle of Russian tanks firing on civilians in Budapest had almost completely wrecked the credibility of Western leftists and the Soviets alike. It has been observed by Marxist intellectuals such as British historian E. P. Thompson, and many other witnesses, that the New Left was born in demonstrations against British involvement in Suez. Israeli irresponsibility in attempting to tie the cart of Zionism to the exhausted horses of French and British imperialism, which even the conservative Eisenhower and Dulles considered unreliable nags on their last legs, was grotesque.

Khrushchev, just when he had been forced to admit in powerful terms the crimes of Stalin and faced global condemnation of Russian rule in Eastern Europe, declared he would send Russian "volunteers" into combat alongside Nasser's forces and would not deter his own son from fighting with them on the Nile. Israeli indiscipline, and British and French arrogance, had quite literally snatched defeat from the jaws of victory at one of the crucial moments in the Cold War.

Some Jewish leaders argued exactly the opposite: that Eisenhower had effectively handed Egypt to the Russians. New York's epitome of the Jewish-Democratic alliance, Herbert Lehman, who had entered the U.S. Senate in 1949 and was about to retire, made such a claim. But the truth remained: strengthening of Soviet ties with Nasser had been encouraged more by the Israeli-Anglo-French attack than by the U.S. disengagement from a neocolonialist policy.

Without Suez, Russian "anti-imperialism" would have remained so thoroughly undermined by the slaughter Moscow perpetrated in Hungary that the influence and even the survival of the Communist empire might have been radically diminished. Poland had already reached an advanced, if uneasy, stage of de-Stalinization by 1956, and in the absence of Suez, the coming of something like the Polish Solidarity movement might have been accelerated.

Thanks to Israel, Britain, and France, Nasser became the outstanding representative of global anticolonial politics, overshadowing more sensible figures such as India's Nehru, and the "nonaligned" trio of Nasser, Yugoslavia's Tito, and Indonesia's Sukarno gained much greater influence over world affairs than they deserved. Nasser was the first of the 1950s nationalist leaders from Africa, Asia, and Latin America to gain widespread sympathy for his youthful charisma, in a world still dominated by old men such as Eisenhower, Khrushchev, Britain's Anthony Eden, and deservedly forgotten politicians in Paris such as Guy Mollet. Suez left Israel, which had sought a place in the nonaligned movement against colonialism, more isolated than before from that global phenomenon.

Meanwhile, Lyndon Johnson, chief of the Senate Democrats, unflatteringly compared threats of United Nations intervention against Israel with the failure of the UN (and the United States) to defend Hungary. The UN could not restrain large states, but it could push small nations such as Israel around. Californian William Knowland, leader of the Senate Republicans, warned that if the United States voted for UN sanctions against Israel, he would refuse to serve in a delegation to the international body. As a firm anti-Communist, Knowland saw things too simply. To him, Russia siding with Egypt was enough to decide the question: the United States should back Israel even if Israeli actions were wrong. Eisenhower, seeming desperate, and viewing any U.S. acquiescence to the anti-Nasser gambit at Suez as an enormous foreign policy error, spoke to the nation, explaining his opposition to Israel's participation in the British-French attack on Nasser. Eisenhower remained isolated in this posture. But finally, U.S. insistence on withdrawal from Suez was accepted by the British, French, and Israelis, all of whom feared losing wider American support and protection.

The degree to which pro-Israel sentiment during the Suez crisis involved the American Jewish leadership or AIPAC cannot be determined. It is clear, however, that the *shtadlan* mentality once again asserted itself, and the lobbies laid low—a wise choice in this instance. Ben-Gurion and the Israeli leadership had committed themselves to the Suez folly without the slightest consultation with or concern for the interests or opinions of the American Jews, their leadership, or even the American aid for which AIPAC lobbied.

During the presidencies of Truman, Eisenhower, and Kennedy, American Jews basked in a glow of liberalism, support for the labor movement and civil rights, and wide social success. Just as Jews had come to the fore of American cultural and professional life after the Second World War, they also achieved new and greater prominence in national elected office. American Jewish leadership in electoral politics was then exemplified by figures such as Abraham Ribicoff, a Democratic politician from Connecticut whose biography bespoke the whole history of East European immigration and the Jewish entry into the New Deal alliance. Ribicoff was the child of an immigrant from Poland who had labored as a peddler and factory hand; the young son earned money for college in a zipper and buckle works. He received a law degree from the University of Chicago without taking a bachelor's, and began a career as an attorney in Connecticut, where he became active in politics.

Ribicoff was elected to the U.S. House of Representatives in 1948 and became governor of the state in 1954. He held that office until 1961, when he was named secretary of health, education, and welfare by President John F. Kennedy—a post reflecting the now-traditional Jewish social component in Democratic politics. Kennedy was the first president to appoint two Jewish cabinet secretaries; Ribicoff was joined by Arthur Goldberg as secretary of labor. Goldberg's career was also emblematic of the New Deal legacy in American and Jewish affairs; he had risen to prominence as a lawyer for the union movement. The next year, however, Ribicoff gained a seat in the U.S. Senate, for which he had once run unsuccessfully against Prescott Bush, father of President George H.W. Bush and grandfather of George W. Bush. Ribicoff remained in the Senate until 1981 and died in 1998. Ribicoff was a typical Jewish Democrat, and heir to the Jewish Socialists, in equating Jewish interests with a broad set of liberal ideals and advancing the former through the latter.

Ribicoff's best-known Jewish contemporary in national politics was a Manhattan Republican, Jacob Javits, whose career reflected the other side of the political mirror: the long survival of Jewish mistrust of New York Democrats. Like Ribicoff, Javits saw Jewish needs as subordinate to the general American concerns of the liberal agenda. Born in the Big Apple in 1904, Javits graduated from Columbia University and New York University Law School, and took a congressional seat in 1946. He served as New York state attorney general beginning in 1954, joining the Senate two years afterward. His legislative achievements included a major role in establishing the National Endowment for the Arts (NEA) and its counterpart the National Endowment for the Humanities (NEH). In 1980, he was defeated in the Republican primary by a more conservative politician, Alfonse D'Amato. Javits died six years later.

Javits was not the last of the prominent Jewish Republicans in national politics: Rudy Boschwitz represented Minnesota for the same party in the U.S. Senate from 1978 to 1991; Warren Rudman similarly held a seat for New Hampshire from 1980 to 1993, as did Jacob (Chic) Hecht, of Nevada, from 1983 to 1989. But these were individual exceptions to the general Democratic hold on the Jewish vote. Arlen Specter of Pennsylvania and Norm Coleman of Minnesota are the only Jewish Republicans in the Senate in 2006, compared with nine Democrats—Dianne Feinstein and Barbara Boxer of California, Chuck Schumer of New York (whom Republicans hate on many issues but who outclasses them all in properly giving the Saudis hell), Russ Feingold and Herb Kohl of Wisconsin, Carl Levin of Michigan, Frank Lautenberg of New Jersey, Ron Wyden of Oregon, and Joe Lieberman of Connecticut.

But none of the Jews elected to the Senate after the Second World War could be said to have done much for the Jews aside from pursuing a liberal or centrist agenda common to most Americans in their time. None were ethnic politicians, and none represented compact Jewish voting groups except, to a minimal degree, Javits and Schumer. They were good for the Jews in maintaining Jewish faces at the summit of American politics and in often (but not always) supporting the labor movement and liberal ideals, more than in their fulfillment of the proposals of the *shtadlan* lobbies or in advocacy for Israel. The California Jewish senators Feinstein and Boxer arguably depended for their success on something very bad for the Jews: ultraliberal Hollywood. In the form of political imbeciles such as Barbra Streisand, Rob Reiner, Miramax moguls Harvey and Bob Weinstein, and the abominable Norman Lear, founder of the misnamed People for the American Way, to mention only the most obnoxious, Hollywood Democrats have wreaked havoc with the image of human sympathy and fairness that all Jewish politicians sought to project. Joe Lieberman, who had to take Hollywood money during his 2000 vice presidential campaign, lashed out repeatedly at the gross immorality and human degradation in Hollywood entertainment.

At the end of 1960, Washington acknowledged reports that Israel, assisted by France, was developing nuclear technology to produce armaments. The Israeli government denied the charge. French involvement was ascribed by the *New York Times* to a need for nuclear fuel, French ambitions for greater international prestige, and the continuation of the French-Israeli alliance at Suez. France remained a major military supplier of the Israelis for years, while the United States played no comparable role. The *Times* reported that U.S. experts, given their focus on Communism, were typically concerned that China would produce a nuclear bomb before Israel would. As the Eisenhower administration came to an end, its dismayed officials expressed the view that an Israeli nuclear weapon would drive the Arabs further toward Soviet influence. As Israel kept mum about the subjcct of its nuke, so did its American lobby, which does not discuss such issues to this day and considers mention of them hostile. Successive U.S. administrations have also kept the matter at arm's length, neither supporting nor criticizing Israel on nuclear policy.

American Jewish opinion remained mostly concerned with domestic issues in the 1960s. Jews played a prominent role in the civil rights movement, especially in the often bloody southern campaign for recognition of African American voters' rights. In addition, Israel was still viewed as liberal, if not leftist. American Zionists of the 1960s still possessed a sense of revolutionary enthusiasm for the collectivist *kibbutzim,* although the frantic way young American Jews adopted such Israeli customs as the *hora,* a Romanian folk dance, seemed in retrospect to mask anguish and guilt over Jewish passivity during the Holocaust.

A certain ardor for the Zionist experiment was kept alive by the sixties-era rise of identity consciousness among younger American Jews. The African American civil rights epic would move every constituency lacking full equality in American social life—Jews, women, Hispanics, American Indians, homosexuals—to assert their own demands. Israel also remained attractive to elements of the European left, even as, after Suez and the Algerian war against the French, Nasser and other Arab militants acquired considerable prestige with young radicals. But the global situation of Israel, and the conditions under which its American supporters had to work, changed with the Six-Day War in 1967.

During the first nineteen years of the Israeli state, the congruence of American and Israeli interests was founded almost entirely on the emotional identification of the American public with victims of Hitler and moral support for Jewish self-defense, as well as for a youthful social experiment. When Israeli politicians came to the United States, they visited their donors and backers in New York and fund-raisers in other cities; they did not focus on Washington as they do today. Many American politicians were happy with this situation and pleased to leave the Jewish state at a polite distance.

While the Middle East was episodically important in the Cold War

scheme of things, American policy makers were content to let the sub-
ordinated British power in the region (which even today is hardly neg-
ligible in many Arab and Muslim states), along with dismally venal Arab
and Muslim rulers, hold the situation in check. The Americans stayed
focused on competition with the Soviets in the Far East, black Africa,
and Latin America. Saudi Arabia in particular would help keep American regional policy in flight on two wings by balancing against support
for Israel. While it was the most reactionary, repressive, and anti-Jewish state in the world, the Saudi kingdom was also fervently anti-Soviet.
The Saudis had an additional advantage over the Israelis in their previously noted relations with U.S. energy companies. Placating both the
Saudis and the Israelis would not be an easy task for U.S. leaders.
Indeed, as seen at Suez, American and Israeli interests could, it seemed,
more easily come into conflict than U.S.-Saudi relations.

In 1967, Israel again took up arms against its Arab enemies. For
some time, Palestinian guerrillas as well as regular forces in Syria had
been firing into Israel. The first indicators of Egyptian preparations for
an attack were received by Yitzhak Rabin, then a military commander,
in mid-May. Rabin, a quiet man with a dry wit, was born in Jerusalem.
When asked for his predictions about the future of Israel and events in
the region, he would reply, "Ask the rabbi, not the Rabin."

In New York City, while war clouds gathered in the Middle East,
life on the Jewish street followed its customary habits. Israel was close
in the heart but distant in terms of active involvement for most American Jews. The seventieth anniversary of the *Forward* newspaper, then
still a daily in Yiddish, was celebrated by a crowd of some 2,400, as
reported in the *New York Times*. One of the few to deliver a speech in
English was Arthur Goldberg, now U.S. ambassador to the United
Nations. Goldberg's affection for the *Forward* reflected his career as a
CIO labor attorney aligned with Dubinsky.

Israeli ambassador to the United States Avraham Harman, who
like many before and after him was something of a nonentity, praised
the *Forward* for its support for the Jewish state. Within a few days,
Rev. Martin Luther King Jr. announced a pilgrimage to the Holy Land
for later in the year, and 500 employees of the Development Corpo-

ration for Israel, retailer of Israel Bonds, with offices in New York and fifty-one other cities, had called a strike. That so important a Zionist asset would be caught up in a labor dispute on the eve of a Middle East confrontation further demonstrated how abstract, at times, the Israeli connection could seem to American Jews.

On May 16, the *Times* reported that Egyptian military forces had been put on a "war footing." Israeli troops were massed on their side of the border. Rumors had ballooned throughout the region of an impending clash. Egypt instituted a naval blockade of Israeli shipping at the straits of Tiran, which was the Jewish state's only access to the Red Sea.

Full-scale war broke out on June 5. On the first of the month, Israeli Labor Party prime minister Levi Eshkol, an immigrant from the tsarist empire to Palestine in 1914 and widely considered in decline as a political leader, had formed a national-unity administration. It included Menachem Begin, a veteran of the terrorist Irgun and an antisocialist conservative, as minister without portfolio, and the one-eyed Moshe Dayan, who was popular with the army's ranks, as defense minister. Eshkol, a dove, had attempted to avoid war, but Israel again faced Egypt, Jordan, and Syria, much as it had during the War of Independence. Rabin was reportedly surprised by the crisis, and to many American and other Gentiles, as well as Jews, Dayan became the favored hero of the moment.

Dayan was born on a *kibbutz* in Ottoman Palestine and at fourteen, around the time of the infamous Soviet-backed Arab anti-Jewish riots of 1929, joined the organized Zionist armed forces, the Haganah. Haganah protected Jewish settlements against Arab attacks—a defense effort widely supported by the European left during the 1930s, when the Arabs were disliked as allies of the Nazis. Dayan was arrested by the British when Haganah was banned in 1939, and spent two years in prison. He then joined the Allied forces in freeing Lebanon from control by the Nazi collaborationist Vichy regime in France. He lost his eye fighting in Lebanon.

Dayan's youthful commitment recapitulated the habits of teenage revolutionaries around the world. Militancy, prison, and armed struggle were their schools and universities. But fourteen-year-olds who join radical movements come in two varieties. Some precocious individuals are socialized in activist ranks, grow up, and move on to normal careers, typically in politics, journalism, or in Israel, the military. Dayan, like Henryk Erlich and Victor Alter before him, as well as the American author Jack London years before all of them, was of that kind. Dayan was also an artist and a lover of poetry. Others who are recruited young to political extremism fall into an amber-like environment in which they are preserved as undiluted fanatics for the rest of their lives. An exemplar of that destiny would be Ayman al-Zawahiri, the vicious lieutenant of Osama bin Laden, who joined an Egyptian Wahhabi cell at fifteen and could best be described as the Peter Pan of bloodthirsty terrorism, a nihilist who never grew up.

Dayan's charisma was famous, as was his courage. He told Shimon Peres, an Israeli Labor stalwart born in Belarus, that when he faced gunfire, he felt "as though I am in a kind of fog. And I am not afraid of fog." Peres wrote that in Dayan's early career Peres "believed that Dayan alone could breathe a new and much-needed fighting spirit into the army." But Dayan's flamboyance nearly caused Peres "a heart attack." In one incident, Peres was working in the Israeli Defense Ministry when he received a call from Ben-Gurion, who said Dayan was standing at an office balcony and firing a shotgun at random. Dayan explained that he had invited some friends for dinner and was shooting pigeons to serve his guests. In 1967, under Dayan's command, Israeli forces treated their work as a pigeon hunt. The Egyptian air force was destroyed in a wave of air raids, and Israeli troops seized the West Bank, Sinai, and the Golan Heights along the Syrian frontier.

In the most dramatic moment of the war, Israel attained control of the Old City of Jerusalem, with the sacred Temple Mount—site of the ancient Jewish Holy of Holies, but also the location of a Muslim religious complex, including the 1,300-year-old Dome of the Rock. On June 7, Eshkol announced that religious sites in the city that is a mother to monotheism would be administered on the basis of history rather than conquest. The Western Wall, the last survival of high, Roman-style outer barriers constructed around the Jewish temple by King Herod, would no longer be known by the demeaning title "Wailing Wall." It would be controlled by the two chief rabbis of Israel, Ashkenazi and Sephardic, representing the established rituals of Judaism. The Muslim structures would be governed by a council of Muslim *ulema,* or scholars, and Christian locations by a clerical council from the different communities of that tradition. Eshkol also praised Israel's Arabs, who "stood by Israel, as loyal citizens, both before and during the severe military test through which we passed." The Muslim holy places on the Temple Mount remain today under the administration of an Arab pious endowment, or *waqf.*

When Israel gained Jerusalem, much of the Western left sided with the Jewish state, just as liberal opinion made up the overwhelming majority in the active pro-Israel constituency in the United States. Since Israel, in this period, was continuously governed by the Labor Party, this made sense. Israel had never gained entrance to the portals of the so-called nonaligned movement, a vehicle that began under the auspices of Nasser and, after being driven around by Tito and other mediocrities, ended up in the hands of moribund and intellectually incoherent Latin American dictators such as Fidel Castro and the illiterate Venezuelan Hugo Chávez Frías. But the Israeli Labor Party maintained its membership in the more powerful Socialist International (SI), founded in the nineteenth century and leftist, but anti-Soviet. At the SI, Israeli Labor sits alongside the ruling party of Algeria, as well as leftist opposition parties from Albania, Bosnia and Herzegovina, Mali, Morocco, Tunisia, Pakistan, Malaysia—all majority-Muslim societies. Fatah, the backbone of the Palestine Liberation Organization, holds consultative status with the SI, and the global Socialist organization has occasionally played a minor role in Israeli-Arab negotiations.

But in 1967, Ben-Gurion had broken with Labor and Eshkol to form Rafi, a new force. Dayan, the young idol of millions inside and outside Israel, was a Rafi supporter. The prominent American personalities and institutions linked to the Israeli political establishment still mainly represented Jewish labor interests centered in New York; AIPAC, the Washington-based Israel lobby, was barely heard from. While the United Jewish Appeal and B'nai B'rith took the lead in collecting millions of dollars for Israel, New York mayor John V. Lindsay, a liberal Republican—like Jacob Javits, a product of the unmentionable dysfunction of the Jewish-Democratic marriage—appeared alongside a minor Israeli official as a key speaker at a massive rally called by the New York City Labor Council. Lindsay praised the Israelis, blasting the United Nations for its pusillanimity and the Arabs for provocative military actions.

Above all, in 1967 Israel was seen as an island of open, Western, and social democratic, if not socialist, values encircled by backward, oppressive, and obscurantist ideological regimes. This was an image that the lobbies—AJC, ADL, and AIPAC—worked hard to maintain in the decades that followed, in advertisements, opinion articles, speeches, and every other form of political advocacy. Israel as the sole democracy in the Middle East, which was more or less accurate considering the susceptibility of Turkey to military usurpation of power, became the basic trope in defining Israel's value to the West. This remained true even as the subsequent rise of the Israeli right indicated that Israel was becoming more "Middle Eastern" in its hardening.

The 1967 war differed from the Suez adventure in that Israel was victorious, but it also had outcomes that were not immediately understood. Israeli control of the West Bank of the Jordan, the war's main consequence, laid the basis for Jewish settlement in what was soon called, as in ancient times, Judea and Samaria, and which would become the main continuing source of Arab grievances. The West Bank had always been a demographic quicksand for the Jews. Inclusion of its Arabs in Israel could, within a couple of generations, reduce the Jews to a minority within the borders of the Jewish state. Earlier Israeli leaders had foreseen this danger and had avoided occupying the West Bank for precisely that reason.

The Israeli victory in 1967 therefore demonstrated conclusively that regardless of who won this or that battle, or even a major campaign, Israel's "Arab problem" would not be resolved easily, if at all. As Ben-Gurion commented in the mid-1940s, "We face a completely new situation. The Land of Israel is surrounded by independent Arab states . . . that have the right to purchase and produce arms, to set up armies and train them. . . . Attack by the Palestinian Arabs does not endanger [the Palestinian Jewish community], but there is a danger, that the neighboring Arab states will send their armies to attack and destroy [us]."

Reading such a statement decades later, one wonders how such a situation could have ever been considered really "new." The immense imbalance in population between Jews and Arabs in the Middle East had always existed, and always would. Unless one believed that the British and French, through direct colonialism, and the United States, through its energy industry, could forever maintain the Arabs in a state of dependency, the outcome described by Ben-Gurion was latent from the beginning of the Zionist movement. If anything, the peculiar dialectic of the Middle East dictated that the gains of Zionism would necessarily stimulate the rise of Arab nationalism and, later, Islamist extremism. This Israeli-Palestinian "mirror effect" had as much to do with an almost unconscious drive to emulate Israeli success as with victimization and anger among the Arabs.

More important in the immediate context, the Soviet Union in 1967 came out aggressively in favor of the Arabs, fulfilling trends that had been visible since Suez, if not before. Israeli president Eshkol told his country that on June 10, Russia, followed by Czechoslovakia and Bulgaria, Moscow's main foreign-policy tools in Eastern Europe, had broken relations with the Jewish state. A largely unnoticed augury of this turn had occurred in 1964, when the Palestine Liberation Organization (PLO) was established with the blessing of Nasser and Soviet patronage, including that of the tiny Soviet-oriented Communist movement in America. Indeed, the Stalinist "old left," although much reduced in influence, was the first political force in America to move from a public attitude of sympathy for Israel to a position holding that Arab complaints were more legitimate than Israeli claims.

Headed by a former Saudi diplomat, Ahmed Shukairy, the new PLO represented the first major step by Palestinians away from years of passivity interrupted only by border raids and other episodic terror actions typically subsidized by Saudi Arabia. Its core cadre was Fatah, the Movement for Liberation of the Palestinian Nation, created by Yasir Arafat in 1959. Its Arabic name is a reverse acronym: it should be abbreviated as HATEF, which sounds like the Arabic word for "death" and was considered unlucky. It included numerous Arab Christians, and its ideology was Nasser's "Arab Socialism," which appeared Soviet-inspired on paper but never moved on to collectivization or related Stalinist-style measures.

In Russia, crude Jew-baiting reminiscent of tsarist times, of a kind that had been absent even during the Stalin-Hitler pact, reappeared in official media. Communism worldwide—including ruling parties in Poland and other Communist states with significant Jewish minorities—expelled Jewish members, or made them irrelevant. The Russians then cut off Jewish emigration to Israel. Those measures inevitably drew new attention to the plight of Russian Jews, who once more were subjected to oppressive quotas in education and other forms of discrimination, six decades after the end of the tsarist epoch. Western interest in the abuse of Russian Jews had last revived, briefly, at the end of the Stalinist era. Then the Jewish Communist leadership in Soviet East Europe had been massacred, and in 1953 a weird "Doctors' Plot" had been fabricated in Moscow to justify an intended mass deportation of Russian Jews to Siberia, a break with the Western left, a new political alignment between Moscow and German and other neo-Nazis, and war on the United States.

The American Jewish leadership and its main media allies had acquitted themselves well at that time. The ADL issued a twenty-page report dealing with the purge trial of Jewish and other Czechoslovak Communist leaders, which ended with the hanging of several among them. The *New York Times* thundered against Soviet anti-Semitism. The West took no action to impede the purges and murders taking place in the Communist states but prepared itself for a possible new war with Russia, like that launched by the North Koreans in 1950.

Then, almost miraculously, Stalin died, the doctors were freed, and Soviet Jew-hatred receded . . . temporarily. Judeophobia never fully loses its grip on the Russian mind.

In the late 1960s and early 1970s, however, the martyrdom of Soviet Jews produced a solidarity movement in the United States that gained some backing from the traditional lobby groups, such as AJC and ADL, but much more reflected youthful, activist discontent with *shtadlan* reluctance to engage with the issue. The campaign for Soviet Jews coalesced in a new group, the National Conference on Soviet Jewry (NCSJ), founded in 1971.

The movement to assist Soviet Jews also had a problem with the most successful *shtadlan* Jew of the twentieth century, Henry Kissinger. As President Richard Nixon's national security adviser, Kissinger had influenced the president toward a discreet but nonetheless sympathetic posture toward Israel, although his fame was more associated with diplomacy toward China than in the Middle East. Still, Kissinger was an exponent of big-power realism. Nixon and Kissinger correctly saw that Israel could be useful in fighting Soviet influence, but both men were inclined to accommodate Soviet power when they thought it would support global order. For them, Israel was a tool, not an end in itself; Kissinger did not evince much familial love for the Jewish people that produced him, or for the state that incarnated their hopes. The aim of the Nixon-Kissinger policy was to integrate Israel into American policy, rather than to enable the Jewish state to pursue its own agenda.

Kissinger therefore was displeased when, in 1974, Democratic senator Henry "Scoop" Jackson of Washington state introduced the Jackson-Vanik amendment into Congress. Jackson-Vanik barred regular trade with any country that impeded emigration, and was applied to restrict improvement in U.S.-Soviet commercial relations unless Kremlin-ordered limits on Jewish departures to Israel were relaxed. The amendment was a solid blow to the Moscow regime, since repeated failures of Soviet-style agriculture, in a land that had exported grain for centuries until the Bolshevik takeover, forced the Russians to purchase food supplies in the United States. Jackson was

more a Social Democrat than a typical liberal, and became another
Gentile who, in the Truman mold, made himself an outstanding
advocate for Jewish issues.

With this development, the Jews reached the highest level of
American policy making in sixty years. Jackson-Vanik marked the first
time since 1912 that a Jewish issue—once again, that of conditions in
Russia—had explicitly set the agenda for U.S. relations not only with
a major power but with *the* major power apart from the United States:
the Soviet Union. Regardless of Jew-baiting legends, U.S. relations
with tsarist Russia, Nazi Germany, and the Arab countries had rarely
been predicated on Jewish well-being. But Jackson-Vanik, like so
many efforts before it, was the product of action by angry, ordinary
Jews in the street, rather than the lobbies.

American Jewish and Gentile outrage over the denial of dignity
suffered by Soviet Jews did something the cause of Israel alone had
not, and which Jews had not experienced since the 1930s: it newly rallied a major share of Gentile opinion. Senator Jackson also attracted
a group of Jewish and Gentile allies, most of whom were Democrats
like himself but who favored a hard line against the Soviets. These
were the group who became known as the neoconservatives, including Norman Podhoretz, originally a literary critic, and his wife, Midge
Decter; political scientist Jeane Kirkpatrick, who is not Jewish; and
others whose trajectory had begun in the general area of activist liberalism. Some of the neoconservatives, such as the accomplished
political journalist Irving Kristol, had been Trotskyists in the late 1930s
and were pioneers in the journey away from radical leftism. Younger
Jackson protégés with no history in radical politics included Paul D.
Wolfowitz and Richard Perle, then minor figures in the American
defense and diplomatic establishment.

It could be described as a stroke of grim luck for American Jews
and for Israel that the Russians decided on a course of brutal ethnic
repression. An unperceived cycle had closed. Israeli defeat at Suez,
which helped resuscitate Soviet influence worldwide, was succeeded
by Israeli triumph, which helped bring Soviet tyranny down. Soon
after Jackson-Vanik passed, President Jimmy Carter was elected and

became a firm backer of the movement for the rights of Soviet Jews. Carter's views appeared to be reinforced by his anger over the Russian invasion of Afghanistan. In an example of historical irony, Jews and Muslims shared a main enemy in Communist Russia, although nobody noticed or mentioned it at the time. Yet while Jackson and Carter would seem to epitomize how good the Democratic alliance could be for the Jews, the New Deal marriage was already in serious trouble.

CHAPTER 4

ESTRANGEMENT

The Agony of the Jewish-Democratic Marriage

The unraveling of the Jewish-Democratic relationship, and the emergence of a new "third force"—the neoconservative intellectuals, who were neither favored children of the New Deal alliance nor functionaries of the Jewish and Israel lobbies—began not in Washington but in the place where the marriage was first consummated: New York City.

The sources of alienation among the political kindred were various. Mainly, the Democrats did not become a party of universal democratic values: genuine equality, common American aspirations, efficient economic guidance, or secure social benefits. Rather, they continued to be what they had always been: a network of urban political machines and what would come to be known as "special interest groups." In the New Deal the Roosevelt administration had crafted an unnatural coalition, joining midwestern and western Progressives and national labor leaders to racist southern white politicians. The latter ruled on a foundation of voting corruption and naked intimidation, but their constituency comprised some of the poorest folk in the country. These disparate elements were drawn together by the urgency of national recovery and Roosevelt's political talent in offering ambitious solutions. Conservatives have condemned Roosevelt for crafting a welfare state, but unlike the proponents of socialism and communism, most New Dealers did not see state intervention in the economy and society as an end in itself. As for the southern Democrats, notwithstanding its debt to this political arm of the white ruling caste, the New Deal held out hope of progress for African Americans. But the distance between these two components of the coalition was never bridged, and in the Truman era the hard core of southern whites began a march away from their Democratic heritage. They would later be brought more widely into the Republican fold by Nixon's "southern strategy."

The Jews of New York had been induced to join this experiment in political polygamy in fulfillment of the universalist ideals most Jews cherished. What was good for the whole of society, they correctly believed, was good for the Jews. But regardless of their attraction to Roosevelt, they had never been completely happy with the arrangement. The Liberal Party slate, the New Deal's successor to the old Socialist movement, remained closer to the Republicans than to the Democrats in New York City, even when Jews voted in their majority for Democratic presidential candidates. New York Jews would, for example, vote for Democratic national and state candidates while supporting a Republican and Liberal Party candidate such as Lindsay for mayor in the early 1960s.

The shadow of Tammany, the disreputable Irish machine, could not be evaded. The Democrats in New York City never shook loose of their heritage of corruption and a style of ethnic patronage Jews found repellent. Jews did not easily accept that they should trade votes in municipal elections for special favors on the Tammany model. But through their history, the Democrats could only offer rewards for ballots, to successive constituencies: to the southern poor and their demagogic politicians, to the ruined midwestern farmers, the insurgent unions, and various ethnic communities—including the Jews. But

most American Jews wanted something different from mere fulfillment of a special, "tribal" agenda, and always had: they sought genuine respect for religious and ethnic differences among all citizens.

The late sociologist Milton Himmelfarb memorably defined the
Jewish dilemma, at the height of the Democrats' ascendancy, as follows: "Jews earn like Episcopalians but vote like Puerto Ricans." But
throughout modern Jewish history, the question persisted: What *is*
good for the Jews, and more to the point, who decides? Uniquely
among the nations, at least since the early nineteenth century, the
great majority have hoped for the disappearance of any need for a
program of Jewish demands, rather than the mere satisfaction of their
own political interests.

Though Jews are viewed by some Gentiles as clannish, insular,
exclusive, and particularist, most American Jews are egalitarian and
generous in their commitment to broader American goals and principles. The political labels have changed from Socialist to Democratic
to liberal, but the sensibility has remained. The permanent tension
between the *shtadlan* habits of the elite and activism on the Jewish
street, whether involving the confrontation with Coughlinites and
America First, the founding of Israel, civil rights protests in the
South, or solidarity with Soviet Jews, reflects the permanent conflict
among Jews between particularist and universalist values. The Jewish
insistence on fairness, and the dissolution of group separatism, was
seen in the avid involvement of numerous Jewish youth from northern cities in the southern civil rights movement of the 1950s and
1960s. Few of the Jewish activists who joined the voting-rights campaigns in the deep South would say they entered the struggle in emulation of their radical forebears, or even as an expression of uniquely
Jewish values. By the 1950s and early 1960s the appeal of ideological
socialism had greatly declined for American Jews, who had largely
moved up into the middle class and out to the suburbs. Yet a Jewish
identification with some kind of social idealism endured. These highly
assimilated, relatively affluent young Jews saw themselves as uphold-
ing an *American* principle, that of equal opportunity, in the civil rights
campaign.

Indeed, this involvement in the civil rights movement of the 1960s, rather than the New Deal, should stand as the moral and emotional high point of American Jewish history. How, for example, can anyone who lived through that time forget the sacrifice of blood by Jewish activists such as Mickey Schwerner, twenty-four, and Andrew Goodman, twenty, slain by the Ku Klux Klan in the infamous "Mississippi Burning" case? Schwerner and Goodman were kidnapped and killed along with James Chaney, twenty-two, a black resident of Meridian, Mississippi. The terrible crime sent a wave of fear and horror through the national liberal and left-wing milieu that supported the civil rights movement.

All over America, thousands of young men and women, many no older than seventeen-year-old Herschel Grynszpan, were also prepared to head south. With secure and promising lives ahead of them, they volunteered to assist disadvantaged and terrorized southern blacks against the most violent and heartless extremist movement America had ever seen—the revived KKK of the 1960s—which further enjoyed the protection of state authorities and local police. As secular Jews, Schwerner and Goodman may never have considered the principles of justice embodied in the faith of Abraham, Isaac, and Jacob. They may never have imagined the fear and courage of the armed Jewish Socialists who defended their communities against the terror of the Russian tsars. But they followed the same path, affirming righteousness and justice for all humanity.

Among Jews themselves, neither of the competing definitions of what's good for the Jews—particularism or universalism—has prevailed. A narrow Jewish agenda has never been thoroughly elaborated in America. If the *shtadlan* lobbies and the socialist agitators differed in their methods, their essential aim was finally the same: the fulfillment of democratic principles. Even the Zionists, though fighting for a Jewish national home, did so less on the basis of particularist than universalist values; they wanted equality among the nations rather than a special status. That was why so much Israeli energy was expended in secular and collectivist projects, rather than reinforcement of Jewish religiosity.

The Jewish-Democratic alliance could never resolve the Jewish contradiction by fostering a sense of America as a successful melting pot, because they kept too many political pots boiling to effectively combine their contents. The shortsightedness in the Democrats' political vision was shockingly exposed in the North just at the time when Jewish labor and the domestic Jewish lobbies, ADL and AJC, were most committed to assisting the African American battle for equal rights in the South. Simultaneous with the southern civil rights movement, the paths of Jews and blacks in New York diverged sharply, beginning a convulsive period that would lead to a deep division between the two communities and the rise of a corrosive black anti-Semitism.

In the late 1950s and early 1960s, the black-Jewish alliance was at its peak. African American intellectuals such as James Baldwin wrote for *Commentary,* the monthly of the American Jewish Committee. A. Philip Randolph and Bayard Rustin, the trusted advisers of Rev. Martin Luther King Jr., were affiliated with anti-Communist Jewish union leaders.

But a traumatic rift opened up in the civil rights alliance as the more militant and separatist rhetoric of the nascent Black Power movement came to dominate the urban African American communities. This conflict emerged as early as 1963, when African American parents in New York organized a boycott of public schools, demanding their full integration through busing of white students to Harlem schools, as ordered by state authorities. Jewish and other white parents were as vociferous in their opposition to busing their children as black parents were in demanding what they called "desegregation."

The Harlem school boycott was the beginning of the long agony not just in the black-Jewish alliance but in the Jewish-Democratic marriage as a whole. Liberal leader Dore Schary, then head of ADL, accurately assessed the problem when he explained that racial imbalance in education was something "northern liberals have been able to contemplate from afar as a circumstance that hadn't affected them. Now it's here." The Liberal Party, backed by Dubinsky's garment workers, opposed busing of students to achieve "instant integration," and predicted it would impede the process of integration by inducing white parents to take their children out of the public schools. Norman Podhoretz, then editor of *Commentary,* said he personally backed the Harlem parents' boycott as "a sort of ritualistic gesture of protest." But he warned, "Any effort to relocate white kids by busing or otherwise will meet massive resistance by parents, including liberals."

Although Podhoretz would not have known it at the time, his comments serve as a historical starting point for the open emergence of neoconservatism: a movement affirming universal, humanistic, and liberal values but sharply critical of the means employed by the Democrats, and the demagogues to whom they have catered, in their alleged fulfillment.

The controversy over busing in Harlem brought a new personality to the forefront of American Jewish affairs. It also anticipated the reemergence of another figure, previously mentioned, but heretofore typically unacknowledged as a significant actor. The first was Albert Shanker (1928–97), elected secretary of New York's United Federation of Teachers (UFT) in 1962. The second was Max Shachtman (1904–72), James Burnham's companion as a Trotskyist agitator in confronting the Nazi Bund in the late 1930s. Shachtman's wife, Yetta Barshevsky, better known as Yetta Barsh, became Shanker's indispensable assistant at the UFT.

In 1961 the union had been granted collective bargaining representation for the city's teachers—the first time American school employees gained labor negotiating rights. Since the 1930s the majority of New York teachers had been Jews. And among the Jewish teachers, most, like the previously described liberal parents, found themselves caught between sympathy for African American demands and the grim daily reality of Jew-baiting and physical danger from black students. This would not be a happy situation for Shanker, who prided himself on his uncompromising defense of teacher rights. His manner was so abrasive that he became famous for, and proud of, a wisecrack by Woody Allen, in his 1973 futuristic movie *Sleeper,* that human civilization was devastated when "a man named Albert Shanker got hold of a nuclear warhead."

Shanker was born on Manhattan's Lower East Side and became an anti-Communist socialist, as a Columbia University graduate student enlisting in the Student League for Industrial Democracy, a moderate Socialist group that would be transformed into the radicalizing Students for a Democratic Society in the sixties. Shanker moved in a direction opposite that of SDS founders such as Tom Hayden, later known as "Mr. Jane Fonda" and a pillar of the ultraleft wing of the Democratic Party. Shanker joined the Yipsels, which had survived under the tutelage of the dissident Trotskyist Shachtman. Earlier, while studying at the University of Illinois at Urbana-Champaign in the late 1940s, he also joined the Congress of Racial Equality (CORE).

CORE organized climactic Freedom Rides to the South at the beginning of the 1960s, in which young whites and blacks together challenged the segregation of interstate bus transport and public accommodations. Freedom Riders were beaten and jailed, and their buses burned, by angry white mobs. CORE was also the organization to which Schwerner, Chaney, and Goodman belonged, and, in the North, it was no less strident in its militancy than Shanker was in teacher advocacy. When Shanker joined CORE in his college years, it was loathed by the Communists as a "Trotskyite-infiltrated" group, and the Freedom Rides of the 1960s were considered a radical challenge to the Democratic administration of John F. Kennedy to prove his party's repeatedly declared support for civil rights.*

Shanker rose to lead the New York Federation of Teachers in his mid-thirties. With Yetta Barsh Shachtman as his confidante, Shanker installed a Shachtmanite cell at the top of the union. Other members included Tom Kahn, who joined the Shachtmanites at seventeen, in

---

* The historian Ronald Radosh, who began as a Stalinist and became anti-Communist after publishing a study of the Julius and Ethel Rosenberg spy case, *The Rosenberg File*, in 1983, recalls that in the early 1960s he wrote an attack on CORE, while the group was leading the Freedom Rides, for harboring the anti-Communist socialists.

1956, when their adult cadre, the Independent Socialist League (ISL), still appeared on the U.S. attorney general's list of subversive organizations. (The ISL was dropped from the list, after extensive legal efforts on its behalf, the next year.) Kahn, when he died in 1992, was international affairs director of the AFL-CIO, after being a speechwriter for prominent figures, including autoworkers leader Walter Reuther; Hubert Humphrey, a long-serving anti-Communist liberal; Rev. Martin Luther King Jr.; and "Scoop" Jackson. Colonization of the teachers' union by the Shachtman group coincided with the end of Shachtmanism as a revolutionary movement and its achievement of influence in the mainstream unions and the Democratic Party.

It was an extraordinary chapter in the history of American radicalism. No other group underwent a long existence, unknown or marginal from 1940 to 1960, only to unpredictably emerge as a major power without a battle for recognition. Every other tendency in the chronicles of American socialism and anarchism had either sunk into oblivion or worked steadily to gain a position of prominence. Examples of the former included the Socialist Labor Party, founded at the end of the nineteenth century by a Sephardic Jew, Daniel De Leon; the Industrial Workers of the World, the fabled "Wobblies," who organized unionists all over the country, but especially in the mines, lumber industry, and maritime trades of the Far West; and the Soviet-line Communists, who never recovered from their political devastation in the 1950s. In contrast, as we have seen, the Jewish Socialists gained unique success in an uneasy alliance with the New Deal Democrats. The meteoric appearance of Shachtman's tiny group as a national political factor was accomplished only because of his personal tenacity and brilliant understanding of politics, both of which remained undiluted through decades in which he was ignored everywhere except among a few New York radicals.

As noted in Chapter 2, Shachtman had remained within the wider left-wing milieu while James Burnham, his fellow dissenter from "official" Trotskyism, departed socialist politics. Burnham followed a path that could be described as "capitalist revolutionism." He was a New York University philosophy professor with elegant manners.

Trotsky's personal secretary in his last years, Jean van Heijenoort, recalled his surprise when he was invited, as a fellow revolutionary militant, to dinner at Burnham's Manhattan apartment, where candles adorned the table.

Burnham gained great but temporary fame with his 1941 book, *The Managerial Revolution,* analyzing the ascendancy of administrative elites in modern society. Burnham argued that, rather than the coming of a liberating social revolution, the 1930s had seen the rise of managerial strata represented by the American class of business administrators, Nazi state bureaucrats, and Stalinist commissars. He was also among the first to predict the onset of the Cold War. In a series of subsequent volumes with such compelling titles as *The Struggle for the World* and *Containment or Liberation?* Burnham called for the United States to undertake an offensive against Communist encroachment, using its military power to free the prisoners of the Soviet gulag, among other ambitious goals. Through some of this period, Burnham was an outstanding Gentile figure in the generally Jewish milieu of *Partisan Review* and a significant forerunner of the neoconservatives.

The former Communist Burnham ended up as a leading member of William F. Buckley Jr.'s founding group at the conservative magazine *National Review*. In Buckley's shadow, he occasionally sparkled, although Buckley favored another ex-revolutionary, the former Stalinist Frank S. Meyer, over Burnham. Elderly *National Review* staff have described with a certain glee how, in editorial debates at the magazine, Meyer's Stalinist insistence on realism in the pursuit of American interests would inevitably trump Burnham's Trotskyist insistence on the power of ideals. Meyer, it is inferred, was a cynic who remained a Stalinist in his psychology. It is unsurprising that *National Review,* representing traditional conservatism, would express a preference for Stalinism over Trotskyism, even though they hired more veterans of the latter than the former. Burnham was joined at *National Review* by another ex-comrade, Suzanne La Follette, who piquantly enough retained some copyrights to Trotskyist material until her death, and by Willmoore Kendall, an early enthusiast of the philosopher Leo Strauss, who had become anti-Communist much as Orwell did, because of his experience in the Spanish Civil War. Burnham died in 1987, having received the Presidential Medal of Freedom from Ronald Reagan in 1983.

Max Shachtman, a childhood immigrant from tsarist-ruled Poland, was of a completely different type, an agitator and organizer from the early Leninist cadre in America, who served as a leading labor journalist and Trotskyist theoretician. He was personally close to Trotsky, having been one of the first and most prominent American Communists to join his dissident movement. Gifted as a writer and speaker, Shachtman accompanied Trotsky on his arrival in Mexican exile from Norway in 1937. After Trotsky's assassination in 1940, Shachtman, although outside the "official" movement, remained close to Trotsky's widow, Natalia Sedova, who like Shachtman also left the Trotskyist movement after her husband's assassination.

Notwithstanding the break with Trotsky, Shachtman kept most of his revolutionary socialist partisans—and their commitment to that ideal—intact. A great many of the Shachtmanites were Jewish; Trotsky himself had been accused of Jew-baiting when, during the internal dissension in the movement preceding his murder, he sneeringly referred to Shachtman's followers as residents of the Bronx, that is, Jews isolated from the mainstream of American society. Trotsky might well have been surprised by the ultimate destiny of the Shachtmanites in reaching the heights of American power. Or he might not. Given that Trotsky sympathized with religious Judaism and Zionism at the end of his life and viewed America in extremely benign terms, it is not impossible that the old man himself might have become a kind of proto-neoconservative. Trotsky was only sixty when he was assassinated, and had he lived twenty years more he would have seen great changes in the world that doubtless would have affected his views. Already in 1939, he predicted a victorious America could reorganize the German economy and become a "very good" global hegemonic power after the Second World War. His widow condemned Communist aggression in the Korean War, and it is tantalizing to imagine how Trotsky and other Bolshevik intellectuals would have reacted to the birth of Israel, the rise of American consumer society, the Tito-Stalin split, and similar events. Shachtman, who was not much less brilliant, certainly evolved in his outlook.

By 1962, it was clear that Sovietism had won the day in the international radical Left. Shachtman and other persistent anti-Stalinists hoped that a new proletarian revolutionary wave would sweep Stalinism aside. But instead of such fresh movements and intellectuals appearing on the horizon, the decade from 1956 to 1966 saw mediocrities such as Nasser and Castro and bloody mass murderers such as Mao Zedong gain the adulation of radical youth. Further, the proletariat as a class, meaning a superexploited and impoverished stratum of factory workers, had disappeared from the Western nations; soon the factories themselves would also vanish. Trotsky himself had warned that if the Second World War did not produce a new upsurge of antitotalitarian socialism, then socialism would have to be considered a utopian fantasy and abandoned—although he also insisted that oppression and exploitation would continue to exist, and that idealistic rebels would have to formulate a new program to oppose them. Trotsky was, of course, largely correct. The old socialism was obsolete, industrial workers no longer looked to revolution as a solution, and labor movements increasingly turned to professionals and government employees in their organizing campaigns.

Shachtman appears to have understood all this, then crafted an alliance that allowed his group to enter the AFL-CIO leadership. This led them inevitably into the arms of the Democratic Party in a spectral reenactment of the original New Deal nuptials. Shachtman's peers and supporters aside from Yetta Barsh and Tom Kahn were hired by numerous anti-Stalinist unions and such related enterprises as the International Rescue Committee (IRC). The IRC had begun by assisting antifascist intellectuals, many of them Jewish, to escape Europe in 1940, and it went on to provide relief for anti-Communist refugees, including Hungarian rebels in 1956 and Tibetan insurgents against Chinese rule, then to general international humanitarian assistance. The IRC was the epitome of antifascism that became anti-Communism out of consistent antitotalitarianism. The path from rescuing antifascists in 1940 to saving anti-Communists two decades later paralleled that followed by Dubinsky and the Jewish Social Democrats as well as Shachtman.

Shachtman himself was viewed with alarm and contempt by the nascent New Left when he moved decisively toward an alliance with U.S. power. Just then young radicals were preparing, at least in their own minds, a new "anti-imperialist" revolt against their own country. While the New Left was hypnotized by the youthful machismo of Castro and his colleagues, who had more in common with Marlon Brando, James Dean, and Elvis Presley than with Marx, Lenin, and Trotsky, Shachtman came out after 1962 as a supporter of the Vietnam War and the removal of Castro. In both cases, Shachtman, still a revolutionary, called for radical opposition to regimes that had suppressed Trotskyists, with special brutality in the Vietnamese instance. Throughout the 1930s and 1940s Trotskyists had led Saigon's struggle for independence from France and then Japan. But with the Communist seizure of power in Vietnam in 1945, hundreds of anti-Stalinists were brutally murdered. Shachtman's position for American intervention to turn back the advance of Communism in Indochina was adopted at a moment when the AFL-CIO overwhelmingly backed such a foreign policy.

The ideological left in the United States preferred to ignore Shachtman's turn, rather than to concentrate too much attention on it and contribute to his importance. A practical labor leader such as Al Shanker was different. Yetta Barsh, Shachtman's wife and Shanker's brain, was a powerful personality in her own right. On her death in 1996, Saul Bellow recalled that she had introduced him to Trotsky's electrifying anti-Stalinist writings. But, he concluded, "I entered into Yetta's enthusiasms for Yetta's sake, for her importance to me was very great. She was one of those persons who draw you into their lives and also install themselves in yours. Even the small genetic accident that made one of her eyes seem oddly placed added warmth and sadness to her look. She always seemed to me to have a significant sort of Jewish beauty. . . . There is something radically mysterious in the specificity of another human being which everybody somehow responds to. Love is not a bad word for this response."

Notwithstanding the shocking nature, to many leftists, of Shachtman's new attitude toward America's role in the world, he and his followers had been slow to give up their association with radical socialism. Burnham and Irving Kristol were more audacious, if not the boldest among the New York intellectuals, in breaking a path from Trotskyism to support for American foreign policy. They and others like them entered the lists for the American center-right earlier in the Cold War while remaining in some degree sentimental about their left-wing origins.

Indeed, Burnham, Shachtman, Kristol, Bellow, and others in a certain sense did not renounce their pasts. They acknowledged that they had evolved quite dramatically away from their earlier enthusiasms. But they did not apologize, did not grovel, did not crawl and beg forgiveness for having at one time been stirred by the figure of Trotsky. In an oft-cited quote dating from 1995, Kristol had praised the internal debates that characterized the Trotskyist milieu: "I have never since seen or heard their equal, and, as a learning experience for college students, they were beyond comparison." There was nothing accidental in a leftist faction with a propensity for such discussion, especially in contrast with the rigid conformism of the Stalinist movement, stimulating some of its participants to a wider skepticism.

That skepticism came to public light in the matter of the Harlem school boycott of 1963, as well as in subsequent contentions that rocked New York—especially Jewish New York. For many New York Jews, the public schools, along with the social service bureaucracies, were ideal places of employment. Their heritage of reading, their belief in the benefits of education, and their commitment to public service were all embodied in the teaching profession. In Jewish families, teaching was considered a prestigious calling.

Samuel G. Freedman, an outstanding commentator on contemporary American Jews, has written that "the history and the mythology of New York's public schools would be inconceivable without the decisive presence of Jewish educators. Barely one generation after the

newly consolidated city created a unified school system in 1898, multitudes of Jewish women began entering the teaching profession. . . .
During the Great Depression, Jewish men actually outpaced women
in seeking jobs in the high schools. The municipal colleges that produced many teachers—Brooklyn, City, Hunter—were nearly 80 percent Jewish in the thirties. . . . Jewish teachers personified New York
schools during the thirties, forties, and fifties, the decades that form
the Belle Epoque of public education" in New York.

The "Belle Epoque" ended with the labor ructions that increased
Shanker's fearsome (to some) stature and pushed intellectuals such as
Podhoretz closer toward neoconservatism. In 1964, Shanker was
elected president of the UFT. Notwithstanding their pro-American
attitudes in foreign policy, he and his Shachtmanite cohort maintained a "confrontational, outsider image" on labor issues, according
to Jerald E. Podair, a historian of the 1968 Ocean Hill–Brownsville
(Brooklyn) school strike, which became a disastrous racial confrontation. In this respect, Shanker was much like Dubinsky, Walter
Reuther of the United Auto Workers, and the leaders of the Sailors'
Union of the Pacific, on the West Coast, who hated the Stalinists but
also outdid them in labor aggressivity. Shanker's union struck the
New York school system for three weeks in 1967, demanding smaller
classes and more spending on education. The strike was joined by
47,000 employees out of a total payroll of 60,000, and it won
improvements in pay and conditions. By New York law, teachers were
public employees without the right to strike, and Shanker spent two
weeks in jail—not the last such experience for him. The union still
enjoyed the full backing of the local labor movement, which saw
Shanker's imprisonment as a violation of workers' liberties.

Quoted in the *New York Times*, however, Shanker eloquently summarized a shift in attitude among the teachers (Jewish and other)
under his command: 1967 had seen the end of "the image of the good
old dedicated teacher who gets kicked around and once a year, on
Teacher Recognition Day, is handed a flower for his lapel." Instead,
under Shanker, the UFT was now more a continuous uprising than a
mere union; Shanker and his Shachtmanite associates were leading

one of the great American strike campaigns. Furthermore, the New
York teachers' strikes marked the unperceived turning point in the
history of the American worker, when the center of gravity of trade
unionism shifted from industrial labor to public employees. But
Shanker's partisans were destined to clash repeatedly and ferociously
with African American parents, aggravating the rift in New York's
New Deal coalition. Shanker was not about to let his members be
intimidated either by demagogy among black school officials and parents or by lawlessness among students. He protested that "a sort of
hoodlum element" had taken over more than a score of public schools
in Harlem, the Bronx, and Bedford-Stuyvesant—all neighborhoods
then known as concentrations of poor blacks. The union leader
referred less to disruptive pupils than to extremist African American
school administrators.

One such facility specifically mentioned by Shanker was Inter-
mediate School 201 in East Harlem, which in February 1968 held an
antiwhite memorial for the slain black nationalist Malcolm X. The
presentation at I.S. 201 was led by the race-baiting poet LeRoi Jones,
who renamed himself Imamu Amiri Baraka—a meaningless pseudo-
Arabic jumble that could be translated as "prayer leader commander
of blessings." Herman Ferguson, an African American assistant school
principal, used the I.S. 201 observance to call on blacks to take up
arms against whites and prepare for "hunting season." Ferguson had
been suspended from his post at a Queens public school the previous
summer on allegations that he plotted to murder moderate black
leaders. But he had become a paid adviser to the I.S. 201 governing
board, under a grant from the Ford Foundation. Among school-
teachers and, implicitly, among schoolchildren, the New York–New
Deal coalition appeared to be in its death throes. In a development
that forcefully expressed the extent of the crisis, CORE, of which
Shanker had been a member, now faced him and his union from the
other side of the barricades.

Resentment between the two sides was sharpened by the murder
of Martin Luther King Jr. in April 1968. The shooting sparked riots
and widespread destruction in urban black neighborhoods around

the country. The following month, the governing board of the Ocean Hill–Brownsville special school district in Brooklyn, which had an African American majority, ordered the dismissal of thirteen teachers and six staffers. The fired personnel refused to leave their jobs. One of them was Fred Nauman, a science instructor at Junior High School 271.

Shanker and the UFT supported the Board of Education in condemning the termination of Nauman and others, whose only offense was their white race, as a violation of school employees' right to due process, specified in their union contract. Shanker further threatened to pull all teachers out on strike in Brooklyn. Ocean Hill–Brownsville became the scene of a near-insurrection as parents, supported by a rival to UFT, the African-American Teachers Association (ATA), occupied the school to prevent the fired teachers from resuming their work. Mayor Lindsay sent police to J.H.S. 271 to keep order. Soon, 350 teachers who supported their dismissed colleagues walked out of eight schools in Ocean Hill-Brownsville.

The radicalized African American parents called for "community control" of schools, regardless of the rights of teachers. "Community control" was de facto segregation. In a grotesque paradox, while blacks in the South sought integration with white society, black extremists in the North demanded separation. The blacks who blockaded J.H.S. 271 to prevent the teachers from returning to the building mirrored segregationist Alabama governor George C. Wallace, who had "stood in the schoolhouse door" at the University of Alabama in 1963 to prevent the entry of African American students. There was and remains, however, a significant difference: Wallace eventually apologized. None of the black militants in Ocean Hill–Brownsville ever apologized. Furthermore, Wallace was defiant in his racism but polite in his language, while the black radicals in Brooklyn were unrestrainedly vile in their Jew-baiting. There was yet another difference: federal marshals pushed Wallace aside, while in Brooklyn, Lindsay's police backed off and told Nauman and his colleagues they would not teach.

But the black racists of Brooklyn were dealing with Shanker, not with a patient apostle of passive resistance such as Dr. Martin Luther

King Jr. When a compromise plan was proposed to the UFT leader, under which the dismissed instructors would return to the school but not teach, Shanker reportedly replied, "Fuck you. I want those teachers in the classrooms now."

The confrontation festered as school authorities grew ever more reluctant to support either side, and Shanker called a series of further strikes. By the end of September 1968, 110 teachers' positions were still at issue in Ocean Hill–Brownsville, and proposals for their return to work included their protection by police officers. When they reported to their jobs, many described an atmosphere of insults, cursing, threats, and mob scenes directed against them. The UFT soon walked out again, shutting down the whole New York system and leaving a million pupils out of school, as Shanker demanded the removal of the Ocean Hill–Brownsville school board.

Shanker, his members, and his organization were accused of racism. Shanker himself defined the 1968 walkouts as seeking "to protect black teachers against white racists and white teachers against black racists." The union once more returned to work and the dismissed teachers were eventually rehired. As a subtext, however, the Ocean Hill–Brownsville chaos posed, above all, the question of what was good for the Jews. Reading the account of Jerald Podair, it is clear that black parents sought a separatist identity and rejected Jewish universalism as a swindle. A black instructor and ATA member, Leslie Campbell, later known as Jitu Weusi, had participated in the black hate rally at I.S. 201 and was then transferred out of his teaching job, charged with insubordination and misconduct. Campbell took to the airwaves of WBAI-FM, the city's premier leftist radio station. Hosted by then-militant black advocate Julius Lester, who later converted to Judaism, Campbell read a poem written by a black pupil from Brownsville and dedicated to Shanker:

Hey, Jew boy, with that yarmulke on your head
You pale-faced Jewboy, I wish you were dead.

Lester himself, as noted, would soon enough become a non-pale-faced Jewboy, and Shanker, a secularist and socialist, was hardly known for wearing a yarmulke. But established Jewish opinion in New York seemed paralyzed with horror at this spectacle (as they also were years later by the murder of Australian rabbinical student Yankel Rosenbaum by a black mob in the Crown Heights section of Brooklyn). Aside from later criticizing Campbell, ADL, which maintains a reputation for actively monitoring outbreaks of Jew-baiting, had little to say about the Ocean Hill–Brownsville war, except to issue a report bemoaning realities everybody already knew existed. ADL noted that black anti-Jewish prejudice had reached critical proportions and was aggravated by the incapacity of Mayor Lindsay and other representatives of the Gentile elite to confront black racism. AJC also remained passive about the collision between Jews and blacks, teachers and parents, union solidarity and racial polarization. The *shtadlan* Jewish advocates seemed less motivated by their traditional caution than by shock, lack of direct contact with the reality of life among New York blacks, and fear of being perceived as bigoted. But how, they asked themselves, could an oppressed people for whom Jews had done so much act in this manner?

Aside from black racism, the school convulsions in New York embodied another issue troubling to Jews: that of quotas in hiring African American teachers and principals. To Jews, quotas for minority jobs to erase past injustices could not be distinguished from the onerous limitations on Jewish entry into schools and other institutions that had been a major grievance in tsarist Russia and a serious problem in Gentile America before World War II. Unfortunately, significant elements of the New York Gentile upper bourgeois classes favored quotas for blacks as a means to "instant integration."

Richard D. Kahlenberg, Shanker's biographer, has noted that "the left," which for Kahlenberg included the *New York Times* as well as the *Village Voice* and the ACLU, joined "business elites" in opposing Shanker and the militant teachers. (By this time, the Jewish-owned *Times* had abandoned its *shtadlan* tradition of groveling discretion to adopt the sixties radical-chic position of collaboration with the enemies of democratic and universalist principles.) Kahlenberg concluded with a crucial point: "Until 1968, when a labor union struck because its workers were fired without due process, liberals knew which side they were on. But in Ocean Hill–Brownsville, the left reframed the issue as white versus black." Jewish parents and professionals in New York had meanwhile begun voting with their feet, as used to be said about refugees from totalitarian nations: they hunted for empty places in New York's private schools (which then had capacity for only 25,000 students) or relocated to the suburbs.

Kahlenberg has written that "Ocean Hill–Brownsville in 1968 devastated American liberalism so profoundly that the effects were still felt" in the first decade of the twenty-first century. "American liberalism" by this definition rests on the New Deal coalition, with its foundation in the vulnerable Jewish-Democratic relationship. Most historians have viewed the radical 1960s as a wild explosion of hormones among the baby boomers, along with yearnings of the unfathomable heart. These, it is often presumed, combined to produce a permanent nostalgia for the era of sexual liberation and the movement against the Vietnam War, along with a propensity for New Age meanderings and professional promotion of tenured leftists. But in New York, then elsewhere, the *yiddishe kop*, or Jewish brain, turned in different directions. With Jewish views on racial issues no longer predictable and support for militant unions suddenly questioned, the known universe of liberal ideology had been thrown into doubt, from the left more than the right. In addition, because of Vietnam, Democrats, with a few exceptions such as Scoop Jackson, had made themselves the party of coexistence with the Soviets, in a revival of Franklin Roosevelt and Sidney Hillman's wartime accommodationism. But the movement for aid to Soviet Jews undermined that trend on the Jewish side of the alliance with the Democrats. The Democrats, nevertheless, increasingly adopted "left isolationism"—opposition to the extension of American power overseas.

The year 1968 saw the peak of radical protest in the United States, and after that "the revolution"—from black nationalist outbursts to campus rebellions reaching the most prestigious universities and the most obscure colleges and even high schools—declined. President Lyndon B. Johnson had decided not to run for another term, and Richard Nixon was elected president, emphasizing law and order at home and the maintenance of American military power internationally. Yet Nixon seemed to possess no means of gaining victory in Indochina. Nixon's unsuccessful Democratic opponent, Hubert Humphrey, lost many votes because he would not follow his party's leftists to a position favoring complete withdrawal from the Vietnam War (a situation that may well be repeated with the Iraq situation in 2008). Humphrey was a classic representative of the anti-Communist, Social Democratic component of the New Deal coalition, and his failure to effectively summon the Democrats to challenge Nixon provided significant evidence that the heritage of Franklin Roosevelt was fading.

By 1972, when Nixon ran for reelection, the lead place on the Democratic ticket was taken by George McGovern. Although he was a veteran of the Second World War, McGovern had been a member of the Stalinist-front Progressive Party in 1948, and his presidential campaign twenty-four years afterward stood for the United States to immediately quit Vietnam. He was the furthest-left candidate on foreign-policy issues the Democrats had yet nominated for president. For some Jewish Democrats, his candidacy was proof that the New Deal marriage could not be saved. Norman Podhoretz, who had evolved considerably from his ambivalent position on the Harlem school boycott of 1963, would comment of the McGovern candidacy, "Never will I get over my amazement at the speed with which the New Left point of view spread from the margin to the mainstream and the Democratic Party caved in to the radical insurgency."

Late in 1972, Podhoretz's *Commentary* published a debate on the looming election, between the sociologist Nathan Glazer—who became known as an early neoconservative while serving as an editor of the *Public Interest*—favoring McGovern, and Milton Himmelfarb supporting Nixon. Podhoretz added his own views in an introduction. He noted that Glazer and Himmelfarb "both expect that Jews will give a smaller majority of their vote to the Democratic candidate this year than they have ever given to a Democratic candidate in any recent Presidential election." According to Podhoretz, a "turn away from McGovern" was "caused not by a sudden access of Jewish enthusiasm for Nixon or his party, but by a steadily mounting Jewish uneasiness over McGovern." Jews, Podhoretz argued, were "bothered in my judgment much more by the general attitudes of the New Politics movement [as McGovern's supporters were known] than by McGovern's stand on Israel—which, after all, as Nathan Glazer points out, is by now as fervent as any friend of Israel could wish—or by his stand on quotas: after all, the Nixon administration has done more to further quotas by deeds than McGovern could possibly yet have done by words." Rather, Jews viewed with distaste the character of the McGovernite Democrats as an "ideologically passionate minority (what the *Wall Street Journal* sometimes calls the 'mass intelligentsia' and sometimes the 'modernist-academic elite')."

Commenting in the *New York Times* on the *Commentary* exchanges, William V. Shannon argued, "Normally, Democratic candidates for the Presidency obtain 80 percent or more of Jewish votes." This was an exaggeration typical of the *Times;* Jews had voted only 64 percent in 1952 and 60 percent in 1956 for Adlai Stevenson, the Democratic standard-bearer against Eisenhower, although the Jewish Democratic vote increased to 82 percent for John F. Kennedy in 1960, 90 percent for Johnson four years later, and 81 percent for Humphrey. According to Shannon's thinly disguised polemic, Jews might prefer Nixon to McGovern because the former was an opportunist who supported Israel and quotas to get elected, while McGovern might "actually believe in something—in this case, some of the wider ambitions of the Women's Caucus or the Black Caucus." Shannon added snidely, "Sincerity is at the heart of this problem that neither Mr. Himmelfarb nor Mr. Podhoretz seems to appreciate." Shannon contributed to a common stereotype about Jews: that they, like Nixon, are political cynics and hypocrites.

But Himmelfarb and Podhoretz possessed a better political sense than Shannon. For McGovern, the Jewish vote returned to its Eisenhower-era level, delivering 65 percent to the Democrats. In his contribution to *Commentary*, Himmelfarb predicted the Jewish vote for Nixon with impressive accuracy: "the forecasts of people whose judgment I respect are between 25 and 35 per cent." Taking the Jewish-Democratic marriage for granted was proving unwise for both partners. But the Democrats also misjudged American voters in general; McGovern won only one state, Massachusetts, and 38 percent of the national balloting. Israel played no role in the 1972 election, which was entirely about Vietnam.

The Democrats proved incapable of correcting their erroneous path, even after the fall of Nixon, his succession by Gerald Ford (formerly of America First), and the election of Jimmy Carter in 1978. Writing in 1984, twelve years after the McGovern debacle, Podhoretz reviewed the recent history of the Democratic Party in bitter terms: "A significant number of life-long Democrats (I myself among them) . . . saw in the Carter Administration—and especially in Mr. Carter's announcement shortly after taking office that it was becoming less and less necessary to contain Soviet expansionism—evidence that the Democratic Party was still in the grip of the neoisolationist forces that had captured it in 1972 behind the candidacy of George McGovern. It was true that after the Soviet invasion of Afghanistan Mr. Carter had repented of his conversion to McGovernism and emerged as a born-again Truman Democrat. Confessing that the invasion had effected a 'dramatic change' in his view of 'the Soviets' ultimate goals,' he even went so far as to proclaim a new presidential doctrine, reminiscent both in spirit and substance of the doctrine bearing Truman's name which had originally committed the nation to the policy of containment in 1947."

Podhoretz recalled how, in the aftermath of the Khomeini revolution in Iran and the Russian assault on Afghanistan, "The new Carter Doctrine of 1979 warned the Soviet Union that 'an attempt . . . to gain control of the Persian Gulf region' would be 'regarded as an assault on the vital interests of the U.S.' and would be 'repelled by use of any means necessary, including military force.'" Further, the captain of *Commentary* praised Carter for a stiffened attitude after the Georgia peanut-farmer-turned-statesman first helped overthrow the Somoza dictatorship in Nicaragua and supported the Stalinist Sandinista government, then condemned the latter when it began suppressing political opposition. But Carter was nothing if not a waverer. The Democratic Party, aside from its commitment to Israel, which still could not be doubted, had left behind the principled internationalism of the New Deal, as well as of the Truman, Kennedy, and Johnson administrations, and had become the exclusive vessel of Vietnam-era defeatism.

Iran's Islamic Revolution reenergized Muslim world opinion against Israel and America. A long and at first slow confrontation had begun between the West, including Israel, and Islamist radicalism. Israel had stood in the front line for the defense of democratic ideals as it contended with the criminal offensive of Arab terrorism. Although the tensions between Israel and the West, on one side, and Arab and Iranian nationalism, along with varieties of radical Islam, on the other, would follow a course predictable by few, after 1978 Israel would never again be a secondary consideration in American foreign policy. In such a context, Republican firmness would make more sense than Democratic delusions about conciliation with democracy's enemies.

The Khomeini revolution was understandably even more alarming to American Jews and to Israel than the difficult conditions under which Soviet Jews lived. Yet the world kept getting more, rather than less, complicated. The election of Pope John Paul II, a Pole and the first non-Italian pontiff in centuries, exacerbated the internal contradictions of the Soviet system, which were even further exposed by Russia's Afghan adventure. These events provided openings for Jews to gain escape from the latest Russian wall placed around them since 1967. The support for Shanker and his teachers a decade and a half before was revived in 1989 by the Jewish elements of the AFL-CIO, inspired by the epic of the Polish Solidarity movement. The Pope's protection of Solidarity sealed the fate of Russian Communism.

John Paul II was, indeed, better for the Jews of the whole planet than any *shtadlan* Jewish leader anywhere, an item recognized earlier by Jewish neoconservatives than by most of their coreligionists. Parallel concerns about Russia and Iran in both the domestic American Jewish and Israeli contexts—and the incompetence of Carter and his Jewish-backed Democrats in effectively dealing with either Moscow or Tehran—propelled more and more American Jews on a rightward path. This was met agreeably by a distinct right turn in Israeli politics following the election of Begin, a graduate of Stalin's concentration camps as well as of the Irgun, as Israeli prime minister in 1977. Begin's Likud was a classic conservative nationalist coalition that anticipated the policies of Margaret Thatcher in Britain and Ronald Reagan in America in clearly distinguishing itself from the socialist and secularist traditions of the long-ruling Israeli Labor Party. Likud favored dismantling of the Israeli welfare state, more religion in public life, and peace through strength. American Jews had an opportunity to gain new political heft in Washington, although it was doubtful it could be realized through cooperation with the Democratic elite.

The 1970s thus proved to be a most challenging decade for American Jews and Israel. Heightened Palestinian extremism further drew the sympathies of youthful radicals around the world, including some Jews, for whom the Holocaust and Israel became "their father's causes." Many younger Jews preferred attending to such pressing matters as sexual libertinism, hallucinatory drugs, simplistic feminism, and the endless discovery of new aggrieved constituencies as pretexts for protests. One can hardly reproach them for these attitudes and activities, given their prevalence in the popular environment, but the refusal of many to move on and to acknowledge their youthful idiocy has been hard to overlook.

On the global level, Arab pressure on the West, after an especially hard-won Israeli victory in the 1973 Yom Kippur War, took the new form of oil diplomacy—boycotts intended to disrupt the sale and flow of energy resources as blackmail against support for Israel. The radical left was increasingly inclined to blame crises in the oil market on Israel; if they turned a blind eye to or excused Arab tyranny and terrorism, they had completely forgotten that the heritage of the American left had once included uncompromising hostility to the Standard Oil trust, the corporate offspring of which stood behind the Arab oil magnates.

Zionism ceased to be perceived by many non-Jewish American leftists, as well as certain leftist Jews, as a wholly progressive enterprise. Between that decade and 2005, when longtime hard-liner Ariel Sharon suddenly swung back to the center, Israeli state policy under Likud governments moved steadily to the right. This trend was visible notwithstanding flings into peace and diplomacy first under Begin, negotiating with Egypt's Anwar Sadat, and again when Labor returned to power in Israel. As an independent country with its own foreign policy and regional needs, Israel had a habit of surprising and even shocking its American Jewish supporters, who could neither dictate nor anticipate swings back and forth from a "hawkish" to a "dovish" position. This sense of dissonance and mixed signals was difficult for American Jews to bear, since with the debacle of New Deal internationalism they increasingly defined themselves by reference to Israel's moral authority and military skill.

Israel was created by universalist Ashkenazi Jews and invested with their values. But in the view of some of its own Jewish citizens, as well as American Jewish liberals, European critics, and Arab protestors, Israel had begun to resemble a garrison state, only concerned to disarm and crush its nearby enemies. What had once been presented as a triumph of self-sacrifice and principled endurance was now seen as an exemplar of power at any cost; the widely praised island of progress increasingly resembled other aggressive Middle Eastern states. A Likud policy of encouraging new Jewish settlements on the West Bank, support for which seemed implicit in the demand for increased emigration of Soviet Jews (many of whom were not actually Jews, and many of whom did not go to Israel after all), further complicated the Western view of Israel as an idealistic experiment. Still, enough American Jews remained liberal and peace oriented to preserve the illusion that a marriage to the Democrats was the best way to help Israel. Jewish liberals wanted an Israel without tears and would not surrender their belief that the Democrats could realize such a goal.

Israel would come to be redefined as a major American strategic asset. As Zionism migrated rightward, a more articulate sentiment in its favor increased among the mass of Gentile Americans, who were and are conservative and internationalist by nature. Such a development would be good for the Jews, even as it increased the dysfunction of the Democratic coalition.

But then came the election of President Ronald Reagan.

CHAPTER 5

JEWISH WASHINGTON

Jews in Power from Reagan to Clinton

In the two decades between 1980 and 2000, American Jews gained power and influence beyond anything they had ever before experienced. These twenty years saw the emergence of Jewish neoconservatives and their Gentile comrades and patrons as a leading force in American policymaking, the extraordinary expansion of AIPAC as America's pro-Israel lobby, the new importance of a solution in the Middle East as a principle of American politics, and an unexpected seduction of certain Jews by the Christian right. American Jews stepped out of the political ghetto in which they had let themselves be lured by the Democrats and took a new position as participants in American democracy.

Jewish political appointments blossomed; Jewish concerns became common American concerns. And yet, tragically, most Jewish leaders seemed unable to break the habit of centuries of *shtadlan* caution. Indeed, their very success seemed, as previously and para-doxically, to thrust them yet further back into a ghetto and *shtadlan* mentality.

In 1980, Jews voted for Ronald Reagan in numbers unachieved by a Republican presidential candidate since Eisenhower in 1956: 39 per-cent. This compared with 45 percent for Carter and 15 percent for a bland independent candidate, John B. Anderson, who, after receiving 7 percent of the national total, immediately sank without trace from popular attention. American Jews had found Scoop Jackson a valu-able helper in dealing with Soviet Jewish issues, and Reagan was one of the few American politicians, Republican or Democratic, who could then outdo Jackson as an anti-Soviet hard-liner. The Reagan administration, although Republican, even increased the power of the Democrat Jackson's neoconservative allies and protégés, some of whom had thought about leaving the Democrats since the McGovern nomination. Others came into the Reagan orbit from the anti-Communist wing of the AFL-CIO, still representing a majority in the unions, as well as from academia and collaboration with leading intel-lectual journals such as *Commentary* and *Public Interest*.

That authentic liberals and even socialists who deeply hated the crimes of Russian imperialism—especially in the new epoch of Polish Solidarity—would prefer Ronald Reagan to Jimmy Carter could only be explained by the left as a "sellout." This bizarre phobia contributed to a polarization that has deeply harmed and cheapened American politics—and is anything but good for the Jews. The ideological ossification of the Democrats led directly to vicious Jew-baiting against the neoconserva-tives during the administration of President George W. Bush.

Indeed, from the perspective of anti-Communist liberals and neoconservatives, the Democrats had become a party of leftist fanat-ics, among whom terms such as *liberal* and *progressive* were empty of authenticity. The Reagan Republicans were never so rigid: since most of academia and media cleaved to the Democrats, the GOP was glad to welcome anti-Communist Democrats, Social Democrats, Shacht-manites, and neoconservatives aboard its ship. And many accepted the invitation gladly.

To emphasize, the rise of the neoconservatives, previously an isolated grouping, to power and status under Reagan was the first of four great turning points in American Jewish politics after the foundation of Israel. Three significant moments in the new Jewish politics followed after this shift: the next was a great political fight between the American Jewish leadership and Saudi interests in Washington over the sale of AWACS aircraft, a major item of ultramodern military technology, which brought about the transformation of AIPAC. Then came the evolution of the Reagan administration's attitudes to Israeli actions in Lebanon in 1982. The last development was the appearance of a new friendship between Jewish and Israeli advocates and Christian conservatives.

Neoconservative influence undeniably exceeded that of any prior intellectual or political trend since the New Deal, in which Jews were prominent—although, as neoconservatives themselves frequently point out, many were and are Gentiles. At the same time, AIPAC, officially America's pro-Israel Lobby, began its expansion into "the premier Washington lobby," as its admirers also would call it. Yet AIPAC would spend the next two decades gravitating between its historic American liberal and left partners, on one hand, and its new conservative friends, on the other—and vacillation, the superlative habit of the *shtadlan* leaders, is never good for the Jews.

The first major indicator of the new role of neoconservatives in the Reagan administration was the naming of Jeane Kirkpatrick— a Gentile political science professor at Georgetown University with an acute understanding of Soviet aggression—as U.S. ambassador to the UN. During the presidential campaign, she had served as a foreign-policy adviser to Reagan. (At the moment of her nomination, an essay on Stalinism in the Spanish Civil War, included in a volume she edited, was about to be pirated as a pamphlet by a small Trotskyist group.) Kirkpatrick in turn drew on the talents of the Shachtmanites, who had reorganized their alliance with the elderly Jewish Social Democrats of New York, and refounded themselves as an organization called Social Democrats, USA (SDUSA). Kirkpatrick appointed Carl Gershman, a functionary of SDUSA beginning in the middle 1970s, as her senior counselor at the UN mission in January 1981.

Some critics described SDUSA as little more than a social network for AFL-CIO bureaucrats of an especially anti-Communist bent, but its milieu would include other influential (and Jewish) figures in American diplomacy at the end of the Cold War, such as Max Green, who served as an emissary between President Reagan and the Jews, and Max Kampelman, destined to become Reagan's arms control expert.

Kampelman was truly an emblematic figure for the rightward journey of Jewish liberal anti-Communists. He was the son of a Bronx hat salesman and New Deal supporter but had a Jewish religious education in childhood and adolescence. While studying at New York University, he worked briefly as an organizer for the ILGWU, Dubinsky's union. In a 1985 *Washington Post* profile by David Remnick, Kampelman recalled, "I was an anti-Communist from the start. They were antidemocratic. That's all I saw in the Communists. I don't know why. It could have been my reading, my professors, it could have been my yeshiva [religious school] training." During the Second World War he was a conscientious objector, but in the mid-1950s, at thirty-five, he joined the Marine Corps Reserve, in which he participated for seven years.

Between his conscientious objection and his service in the Reserve, Kampelman wrote a doctoral dissertation in political science at the University of Minnesota on Communist efforts to dominate the CIO unions. His adviser was Professor Evron Kirkpatrick, husband of Jeane. Kampelman then joined Hubert Humphrey in actively removing Communist control from the Minnesota CIO and the state's Democratic-Farmer-Labor (DFL) party, a New Deal "halfway house" not unlike the American Labor Party in New York—but which still exists today, more leftist than ever. In 1947, the task of liberating Minnesota from direct Muscovite influence was accomplished. Humphrey was elected to the U.S. Senate the next year, and hired Kampelman as his legislative counsel in 1949.

Though Kampelman remained a Democrat, he was deeply disaffected by the McGovern presidential candidacy of 1972, in which he admitted he was "deliberately not active." Instead, he grew closer to Scoop Jackson. When he was selected by Reagan to serve as his main arms control adviser, the nomination was viewed by Remnick as "a victory for Norman Podhoretz, Midge Decter, Irving Kristol," and other neoconservatives. Kampelman remarked, "I don't know why being in favor of a strong national defense or highlighting a perception of the Soviet Union as a danger to democracy and our liberty should be called conservative. I think my position is consistent with the traditions of the Democratic Party and American liberalism."

Ambassador Kirkpatrick, for her part, was widely said to have gotten her job at the UN thanks to an article in the November 1979 issue of *Commentary* titled "Dictatorships and Double Standards." There she sharply condemned the record of the Carter administration, which had encouraged Soviet expansionism and brought disaster to American interests in Iran and Nicaragua. Kirkpatrick's article presented neoconservative principles in a militant tone, and served the Reagan administration as a foreign-policy manifesto, remaining in some part relevant in guiding U.S. international action a quarter of a century afterward: "The United States is not, in fact, a racist, colonial power, it does not practice genocide, it does not threaten world peace with expansionist activities," she wrote. "[A] posture of continuous self-abasement and apology vis-à-vis the Third World is neither morally necessary nor politically appropriate. . . . Liberal idealism need not be identical with masochism, and need not be incompatible with the defense of freedom and the national interest."

Kirkpatrick's article became better known for its argument that authoritarian regimes such as that of Anastasio Somoza in Nicaragua could be friends of the United States and that right-wing autocracies could evolve into democracies but leftist dictatorships would not. The first proposition had long been obvious; the second was proven by the next twenty-five years of peaceful transitions from authoritarianism to democracy in Spain, in many Latin American countries, and in Far Eastern states. Kirkpatrick could be faulted for failing to understand that support for the United States by dictators did not justify support of dictators by the United States—that clarification would not be adopted by an American president until the administration of George W. Bush.

Kirkpatrick, of course, could not have anticipated her other oversight: she failed to foresee that Communist nations in central Europe, most of them with a Catholic and Protestant heritage, would also accomplish peaceful transitions to capitalist democracy. The road to freedom and prosperity would be blocked in the Orthodox Christian nations—Russia, Belarus, and Ukraine, as well as in the Russified Muslim countries from Azerbaijan to Uzbekistan. Finally, culture and tradition were more significant than ideology in the Communist world. The Catholics in Poland, Hungary, Lithuania, the former Czechoslovakia and Yugoslavia, and the East German and Baltic Protestants had never surrendered their souls to Communism, while the Orthodox embraced it. The Muslims, like many Jews and Catholics, were beaten, starved, murdered, and deported to force their acceptance of it.

The liberation of the Communist empire was made possible by Reagan and the neoconservatives, both in and out of his administration. The Reagan White House would not flinch from a serious challenge to global totalitarianism. Because he had experience as a disillusioned liberal fighting against Stalinists in the Hollywood cinema unions in the mid-1940s, the new president viewed the Soviet dictatorship and its political surrogates around the world as overweening bluffers likely to fold in the face of serious resistance. Reagan, a popular leader of the Screen Actors Guild, shared that perception with anti-Communist trade unionists such as Dubinsky. Kirkpatrick and other neoconservatives, reflecting the legacy of their anti-Stalinist forebears, whether Social Democratic, Shachtmanite, or Shankerite, as well as their own analytical evolution, agreed with Reagan's analysis of Soviet impostures and provided his policy instincts with an elaborated rationale.

In the relationship between Reagan and the neoconservatives, Kirkpatrick at the UN and Podhoretz at *Commentary* were the key elements. *Commentary* would become, through this period, the main print barometer of neoconservative politics and the bellwether of a possible recasting of American Jewish politics in the direction of a permanent coalition with the GOP—or at least a move away from the false Promised Land of the Democrats. In February 1981, Podhoretz's wife, Midge Decter, launched the Committee for the Free World (CFW), a grouping of 400 anti-Communist "writers, publishers, academic figures, scientists and labor leaders from a dozen countries, including Britain, Canada, Australia, France and West Germany," according to the *New York Times*. Its membership was the most complete roster ever assembled of neoconservatives and their allies, some of whom would later fall away from the movement. CFW included Sidney Hook, Irving Kristol, Nathan Glazer, and Seymour Martin Lipset, along with Podhoretz, of course, and Ambassador Kirkpatrick, who had to remain a member on suspension because of her diplomatic post. Decter was its main activist.

A new political migration of American Jews proceeded, much slower than any previous exodus, either to the Progressive Republicans at the beginning of the twentieth century or to the Democrats in the New Deal era. The section of Jewish opinion that Reagan elevated to a new position, like their Progressive and New Deal predecessors, represented an outspoken constellation of personalities with only formal relations to the *shtadlan* elite. But the Progressive Republican and New Deal Jews had been representatives of consensus in their community, and individuals such as Oscar Straus and Sidney Hillman were objects of broad popular adulation.

Not so the neoconservatives, who because of their dissent against domination by the Jewish-Democratic alliance were denied the collective approval of American Jews and (with the qualified exception of a Gentile, Daniel Patrick Moynihan) did not immediately produce a successful outstanding public representative for their platform. Yet the neoconservatives, like the "New York intellectuals" from whom they emerged, had their revenge. New Deal Jews who preceded the neoconservatives at the summit of American power had helped craft domestic policy, on which the Jewish-Democratic marriage was founded, but never guided foreign affairs. The neoconservatives made such an advance over the objections, at times, of the *shtadlan* lobbies.

In an example that produced much gossip among leading Jews as well as Gentile neoconservatives, the American Jewish Committee, publisher of *Commentary*, became deeply discontented with the pro-Reagan line adopted by Podhoretz and tried to sever relations between the AJC and the monthly. The neoconservatives, according to AJC, were too harsh, too eager, and too right-wing; the AJC identification with them was compromising. They were also newly powerful rivals to the *shtadlan* leaders. But mainly, their style was gratingly opposite that of the *shtadlan* tradition. AJC finally compelled the editors of *Commentary* to search for independent financing, and although the relationship between the magazine and AJC remained officially in effect, every issue would carry a disclaimer, included to this day, stating that the views expressed in its pages should not be construed as representing those of the American Jewish Committee.

Neoconservative success would not, however, ensure deference by the White House to Jewish or Israeli positions. Thus within three months of Kirkpatrick's appointment in 1981, the Reagan administration began advocating for the sale of AWACS (Airborne Warning and Control System) warplane technology to the kingdom of Saudi Arabia, i.e., to the most anti-Jewish, reactionary, repressive, obscurantist, and violent Muslim country in the world. The dynamics of the Cold War had brought about the most severe test ever faced—even in retrospect—by the American Jewish leadership.

The Saudi request to purchase AWACS was a result of the extraordinary growth of that country's oil wealth following the dramatic rise in petroleum prices in the 1970s. With almost inconceivable financial resources, the Saudi establishment had gone shopping. The Saudis had little real need for elaborate military technology; rather, like a newly employed teenager with his or her first paycheck, they wanted to show off their sudden wealth and test their influence. At the end of the Carter administration, the Saudis asked about AWACS, then the most advanced military hardware on the American market. Carter approved the sale of five AWACS aircraft to the kingdom but left office before the deal could be consummated.

Reagan proved a supporter of the sale, with the backing of the Pentagon and the Boeing Corporation, the main firm involved in developing AWACS. Many other corporate interests were significant for the AWACS deal and its peripheral business activities. They included, of course, the Standard Oil successors, additional energy companies, banks, and law firms making money in the Saudi kingdom.

To block the AWACS deal, American Jewish leaders mobilized their constituents as never before. Norman Podhoretz wrote with uncharacteristic delicacy in the *Washington Post*, "The decision to sell the electronic surveillance planes known as AWACS to Saudi Arabia is puzzling and disheartening to many of us who have looked to the Reagan administration for a new approach to the greatest of all dangers facing the United States: the danger that the oil fields of the Persian Gulf might fall under Soviet control. Instead of developing a new approach, the administration seems to be returning to old illusions and discredited policies of which President Reagan himself was once the strongest critic."

It was exceedingly strange that Podhoretz and his allies should view the Saudi kingdom as threatened by a leftist takeover. While the Khomeini revolution in Iran had given rise to such fears about that country—and created a permanent Jewish and Israeli anxiety over Tehran, sometimes justified, sometimes exaggerated—Saudi Arabia at the beginning of the 1980s was hardly a candidate for major political convulsions. Indeed, in the debate over AWACS, an argument that selling advanced military technology might help the Saudi state beat back Soviet expansionism made more sense, in reality as on paper, than a claim that the kingdom and any weapons it possessed would fall into Muscovite hands. Objections to selling AWACS to the Saudis would have been more compelling if one accurately viewed the monarchy as an aggressive radical Islamist power with a potential, on its own, for generating threats to the world. Few Westerners knew enough about the Saudis and Islam to grasp this, however, and that knowledge gap afflicted allegedly omniscient Israel and its intelligence services no less than the United States. But the early neoconservatives were better at anti-Communism than at analysis of Islamic politics, which dictated the content of their objection to the AWACS deal.

The AWACS donnybrook also commenced the great change of AIPAC from one among countless Capitol lobbies, known for little more than its aggressiveness, into the brightest star shining over the Hill. Before the AWACS battle, AIPAC was believed by many people to possess great power; but its officers and other Jewish leaders correctly argued that much of the clamor about its clout was Arab propaganda against a purported "Jewish takeover" in America. An unidentified source in the Jewish community told the *Washington Post,* "It isn't that Jews do anything different or better than other lobbies, it's just that our grass-roots support is much stronger." AIPAC could depend on Jews around the country to take action for Israel, while aside from Irish Americans, other lobbies or "special-interest groups" were mainly limited to their own efforts in Washington. By American rules, the Saudis should have been at an extreme disadvantage in this contest: there were then fewer than 2 million Arabs in America, compared with some 6 million Jews. Arab Americans were Christian in their majority, which divided them over issues such as Lebanon. And Arab Americans lacked the Jewish tradition of political commitment in the American context.

Before AWACS, a battle it lost, AIPAC's main achievement had been the passage of legislation in 1977 banning American involvement in the boycott on Jewish goods adopted by the Arab states in 1945, three years before Israel declared its independence. The boycott in its complete form was so unwieldy as to be unenforceable. It forbade direct Arab trade with Israel, then at a secondary level trade with non-Arab companies that did business with Israel, and at a third level, barred commerce with any firms that had relations with enterprises in the second category.

Many European and Japanese enterprises, as well as economic institutions in Communist states, complied with the boycott. North African Muslim states observed the first level, barring business in

Israel, but ignored the rest. Non-Arab Turkey did not join. Egypt and Jordan, which recognized Israel, dropped their involvement. In recent years, Kuwait, Qatar, and Oman edged away from the boycott, returned to it during Palestinian violence, and have lately drawn away again from its observance. American antiboycott regulation prohibited direct discrimination against Israel but did not block U.S. trade with countries that participated in the boycott. The situation was and to some extent remains absurd, but one point cannot be argued: boycott or no boycott, law or no law, even as the Saudi rulers have been the champions of the anti-Israel boycott, ExxonMobil and its peers conduct their affairs in the Saudi kingdom unmolested by the U.S. government.

AIPAC led the anti-AWACS charge in Washington, while its strategic work was supplemented in cities across the United States by the National Jewish Community Relations Advisory Council (NJCRAC). NJCRAC, now known as the Jewish Council for Public Affairs (JCPA), brings together local community relations groups that coordinate when necessary with the bureaucracies of ADL and AJC—which is not very often, because each of the *shtadlan* groups runs its own show and controls its own turf. Jewish Community Relations Councils (JCRCs) are mainly concerned with organizing interfaith colloquies and similar publicity events. Most are top-heavy with do-gooders, and therefore Democrats, although they may not contribute directly to maintenance of the Jewish-Democratic marriage.

Norman Podhoretz had it wrong: Opposing AWACS was not about Communism. In a 1993 *Frontline* television documentary, "The Arming of Saudi Arabia," journalist Steven Emerson commented, "The 1981 AWACS debate was essentially a face-off between two very powerful constituencies—the domestic American Jewish community, which was fearful that the AWACS would fall . . . in enemy hands against Israel, and the American corporate community, which was lobbying essentially at the demand and control and direction of the Saudi government. American corporations . . . were told in no uncertain terms that unless they lobbied their Congressmen and Senators, they would not receive renewals of [Saudi] contracts." Aside from Boeing, principal players would include the predecessor units of ExxonMobil (the primary Standard Oil successor). What was then Mobil Corporation manned a forward post for the Saudis in the media campaign.

The broader American public perceived the AWACS confrontation as little more than lobby vs. lobby. Paul Taylor, a writer for the *Washington Post,* described AIPAC's then executive director, Thomas A. Dine, as "the point-man for the nation's 'Jewish lobby.'" During a single afternoon in September 1981, Dine visited eleven senators to argue against the AWACS sale, which Taylor called "an impressive day's work." In contrast, the Saudi lobbyist Frederick Dutton, a former aide to Jack and Bobby Kennedy, had "been a virtual stranger on the Hill these past few months," according to Taylor.

Saudi Prince Bandar bin Sultan bin Abd al-Aziz Al-Saud had come to Washington to secure the AWACS deal; two years later he would be appointed Saudi ambassador, a post in which he served until 2005. The Saudis signed a contract with a public relations firm for a half million dollars and paid a $200,000 annual retainer to Dutton for the AWACS campaign. The desert clan understood, according to Taylor, that they could remain apart from direct involvement in the fray while the Reagan administration would "navigate the package through Congress." Bandar had been instructed "not to speak above a whisper" when dealing with Americans; he limited himself to low-key visits at congressional offices, parties at his residence, and what would become his favorite form of intrusion into the affairs of Americans, "sitting in on administration strategy sessions."

Taylor reported, in words that should have startled and alarmed every American, that the bandits ruling the Saudi monarchy believed "having to lobby for the [AWACS] sale themselves would defeat part of the rationale for the purchase." Dutton averred that the Saudis took "the position that this is a battle for the administration to fight, not them." For his part, Dutton wanted to "take the muzzle off" and launch an open Jew-baiting campaign. "I'd have bumper stickers plastered all over town saying 'Reagan or Begin,'" he leered. Incarnating the Coughlinite spirit of five decades past, Dutton railed against "a foreign chief of state"—the prime minister of Israel—holding a veto over U.S. policy. "That kind of stuff [i.e., bashing the Jews] really plays in Peoria," he exulted.

Reagan echoed Dutton, affirming, "It is not the business of other nations to make American foreign policy." The reference to Israel was obvious; nobody wanted to say that in the AWACS game, Saudi Arabia was also an "other nation" attempting to dictate American policy. And if Reagan was cautious in his comments, Dutton's prattle was echoed more loudly and egregiously by then-Congressman Paul N. "Pete" McCloskey, a California Republican who became one of the country's most offensive anti-Semites. (Soon after September 11, 2001, the wretched McCloskey felt no shame in publishing a 2000 speech to a convention of Holocaust deniers. He referred to "the so-called Holocaust," stated, "It was as if 'Israel über Alles,' or 'Israel above all,' became the watchword," and described Yasir Arafat as "a man of peace.")

An Arab American advocate, David Sadd, predicted that Israel and the Jews would suffer enormously with Gentile Americans if the AWACS deal was not settled in favor of the Saudis. Unsatisfied with merely grabbing the West by the throat and extorting more money for oil, they would also demand an open door to America's economic storehouse, to come and go and use the premises however they wished. From the other side, the *Post*'s Taylor quoted AJC's Hyman Bookbinder verbalizing the eternal *shtadlan* dilemma: "if we lose we lose and if we win we lose." Defeating the AWACS sale, according to some Jewish leaders, would simply provoke more hatred of Jews.

The Saudis were correct, if immoral, in their strategy. The Jewish leadership lost the AWACS fight. The planes were sold to Saudi Arabia.

The Senate voted for the AWACS sale by only fifty-two to forty-eight, but the deal was approved. America remains Israel's friend but Saudi Arabia's servant. AIPAC lobbied for what it wanted; the White House lobbied for what the Saudi princes wanted. Israel and its Jewish supporters offered votes and the continued satisfaction of the Western conscience. Saudi Arabia offered multibillion-dollar profits to American corporations. Any other eventuality than a Saudi triumph was unimaginable. Looking back across the quarter century since AWACS, it is obvious that the claims of Osama bin Laden and others that Saudi Arabia is a pawn of the United States are ridiculous. America remains a hostage of the Saudi monarchy and its corporate oil partners. And while America in 2001 began a campaign to liberate the Arab and Muslim world from corruption and fear, the outcome must eventually be settled in Mecca and Medina, through the transformation of the Saudi state.

Much more than Suez in 1956, AWACS revealed the gap between public insistence that Israel was a major American ally and the silent but continuing servitude of the Beltway to Arab interests. AIPAC would try, as a "single-issue" movement, to resolve the problem. Such was the beginning of AIPAC's maturity as a leading element of the broader Jewish leadership. AIPAC began to overshadow the Anti-Defamation League and the American Jewish Committee as a representative of "the Jewish lobby" in America. Although defeated over AWACS, AIPAC used the opportunity to expand its support networks and increase its focus on Washington. From then on, AIPAC partisans would be kept in a state of permanent alert through directives from the national headquarters and more extensive organizing on the national Jewish circuit.

Perhaps the most bizarre aspect of the AWACS affair was that both AIPAC chief Tom Dine and Saudi flack Fred Dutton were liberal Democrats and former political operatives for the Kennedys. The brother of the noted pop artist Jim Dine, Tom Dine had served as an aide to Senator Ted Kennedy and joined AIPAC in 1980, the year before the AWACS debacle. He was forced out as AIPAC chairman in 1993; he had insulted ultra-Orthodox Jews, commenting to Israeli journalist David Landau, "Their image is—smelly. That's what I'd say now that you've got me thinking about it. Hasids and New York diamond dealers." Dine was saved by the Clinton administration. He was appointed to run the U.S. Agency for International Development's projects in Central/Eastern Europe and the former Soviet Union, then took over management of Radio Free Europe/Radio Liberty, a U.S. government broadcaster serving the same area. In 2005, he moved to San Francisco to manage the local Jewish Federation.

Dine and other AIPAC bosses have had a long reach as well as a sharp tongue. Larry Cohler-Esses, a New York Jewish journalist known for his daring and enterprise, has recalled that Dine and AIPAC tried to get him and another leading Jewish community reporter, Andrew Silow-Carroll, fired from the *Washington Jewish Week,* a community paper, in 1992. "They never came to me with complaints about my coverage (with one or two exceptions)," Cohler-Esses said. "They didn't even go to the editor. They went to the owner and publisher. . . . The board members of AIPAC would never agree to speak with me (with a couple of brief exceptions when I caught them on the phone at home)." According to Cohler-Esses, Dine objected to the journalists' normal and ethical insistence on reporting candidly on the Jewish domestic and pro-Israel lobbies.

Of the ignominious Dutton, the less said the better. He had once been chief of staff for Edmund G. "Pat" Brown, the last authentic representative of the Progressive tradition to serve as governor of California. But Dutton had found the path of ex-Progressives such as the Nazi-loving Lindbergh and Wheeler best suited to his character.

The AWACS debacle marked the second major shift, following the ascent of the neoconservatives, for Jews in Washington since 1948; everything that happened within the communal leadership after AWACS reflected the reorientation it forced on AIPAC. AIPAC was now a better-recognized player in Washington, and although it had been defeated, it would reform its ranks and rethink its strategies to prevent such a reverse from being repeated. It went about its business with a new élan, and its membership soon included an energetic activist, Steven J. Rosen. Rosen was born into a radical leftist family and shared the Stalinist proclivity for political manipulation. He came to AIPAC in the summer of 1982, having worked since 1978 as a social science analyst for the RAND Corporation. In the years after AIPAC hired him, Rosen never took a position above that of policy director, supposedly because of his difficult personality, but he was said by many to be responsible for the mutation of AIPAC into the King Kong of the Hill, as Washingtonians would inevitably see it.

When Tom Dine left AIPAC in 1993, it was ten times bigger in financing and five times larger in its staffing and other numbers compared with its assets and size when he began thirteen years before. During the AWACS debate, AIPAC had 30 employees, a budget of $1.3 million, and 12,000 members around the country, with its information network reaching some 200,000 people—not, in the end, very many. By the time of Dine's ejection, it had some 150 people on its staff, as many as 50,000 members, and a $15 million budget. It also had much greater influence in the White House. But it was Rosen, more than Dine, who may be credited with this achievement.

Rosen oriented the lobby less toward congressional legislation and foreign aid for Israel than to contact with the White House and cabinet staff. He became the organization's political brain. But almost from his joining AIPAC, Rosen also involved the lobby in penetrating the higher, classified reaches of government and obtaining secret information. Already in 1983, according to a memo reportedly found twenty-two years later by the FBI, Rosen bragged to Dine that he had access to National Security Decision Directive 99 (NSDD 99) on the Middle East, classified Top Secret. Rosen's exultant memorandum, in which he boasted of his access and capacity to influence policy toward Israel, was also sent to Guilford Glazer, a shopping mall magnate, Israel Bonds campaigner, AIPAC donor, and close associate of Armand Hammer, the energy billionaire and Soviet agent of influence, whom, as it happened, President Reagan despised.

Rosen would come to exemplify the AIPAC pattern of traveling back and forth between left and right in search of advantages for the lobby. But he was, if nothing else, a fighter, and he had come to the organization at the right time. Although it had opposed the Reagan administration over AWACS, AIPAC evinced something of the fresh, combative attitude of the Reaganites and their neoconservative allies. This tendency became ever stronger in AIPAC as the 1980s wore on.

The lobby's staff, previously made up of liberals and Democrats such as Dine, gave way to conservative Republicans such as Howard Kohr, AIPAC executive director since 1996. Kohr is a colorless personality who served an eight-year apprenticeship at the lobby, preceded by work at AJC, and has been seen as a tool of Steve Rosen.

In the Reagan era, Israel was an important friend of the United States, but even at the new height of their influence, American Jews could not avoid the historic contradictions of U.S. policy in the Middle East. Still, as Reagan and the neoconservatives marched rightward, with the main aim of turning back Russian expansionism in Latin America, Africa, and Asia, first AIPAC rushed, and then the *shtadlan* leaders in ADL and AJC tiptoed, in the same direction. While the White House and the neoconservatives kept their focus on Communism, the big three Jewish advocacy groups concentrated on domestic issues as well as on Israel. But the Reagan neoconservatives had little direct effect on the development of the American Jewish leadership. In pushing Jews in a conservative direction, the place of the American neoconservatives was taken by the leaders of Israel itself, who continued their own march to the right.

The first year of the Reagan presidency turned out to be trying in the extreme for the American Jewish leadership. By the end of 1981, Jewish anguish over the AWACS sale was complicated by the effects of the Israeli legal annexation of the Golan Heights, Israeli raids in Lebanon, and the Israeli bombing of Iraq's nuclear reactor. The Reagan administration imposed a boycott on military sales to the Jewish state and suspended strategic cooperation between the two countries. Finally, Begin lashed out, protesting American policy to United States ambassador Samuel Lewis. Begin described the United States as persecuting Israel and treating it as a "vassal."

For a time, the Reagan administration seemed to have adopted the traditional State Department orientation, seeking to curb Israeli influence with the goal of Arab accommodation. Howard M. Squadron, chairman of the Conference of Presidents of Major American Jewish

Organizations, a pro-Israel umbrella organization even more discreet than the *shtadlan* groups that mainly compose it, echoed Begin. Accusing the United States of "punitive action against Israel," Squadron praised Begin's angry words. According to Squadron, "No self-respecting leader of any independent country in the world would react differently."

The situation became most challenging in June 1982 when Israeli armed forces mounted a general invasion of Lebanon. Begin and his Likud Party had gained power in Israel in 1977, even before the commencement of the Reagan presidency. They decided to act in Lebanon, with Ariel Sharon holding the defense portfolio and Yitzhak Shamir as foreign minister in Begin's cabinet. All three were hardliners, although from differing political backgrounds.

Begin was well known as religiously observant and as a proud commander of the Irgun during the war for Israeli independence. Shamir, born in Poland during the First World War and a veteran of the Stern Gang, was even more truculent than Begin. Both were Eastern European extremists of a nineteenth-century kind. In 1948, with Soviet and Czech backing for Zionism, the militants, as previously noted, were idolized by the global left. Shamir's adventures were reminiscent of Dumas' *Count of Monte Cristo* no less than of Russian revolutionaries a century before. He had been interned by the British in a camp in northeast Africa but escaped to a French colony and to France itself, where he gained asylum. He then returned to the urban war front in Palestine.

Sharon, born in a Jewish town in Palestine, was a patriot who worked his way up the ranks of the mainstream Jewish military organization, the Haganah, which he joined during the Second World War. The attainment of power by Begin, Shamir, and Sharon, then known as the three hardest leaders of Israel, was an expression of the crisis of the Zionist-socialist alliance in the Jewish state. The Israeli political change paralleled the difficulties of the Jewish-Democratic coalition in the United States but had a much more volatile character. Likud had taken power as a conservative force determined to reverse the policies established during the long tenure in government of the Israeli

Labor Party. But a strong social welfare order had been the foundation of power in Israel since its declaration of independence. It was no less embodied in the vast economic role of the Histadrut union federation. Yet this dominant political tradition of the Jewish state was undermined by class differentiation in Israel, just as the Jewish-Democratic marriage in America had been afflicted by issues of race and the radical liberalism of the "new class."

The post-1948 inrush of Arab-speaking Jews, known as Sephardim and Mizrahim, had produced an unskilled proletariat and underclass that voted for Begin and Likud as a protest against discrimination by the Eastern European elite that created Israel and its socialist image. Jews from Arab countries were also more intransigent in their view of their former neighbors. Having experienced the 1948 convulsion in their own flesh, in Arab lands where they had lived for centuries, they were sometimes no less aggrieved than refugees from the Nazi Holocaust in Europe. The rightist Sephardim and Mizrahim were additionally more religious than the secularized, even antireligious East Europeans.

The Israeli invasion of Lebanon in 1982 was provoked when an Arab leftist terror group headed by Abu Nidal, then among the most famous terrorists in the world, attempted to assassinate the Israeli ambassador to London, Shlomo Argov. The Israelis bombed selected Palestinian targets in Lebanon; the Palestinians carried out an artillery assault on the Galilee region of the Jewish state. A massive Israeli incursion in Lebanon began, directed by Sharon. In addition to the Palestinians, Syrian troops, sent into Lebanon during the latter country's civil war, engaged with Israeli forces.

In the new atmosphere of neoconservative initiative and Reagan's anti-Communism, the United States could not refrain from a more direct involvement with Israeli affairs. This was the period's third great change in American Jewish politics after 1948. Responding to the Likud trio's action in Lebanon, Reagan sent American diplomat Philip Habib to the region to craft a ceasefire, but Palestinian combatants remained on Lebanese territory and continued attacking the Jewish state, while also interfering significantly in the Lebanese civil war that began in 1975.

By the end of summer 1982, three months after the Israelis crossed their northern borders in force, Habib had negotiated a Palestinian withdrawal from Lebanon. The Palestinian political leadership under Yasir Arafat relocated to Tunisia. American and French troops oversaw the Palestinian retreat, but it was followed by a new and worse Lebanese crisis when Sharon led the Israeli army to the seizure of West Beirut—without authorization from the Israeli cabinet. Then came atrocities at Sabra and Shatila, refugee camps into which Lebanese Christians erupted and murdered hundreds of Palestinians. Israel was perceived as having encouraged the horror, and the U.S. government demanded that the Jewish state withdraw its military from its northern neighbor. Reagan sent U.S. Marines into Lebanon, along with French and Italian forces, in a bid to calm the situation, while the Sixth Fleet patrolled offshore.

On October 23, 1983, a car bomb exploded at a barracks in Beirut, killing 241 American Marines. Shia Muslim militants from Hezbollah, a militia subsidized by Iran, were blamed—an accusation Americans would not forget. In March 1984 the Marines were withdrawn and a Lebanese peace accord with Israel collapsed. Ordinary Americans remained outraged at the Marine barracks bombing and, following their frustration over oil boycotts and fluctuating gasoline prices, tended to side against the Arabs and Iran. But the image of Israel had become even more aggressive, and the acceptance of Israeli policies in Washington was not automatic. If Reagan and Begin had a certain boldness in common, and shared friends among the neoconservatives, Reagan did not cut American policy to suit Begin. In 1983, however, mutual interests prevailed, along the lines of NSDD 99, the secret document to which Steve Rosen had claimed access. NSDD 99 presented a thorough analysis by the National Security Council of U.S. policy in the Middle East. It led to a reinstatement of the U.S.-Israel military coordination, disrupted by the Lebanon invasion, and upgraded Israel as a regional asset against Soviet expansionism.

Begin still did more to drive American Jews to the right than Iran, Reagan, or the neoconservatives. But even after Begin assumed power, the *shtadlan* lobbies continued to promote Israel as a paragon of liberalism, social progress, and commitment to peace, based on the long governing record of the Labor Party and its social welfare system. The situation remained a mirror image of that in the United States, where the Jewish-Democratic alliance similarly evoked the New Deal consensus.

American Jews meanwhile faced more trouble inside the Democratic household. In 1984, the African American leader Jesse L. Jackson, a shameless demagogue who had been touring the Arab nations and cuddling with murderers such as Arafat (something even the head of the secret police in benighted Communist Romania found distasteful), emitted a series of vulgar comments that deeply wounded Jewish sensibilities. "I am sick and tired of hearing about the Holocaust and having America being put on a guilt trip," Jackson blurted. "We have to get on with the issues today and not talk about the Holocaust. The Jews do not have a monopoly on suffering." "Reverend" Jackson further demonstrated his respect for interfaith comity by attacking rabbis who dared criticize him. What American Jewish leader had ever suggested he or she was sick and tired of hearing about black slavery and America's "guilt trip" about it? As the Ocean Hill–Brownsville radicals had imitated George Wallace by blockading the entrance of a school to prevent Jewish teachers from working, Jackson had borrowed the idiom of David Duke, the KKK activist, to stir up his constituency against the Jews.

Jackson also gained backing from the Saudi kingdom, in which the slavery he allegedly hated still continued long after its disappearance from the United States. Finally, it was reported that Jackson privately referred to Jews as "Hymies" and to New York as "Hymietown." Jackson responded with an impressively novel if logically ridiculous attempt at denial: "I'm not familiar with that," he said when asked if he used such vocabulary. Jackson went on to accuse the Jews of "hounding" him, as if he should not be held accountable for his statements. Within two weeks, however, he admitted the slur. But he added yet another improbable note to his attempt at self-justification—the only form of communication Jackson knows—when he claimed unconvincingly that "Hymie" was a commonplace term for Jews in South Carolina, where he grew up. Jackson was backed up with threatening language by the former musician "Calypso Louie" Walcott, alias Louis Farrakhan, trash-talking head of the so-called Nation of Islam—a cult universally rejected by real Muslims for its black racism, and more resembling an African American variety of Freemasonry than a religious sect.

Jackson's insults were most shocking for liberal Jews, who wanted to preserve the illusion that Jews and blacks could still be loving participants in the New Deal coalition. Jewish leftists have long wished they could vote for a serious African American presidential candidate—which is one reason they would later adulate Colin Powell. Such a politician would, it seemed, have to be a Democrat. But how many Jews could be expected to cast their vote for Condoleezza Rice as a Republican presidential standard-bearer if she was to run in 2008?

In domestic affairs, the widening breach in the alliance with African Americans significantly undermined Jewish liberal self-confidence. In the "culture war" that began to take shape during the 1980s between right and left, affirmative action—bluntly put, racial quotas in hiring—still alienated Jewish opinion even more than Jackson's bumptious insults. With the corruption of the civil rights heritage and replacement of African American leaders such as Rev. Martin Luther King Jr. by crude demagogues including Jackson and, later, Kweisi Mfume and Al Sharpton, Jews were again made to feel unwelcome by their supposed African American allies even inside the Democratic Party.

More American Jews, who were already attracted by the Israeli ascendancy of the militant Likud, became disenchanted with the Democrats. But in the short term, they were still reluctant about a new association with the Republicans. Serious consideration of the latter option would be delayed until the aftermath of September 11, 2001, and the stark choice between firm leadership of an America and a world in which Jews would be respected and secure and the abandonment of the Jews by leftist Democrats.

But something much worse for the American Jews than Jackson's insults came late in 1985. An unknown American Jew and civilian analyst for naval intelligence, Jonathan J. Pollard, was arrested by the FBI and charged with selling classified information to the Israeli government. Israel joined the United States in investigating the case, and found that Pollard had been recruited by a small scientific analysis group, independent of Mossad and the other agencies of the main intelligence apparatus in the Jewish state. The group was declared a rogue operation by the Israelis and the documents purchased from Pollard were returned to the United States.

Pollard and his wife took refuge in the Israeli embassy in Washington but were turned over by the diplomats there to the FBI. Pollard was tried and sentenced to life imprisonment. A small minority of Jewish leaders advocated a pardon and release of Pollard on the grounds that he assisted a friendly power, not an enemy. Pollard himself asserted that he had handed over only information that was relevant to Israeli security but held back by the Pentagon. This data involved Russian aid to Syria, chemical weapons technology possessed by the Iraqis and Syrians, the development of a so-called Islamic nuclear bomb by Pakistan (with Saudi encouragement unperceived at the time), and air defense systems operated by Libya. But the Pollard case gave major credibility to the defamatory claim that American Jews had divided loyalties, or a superior loyalty to the Jewish state.

Jews had in the past been accused of holding themselves apart from the Christian world as a hostile and hateful force, of various unethical business practices, and of a conspiratorial effort to control and manipulate Christendom. When, for example, Captain Dreyfus was falsely accused in France at the end of the nineteenth century of serving as a spy for Germany, the alleged motive had been Jewish self-interest, with the specter of global plotting for aggrandizement of the Jews barely hidden in the charge. But the existence of a Jewish global conspiracy could not be proven. Decades later, however, the very presence of Israel in Middle Eastern affairs had become a powerful element in the American consciousness and seemed to add substance to such charges.

The might of Israel, and the accusation of dual loyalty against Pollard, reinforced allegations, from the disreputable fringe of American politics, about international Jewish scheming. The aim of the supposed connivance shifted, however, from global financial domination, the favored motif at the time of Dreyfus, to control of American policy in the Israeli interest—finally, not much of a difference. The composition of the venom, so to speak, had changed, but its deadly effect remained the same: the Jews were suspected of deception. For the Pollard case, however, there was no cure. The damage was done, and there was nobody to blame but Pollard and those who recruited him. Yet unlike the gain in responsibility for the neoconservatives, the maturation of AIPAC, and the new American activism in the Middle East, the Pollard case had little impact on American Jews. Notwithstanding the scurrilous charges advanced by febrile Judeophobes, the wider American public saw Pollard as an exception rather than an exemplar of the American Jewish community.

Jewish neoconservatives established a coherent, cohesive, and compelling presence in American politics under Reagan, but they were viewed as hard-line anti-Communists first and Jews or Zionists second. By the time George H. W. Bush ran for president on the Republican ticket in 1988, the Soviet empire was already manifestly crumbling. The neoconservatives had been eclipsed in the Reagan administration as the Cold War approached its end and the Jewish-Democratic alliance began a revival. In 1984, the Jewish Republican vote in the presidential race had only slipped from 39 percent to 31 percent for Reagan, but the Jewish Democratic share had leaped back to 67 percent for Walter Mondale, a leftist in the northern-midwestern mold of McGovern, if somewhat more dense. In 1988 Bush won, although he got only 35 percent of the Jewish ballots against Michael Dukakis, the Democratic standard-bearer.

George H. W. Bush noticed the numbers, and became the first

U.S. chief executive to manifest a positive desire to roll back Jewish influence in Washington. Bush 41 (as his family calls him) opposed the expansion of Israeli settlements in the occupied West Bank but said publicly that his hands were tied in Middle East policy by the Jews. His secretary of state, James Baker, is reputed to have declared, "Fuck the Jews. They don't vote for us anyway." In a well-remembered 1989 speech to AIPAC, Baker called on Israel to move past the "unrealistic vision of a Greater Israel" that would include Gaza and the West Bank. In reality, neither any Israeli government nor, certainly, AIPAC had ever publicly proclaimed such a goal, and promiscuous use of the phrase, with its overtones of the Hitlerian "Greater Germany," was disturbing. Jewish newswriter Larry Cohler-Esses claimed that AIPAC's Tom Dine had tried to have him fired from *Washington Jewish Week* after Baker made this offensive statement. Cohler-Esses had described a comment by "an AIPAC *macher* from Iowa . . . saying 'That speech was garbage.'" Dine sent the newspaper's publisher a letter from the Iowan disclaiming the quote and charging that Cohler-Esses had never interviewed him. But Cohler-Esses had kept the interviewee's business card, on the back of which he had written the quote. The journalist kept his job. Cohler-Esses also described the hilarious fact that Israeli diplomats treated him as if he were an Israeli reporter— that is, as an enemy, who because he was interested in news rather than fulfillment of an official agenda could not be trusted to suppress the truth. That comment reflected extremely well on Israeli journalism but very poorly on Israeli diplomats.

It was obvious throughout the history of the Bush/Baker administration that because of the energy factor—including the Bush family's own affiliations with the oil industry—Bush 41 esteemed the Arabs and resented Jewish/Israeli pressure. Nevertheless, this period of challenge and confusion saw the same Republican president reaffirm American readiness to stand by Israel as an ally, regardless of Jewish voters' loyalty to the Democrats. Recognition of and support for the Jewish state were so embedded in American policy that to really break with these habits would have been an extremely radical act. In sum, the American Jews and Israel could be criticized, snubbed, and cheated but could not be ignored or abandoned. Unfortunately, the *shtadlan* leaders of the lobbies, as well as AIPAC, typically seemed more cowed by bad treatment than encouraged by their now undeniable standing.

In 1991, Kuwait was invaded by the armies of Saddam Hussein, and the United States joined with the Saudi kingdom to restore the rule of the Kuwaiti monarchy—the former ally of Saddam and then no friend of Israel. The territory of the Jewish state was struck by Saddam's Scud missiles, but Bush 41 restrained the Israelis from serious retaliation, to diminish discontent among the Arab members of the first anti-Saddam coalition.

During the Kuwait war, however, the propagation of mistrust for the Jews found an outstanding new exponent, louder and more aggressive than any since Father Coughlin, in the person of former Nixon speechwriter Patrick Buchanan. A Catholic from Chevy Chase, Maryland, Buchanan had a reputation as a bully since adolescence and a particularly loose pen when it came to political and ethnic obloquy. Buchanan distinguished himself by launching a freshly libelous charge. He argued that the Kuwait war was fought in the interest of the Jews and supported in Washington by "Israel's amen corner," meaning the group of American Gentile politicians known for sympathy with the Jewish state. But while Israel unquestionably feared and despised the Saddam regime, it and AIPAC, as well as the *shtadlan* Jewish groups, played almost no role in the Kuwait conflict, except to insist on the right of Israeli self-defense against the terror of the Scuds—a right never exercised. Buchanan had revived vulgar Jew-baiting for purely cynical motives, gambling that it might provide a useful means to summon up a nativist and bigoted constituency in the American body politic. The Bush 41 administration, which prosecuted the Kuwait war, paid little or no attention to Buchanan; oil was at stake in Kuwait, not in Israel.

Yet in the fight against Saddam, Israel had became the Iraqi dictator's target, and in defeating Saddam, the U.S.-led coalition had saved Israel from further harm. There now seemed more irony than analysis in the question "Is it good for the Jews?" The issue previously posed by Podhoretz assumed new gravity—why should Jews remain aligned with a Democratic Party that loudly proclaimed its pro-Israel sentiments but whose program would obviously become increasingly isolationist, ideologically rigid, corrupted by identity politics, and bereft of historical imagination? Would Jews shift their allegiance to a Republican Party that seemed, even after AWACS and the crude behavior of Bush and Baker, still better at protecting universal security, which included American Jewish and Israeli needs, at least in foreign policy?

Bush 41 was, unfortunately, poison to the Jews. If his partiality to the Arabs and his irritable attitudes were not enough, he gave off an air of the East Coast Protestant ascendancy, with its old traditions of anti-Semitism. American Jews did not allow the outcome of the Kuwait war to affect their voting patterns, and in 1992 they cast 80 percent of their ballots for Democratic candidate Bill Clinton and only 11 percent for Bush (the rest was donated to the eccentric third-party candidate Ross Perot).

The Democrats came back to rule Washington, but signs of fracture were ever more visible in the Jewish leadership. AIPAC had moved far to the right, so far that by 1992 America's Pro-Israel Lobby had begun involving Christians in its work. Thus came the fourth major seismic event for the American Jews in the second half of the twentieth century. Such a development was inconceivable in the *shtadlan* lobbies, ADL and AJC, and reflected the Reagan-era convergence of the neoconservatives with Christian conservatives, only partly based on support of the latter for Israel. But AIPAC, based in Washington, understood the political evolution of the United States far better than ADL and AJC, which remained headquartered in a Manhattan that, not least because of its Jewish history, was still considered by many people a separate country from America.

A turn to Christian conservatives by AIPAC as well as by Norman Podhoretz and some other neoconservatives has endured and remains deeply divisive among Jews. In 1981 Seymour Martin Lipset and Earl

Raab, a fellow student of Lipset when they were under Trotskyist influence at the City College of New York, published a brief but important *Commentary* article, "The Election and the Evangelicals." (Raab was also an outstanding figure in the movement for solidarity with Soviet Jews in the 1970s.) They pointed out that while conservative Protestants had been susceptible to radical anti-Semitism in the 1930s, "today's evangelical groups have made it a point to avoid this kind of hatemongering." Indeed, Moral Majority, an entity then dominant in Christian conservative politics, had expressed its desire for "dialogue" to assure Jews that "we are not an anti-Semitic group and . . . are probably the strongest supporter of Israel in the country."

Evangelicals and other conservative Christians gravitated toward Jews, but most of the latter were repelled. In 1994, ADL shed its *shtadlan* habits and, in a report titled *The Religious Right: The Assault on Tolerance and Pluralism in America,* attacked Christian conservatives for allegedly seeking to violate the American constitutional requirement for separation of church and state, and for embodying "conspiratorial, anti-Jewish, and extremist sentiments." Midge Decter replied sharply in another *Commentary* article, titled "The ADL vs. the 'Religious Right.'" Decter claimed ADL had employed a "breathy, triumphal tone in which it offers some supposedly shocking revelations . . . Christian conservatives have never concealed their view that when the Constitution says there shall be no established church, it does not intend that there shall be no expression of religion in public life." She added pointedly, "Christian conservatives are by no means alone in this view." Decter also charged ADL with a "disquieting" and "nasty" attitude toward the Christian right, arguments vaguely sourced from hostile media, distortions of the record, and charges based on guilt by association. ADL had, she said, portrayed Christian preacher and broadcaster Pat Robertson as a crony of Jew-haters, when it was clear that Robertson was extremely pro-Israel.

The alliance of Jewish neoconservatives and conservative Christians had encountered trouble after Robertson in 1991 published a book of bogus history, titled *The New World Order.* The volume offered a stale buffet of disreputable and unfounded antileftist, antiliberal, and antimodern legends dating back to the aftermath of the French Revolution. In this system of magical thinking, all the chaos, bloodshed, lost illusions, radical fantasies, and other troubles of the post-Enlightenment world were blamed on malign financiers seeking to establish a single global state. The specter of the Illuminati, a tiny eighteenth-century revolutionary faction, appeared on page 6, with the well-known name of the Rothschilds, the quintessential Jewish investment bankers, on page 7. Robertson went on to name the Warburgs and Jacob Schiff, other outstanding Jews, as participants in this fearful conspiracy, along with Karl Marx and the Trilateral Commission. But the Jewish promoters of the scheme were not identified by their religion or ethnicity, only as Germans or Europeans.

Given Robertson's repackaging of such a toxic commodity, how could any Jews ally with him, regardless of his views on Israel? Into the breach stepped Norman Podhoretz, who was prepared to offer an apologia and full absolution for a book as disgraceful and shoddy as any other such product. Four years after Robertson's ridiculous tome appeared, Podhoretz wrote "In the Matter of Pat Robertson" for *Commentary,* an article as controversial as its subject. Podhoretz reexamined the ADL's 1994 report and found it yet worse in its treatment of the television evangelist. Podhoretz admitted that Robertson's book had restated "a crackpot theory" according to which Jewish bankers sought world domination, and was reluctant to give Robertson the benefit of the doubt on these matters. Podhoretz argued that Robertson had "knowingly or unknowingly . . . subscribed to and purveyed ideas that had an old and well-established anti-Semitic pedigree." But Podhoretz finally came down on the side of Robertson, who, regardless of his shortcomings as a historian, had eloquently declared his commitment to defend and assist the Jewish people, including the Russian Jews and the state of Israel. Podhoretz also noted that the ADL had become "rather different" in its manner than it had been in the past. He was right; ADL had abandoned *shtadlan* discretion to embark on a sustained and strident campaign against Jewish involvement with many Christian conservatives.

Podhoretz summarized his judgment on Robertson, citing a rabbinical argument having to do with the unintentional and trivial impurity of portions of food, according to Jewish religious law. The food could still be consumed because of the small measure of the contamination. Podhoretz declared, "Robertson can and should be absolved on that basis of the charge of anti-Semitism." The same could not be said, Podhoretz warned, of "the other Pat, the secular one [i.e., Buchanan], who has now, alas, become rather more prominent on the Right than Robertson."

Podhoretz was certainly correct that Buchanan was worse than Robertson, but Podhoretz's apologia for Robertson was, to say the least, disingenuous. Robertson's book had the compelling illogic of a familiar Jew-baiting paranoia, even if Jews were never singled out for blame. It is difficult to imagine Robertson actually writing it; rather, it gave the impression of being a clip job assembled by a professional editor drawing on the standard protofascist literature read by cranks and illiterates for a century and a half. In terms of historical inquiry, the book was ridiculous. Paranoia about the French Revolution and the Jews had once been a Catholic rather than a Protestant staple. After all, without the Protestant Reformation there would have been no French Revolution. The Jews and Israel had been left out of Robertson's script as an expression of politeness, but it was absurd to ascribe to mere stumbling naivete the association of the proclaimed Judeophile Robertson with such an abominable rehash.

Podhoretz was a sophisticated critic and essayist who knew the difference between inept ruminations and evil propaganda, and certainly should have been familiar with this dreadful genre. Robertson has since become known for his eccentric views on everything from the State Department (which he said he would like to blow up) to state-sanctioned assassination of foreign leftist rulers. But whatever the context, the distortion of history could not be good for the Jews, who did not need such friends. Podhoretz did not end his romance with the conservative Christians there; nor did ADL cease its agitation against them. Few American Jewish leaders recognized in the Protestant friends of Israel a recrudescence of the noble Dutch Renaissance, in which a rural Christian preacher was painted, pointing to the

Hebrew *Torah* as his guide, and the works of Rembrandt celebrated Amsterdam's rabbis. Along with its achievements, greater power in Washington since the election of Reagan therefore produced a new and deep split in the Jewish leadership, soon to be complicated by more fissures.

In 1996, *Commentary* published Podhoretz's essay "How the Gay-Rights Movement Won," in which he sounded a great deal closer to Pat Buchanan than to Pat Robertson. Robertson, as a fervent Christian, disapproved of gays but did not make their harassment a primary element of his sermons. Buchanan abandoned himself to a gay-bashing rhetoric almost as lurid and inciting as his Jew-baiting. Much of Buchanan's ire was directed against the National Endowment for the Arts, which had admittedly paid for exhibits of some grossly offensive artworks. Podhoretz chimed in, cautioning that "the approving attitude of the culture toward homosexuality is overcoming the resistance of majority sentiment" in America. *Commentary*'s turn to antigay rhetoric may have appealed to conservative Christians but cost it some support among younger neoconservatives who did not share the prejudices of their elders. However, Podhoretz was once again prescient insofar as gay marriage would become a major political issue after 2004, although few Jewish conservatives would express enthusiasm for gay-baiting.

If Podhoretz downplayed problems with Christians, the ADL exaggerated them: The high-pitched hysteria of its "crusade" against conservative Christians continues today. Abraham H. Foxman, ADL's national director, led a campaign against Mel Gibson's 2004 film *The Passion of the Christ* with an alarmist allegation, expressed in an op-ed cosigned by his "interfaith consultant," Rabbi Gary Bretton-Granatoor: "For those who will see this film, the poisonous accusation that the Jews were responsible for the killing of Jesus will be unambiguous and clear." Foxman seemed convinced that Gibson's film would produce new anti-Semitic outrages in the United States. But *The Passion of the Christ* was a movie, and no more. It did not have the power to create grievances where none existed, and by 2004 complaints against Jews were to be found among isolationists of both the left and right, not among sincere Christians.

And yet the ADL offensive wears on. As 2005 came to an end, Foxman accused conservative Christians of harboring a sinister goal: "To Christianize America. To save us!" He argued that Jews could be "major victims" of conservative Christian intentions and called on AJC to join ADL and Jewish religious leaders in a united front to turn back the tide of "Christianization." Many Jewish leaders, however, simply yawned and wondered publicly if Foxman and ADL had lost their effectiveness, if not their bearings. Rabbi Jerome Epstein, executive vice president of the United Synagogue of Conservative Judaism, noted that the ADL chief "sometimes overreacts." To abandon *shtadlan* reluctance for unrestrained "ethnic panic" was to turn from one woeful extreme to another. The enemies of the American Jews have always been political rather than religious. And to be mistaken in recognizing one's enemies is the worst thing that can happen to Jews. But Foxman's underlying aim appeared to be to frighten Jews away from conservative Gentiles, that is, Republicans, and to keep them toiling on the Democratic plantation. As it happened, the twenty years that began with the election of Reagan and the enfranchisement of the neoconservatives ended with the Jews back in bondage.

The Democrats, who know more than anybody else about running plantations, found a natural leader in Bill Clinton, a southern populist who seemed made for the role of benevolent master. With Clinton in the White House, the residents of the plantation, both house servants and field hands, could spend a good deal of time relaxing. The Jewish political capital accumulated over twenty years did not diminish; it was simply left fallow. As a result, the American Jewish leadership fell into lassitude and even disarray. They could expect to get what they wanted, thanks to their votes, and felt little need to struggle for anything. Instead—in the worst *shtadlan* tradition—they deferred their interests to Clinton, who saw the achievement of peace in the Middle East as a grand performance starring himself. In this tragicomedy Jews would play only bit parts, and AIPAC, no less than the *shtadlan* lobbies, would seldom be heard.

Indeed, the main organizations drifted in different directions. AIPAC, although favorable to hard-line Israeli policies, vowed to grit its teeth and let Clinton have his chance. Furthermore, AIPAC was expressly committed to whatever options Israel adopted, and even if some American Jews were highly enthusiastic about rightist Likudniks such as Begin, Shamir, or, between 1996 and 1999, Benjamin "Bibi" Netanyahu at the head of the Jewish state, AIPAC also worked to defend the less militant Labor governments of Shimon Peres, Yitzhak Rabin, and Ehud Barak.

But with AIPAC on the right, ties with Israel under Clinton came to be influenced by minor left-liberal Jewish groups such as Americans for Peace Now (APN) and the Israel Policy Forum (IPF)—which were also affiliated with AIPAC, although they played so little a role in it they were considered outside its tent. These small factions benefited from their involvement with the Clinton administration but could never challenge AIPAC for leadership of American Jews on Israeli issues. They seemed more a relic of the radical 1960s, with a sentimental dedication to peace and reconciliation, than organizations appropriate for political affairs in the 1990s—although that could be said of many components of the Democratic-led coalition.

As Clinton began his peacemaker dance, ADL and AJC pursued their own concerns. ADL was held in the grip of its new obsession with alleged Christian threats to church-state separation in America, and AJC focused on issues of equality and social welfare. Both groups studied Arab and Islamist terrorism and extremism, in the Middle East and in the United States, where Saudi-financed Wahhabism became dominant among American Sunni Muslims, but neither agency understood or could do much about these issues. None of the major American Jewish organizations had, by the end of the twentieth century, produced new, charismatic leaders. The days of the Dubinskys and Shankers seemed to have passed for good. AJC's David Harris, and AIPAC's Dine, Kohr, and Rosen were still seldom heard in the broader American dialogue. Such figures had become quintessential bureaucrats, comparable to the third-generation proprietors of family businesses. A bland sort of "Jewish Washington" emerged in the culture of the lobbies under Clinton, based on a pose of mutual good feelings, but beneath it lurked unavoidable and bruising conflicts.

Only among the neoconservatives did signs of a critical spirit persist. Some of them had voted for Clinton against Bush in 1992, and Shachtmanite Social Democrats, who stayed in the Democratic Party as well as in the AFL-CIO bureaucracy, gained minor posts in the Clinton administration. Carl Gershman, former assistant to Jeane Kirkpatrick, had become head of the National Endowment for Democracy (NED), a federally sponsored global democratization program, in 1984. He remained in that post through successive administrations, although the NED, a major institution in the age of Reagan, was drained of vision and force under Gershman's stewardship. After the shock of September 11, 2001, the NED sought to become a major element in assisting moderate Muslim intellectuals, but lacking inspiration as well as knowledge of Islam, the NED established a close alliance with a highly questionable entity, the Center for the Study of Islam and Democracy (CSID) at Georgetown University. CSID has served as a shelter for a range of Islamist ideologues that reinvented themselves as putative Islamic reformers. Cooperation with CSID by the NED is public money wasted. Rachelle Horowitz, another Shachtman Social Democrat, rose to a high position on the Democratic National Committee.

Such individuals walked as confidently in the halls of power under Clinton as under Reagan. The Shachtmanites had come a very long way indeed from the streets around Madison Square Garden, where in 1939 they fought the New York police and the German-American Bund. But their presence in Washington was finally more symbolic than effectual, at least with the Democrats in power, for whom they were little more than a fifth wheel. Other neoconservatives argued that their standing as a separate group among conservative Americans had dissipated. In a 1999 declaration that a half dozen years later would seem absurdly shortsighted, Midge Decter claimed, "I am a neocon no longer. . . . Since I can find no significant difference from the basic views of most serious conservatives . . . it is long since time for me to drop my original designation."

But the long Israel-Arab peace festival known as Oslo, mainly and ineptly sponsored by Bill Clinton, was a real source of discord in the house of Abraham, Isaac, and Jacob. Oslo became possible when U.S. intervention in the Kuwait war was followed by the collapse of the Soviet Union in 1991. The Labor Party regained power in Israel, led by Rabin, the first native of the country to become prime minister of the Jewish state. Sudden American world hegemony, along with Israeli optimism, impelled Rabin to believe a peace agreement could be reached between Israel and its Arab foes. The apparent disappearance of Russian backing for Arafat and the PLO greatly encouraged Rabin.

Rabin was also buoyant about the election of Clinton. In the domestic context, Clinton appears as the most assiduous of the Democratic presidents in seeking to prove that the Jewish-Democratic marriage was good for its Jewish partner. Clinton's cabinets included a high rate of Jewish membership. In his second term, Madeleine Albright served as secretary of state—a woman who acknowledged her Jewish background later in life; Robert Rubin was treasury secretary from 1995 to 1999; Robert Reich was first-term secretary of labor; Dan Glickman was second-term secretary of agriculture; and Mickey Kantor was commerce secretary in 1996. (William S. Cohen, defense secretary after 1997, is a Unitarian whose father was Jewish but not his mother, leaving him outside the Hebrew people.) Jews were prominent at every level of Clinton's and the Democratic Party's bureaucracies, and well represented in other appointments.

For example, Clinton named forty-four Jews to the federal Appeals Courts, far outpacing his predecessors, and reflecting higher-than-ever Jewish participation in the legal profession. By contrast, Bush 41 made only twelve such appointments, and Reagan had selected twenty-seven. During Clinton's presidency, the group of Jewish Democrats in the Senate rose to seven, nearly doubling the total when compared with previous administrations. (In 2006, eleven Jews sit in the Senate, of whom only two are Republicans.)

Jewish involvement in the Democratic leadership fused with Clinton's Arkansas populist messianism—a vanity that often resembled the "Christian Zionism" of Pat Robertson and other pro-Israel fundamentalist Protestants, since it emerged from a common southern white culture. With these factors driving him, the Oslo agreement in 1993 allowed Clinton to forever revel in a famous photo image where he stood between Rabin and Arafat as they shook hands to seal the new hopes for peace. The Hebron massacre of Muslims by an American-born doctor, Baruch Goldstein, in 1994 and Rabin's assassination the following year by another deranged opponent of Oslo were traumatic for American Jews, Israel, and the world but had no impact on the peace process itself.

Oslo originally had three essential points: Israeli withdrawal from Gaza, plus economic development and international aid for the Palestinians. In its final form Oslo envisioned continued Israeli control of Jerusalem and no removal of settlements in the West Bank, recognition of the Palestinian Authority (PA) as a governing power, and a Palestinian pledge to stop anti-Israel violence.

But Oslo was a mere revival of the theater piece associated with the Camp David Accords, accepted by Begin and Egyptian dictator Anwar Sadat with Jimmy Carter hovering as their angel, beginning in 1978. If ever there were proof of Karl Marx's famous dictum that history repeats itself tragically, it was visible when "the spirit of Camp David," embodying an artificial conciliation between Israel and Egypt, was resuscitated, after fifteen years, in the form of Oslo.

The 1978 accommodation at Camp David had also revitalized the Jewish-Democratic alliance and cheered up peace-hungry Israelis. But it had a different impact on Egypt and among the Palestinians. In the ranks of Arabs, an extremist Islamic subculture originally fostered from the 1930s to the 1950s by the Muslim Brotherhood, or *Ikhwan*, had been nurtured with generous Saudi financial help. Sadat's acceptance of peace with the Jewish state became a pretext for Egyptian Muslim fundamentalists to produce new and more violent forms of protest. This phenomenon culminated in the emergence of Egyptian Islamic Jihad, a forerunner of al-Qaeda, which assassinated Sadat in a terror orgy in 1981. By 1987, the same movement—the Muslim Brotherhood—would provide the organizational basis for the Islamic radicalism of Hamas, while Saudi Arabia paid its bills.

Arafat was not Sadat, which was a defining aspect of Oslo and of its insubstantial quality. Arafat could never make his word good, as Sadat could, even if briefly. Sadat had sympathized with the *Ikhwan* at the time of the Nasser revolution, in which he was a leading participant. But Sadat ruled an Egypt possessing an industrial infrastructure that, notwithstanding frightful corruption, could absorb an immense quantity of U.S. military and economic aid. American economic help to Egypt has averaged $2 billion per year since 1979, thanks to Carter and Camp David. Sadat had reason to believe he could curb Islamic extremism by business incentives along with a crackdown, and he was no stranger to the application of harsh repression.

By contrast, Arafat could not assimilate foreign aid for productive use or stiffen his forces to suppress terrorism. Always reminded of Sadat's gruesome death, Arafat would soon bow to the volatile Israelophobia of the Saudi-backed Hamas. Oslo brought to an end the first *intifada,* or Palestinian uprising. That internal Arab assault in Israel and the West Bank, originating in 1987, had already slackened off after the defeat of Saddam in 1991. But after the signing of Oslo, Hamas soon raised the level of terrorist aggression anew.

A part of the American Jewish intelligentsia, including neoconservatives charmed by Bibi Netanyahu and other articulate elements of the Likud right, were never reconciled to Oslo. Throughout the Clinton period, the more militant section of Jewish Washington, including such mainstream adornments of the Jewish-Democratic marriage as the *New Republic* magazine, accused Clinton's diplomats and Jewish advisers, from chief negotiator Dennis Ross and his main assistant Aaron Miller (an Orthodox Jew) to Martin Indyk, the first Jewish U.S. ambassador to Israel, of "Arabist" sympathies.

"Arabism," meaning academic or political training resulting in pro-Arab sentiments reminiscent of those historically associated with the British Foreign Office, had long been a problem in the State Department. But American policy under Clinton, which strove for fairness to both sides, was repeatedly depicted by the Israeli right and

its partisans in Jewish Washington as deliberately aimed at selling out
Israel. The level of rage and invective expressed in these polemics was
extraordinary. Urbane and perceptive Martin Indyk was a particular
target. Born in London and raised in Australia, he had worked on
Middle East problems for the Australian government. He was brought
to Washington to work at AIPAC by none other than Steve Rosen, an
example of Rosen's organizational gift and political savvy. Indyk
became the first executive director of the Washington Institute on
Near East Policy (WINEP) and served in various posts in the Clinton
administration before being named ambassador to Israel in 1995. The
latter posting was a triumph for AIPAC, and Indyk came under major
attack from Arab advocates in the United States because of his experience with the Israel lobby.

He proved a loyal servant of Clinton's peace ambitions and found
himself subject to humiliating and gross insults from Jewish right-
wingers. Indyk was personally vilified as a traitor to the Jewish people. Reappointed as ambassador in 2000, Indyk told a Reform Jewish
group that Jerusalem "is not, and cannot, be the exclusive preserve of
one religion, and the solution cannot come from one side challenging or denying another side's beliefs." President Morton Klein of the
small but vociferous Zionist Organization of America (ZOA), considered by the *shtadlan* leaders and AIPAC an annoyance more than a
serious force, claimed that Indyk had called for the division of
Jerusalem, a source of great anxiety for the right wing of Israel's supporters. An Israeli legislator referred to Indyk as a "Jewboy."

The same vulgar manner would be employed against the man
who succeeded Indyk as ambassador to Israel in 2001, Daniel Kurtzer,
another Orthodox Jew. Kurtzer, a Foreign Service employee and academic Middle East expert, had already passed a more serious test
when he became U.S. ambassador to Egypt in 1997—the first Jew to
represent the United States in an Arab state. He was viciously carica-
tured in Egyptian media, known for their gutter proclivities. Yet
behind the scenes, as early as 1991, at the Madrid conference convened
by Secretary of State Baker that laid the basis for Oslo, some right-
wing Israelis labeled Kurtzer, along with Ross and Miller, "Baker's Jew-

boys." Considering Baker's objectionable views, it was difficult to imagine a worse reproach.

In 2001, Clinton's second term ended. At the close of the epoch that began with Reagan's election, Jewish power was more formidable than ever in Washington, but the global situation had turned very bad for the Jews, and the Jewish-Democratic alliance had suddenly undergone new strains. Another Palestinian uprising began, known as the second *intifada,* seemingly caused when Ariel Sharon undertook a walking tour, in September 2000, to the al-Aqsa mosque and the Dome of the Rock, the Islamic precincts of the Temple Mount in Jerusalem. But the insurrection had really followed Arafat's rejection in July of the Clinton-sponsored effort, accepted by Israeli Labor prime minister Barak, to arrive at a new peace agreement at Camp David. The first Camp David agreement and Oslo should have made such an effort obviously dubious, but Clinton had a perception of his own glory and would not hold back his ambitions; unfortunately, neither would Arafat, and their conceptions were highly dissimilar.

Prior to Arafat's refusal of an agreement and Sharon's well-publicized stroll, Israel had withdrawn from southern Lebanon, occupied by Hezbollah, in May 2000. Leaving Lebanon was viewed by many Israelis and American Jews as a much greater incentive for the violence of the second *intifada* than Sharon's visit to the Temple Mount. Although Sharon was seen as asserting a Jewish right of access to the area, religious Jews are barred from gathering on the top of the Mount until the coming of the Messiah. Sharon's action reflected his secular upbringing as well as his provocative personality.

The second *intifada,* which produced waves of Arab violence, had significant economic as well as political and psychological effects on the relations between Israel and American Jews. Israel's vital tourism industry had for years been a mainstay of support for Zionism, attracting increasing numbers of American Christians as well as Jews, and becoming as political as pleasure driven. Israeli tourism was shaken by the impact of the new fighting, with some Israeli and

American Jewish tourism officials charging that one of their biggest problems was the U.S. State Department, which warned American citizens to steer clear of Israel and the occupied territories. In this context, at least, the Clinton administration could not maintain its commitments to Israel and the American Jewish leadership, however it might have wished to do so.

The main item of complaint by Israeli officials was an October 24, 2000, State Department travel advisory urging Americans to "defer" travel plans to Israel, the West Bank, and Gaza. The advisory "caused an immediate collapse of tourism in Israel," said the Jewish state's tourism commissioner for North America, Aryeh Sommer. "We estimate that around 80 percent of cancellations—a loss of $1 billion—were caused by this warning," Sommer said. "People took the warning seriously and preferred to postpone their trips. This included Christian groups as well as Jewish groups and individuals."

A State Department representative said the advisory was warranted by increased risk in the area. But Israeli tourism experts insisted it was unjustified. Amnon Lipkin-Shahak, Israel's tourism minister and Sommer's boss, described the crisis in dire terms in a speech in Chicago early in November 2000. Addressing the General Assembly of the United Jewish Communities, the national body coordinating Jewish charities, Shahak painted a dramatic picture of empty hotels, idled workers, and a devastated economy. He begged the community leaders to organize group visits, to show solidarity with the Jewish state and pour dollars into its tourism industry. "We need you," he said.

But while local Jewish federations and other groups pledged to send symbolic delegations, there were few signs of any organized effort to have the State Department travel advisory lifted. Indeed, some key Jewish activists said they hesitated to question the State Department's judgment in a matter where American citizens' safety was at issue.

At least one Jewish leader, perhaps predictably, read darker motives into the advisory. "All too often the State Department has used travel advisories against going to Israel as a form of political pressure," said ZOA's Mort Klein. Israel had expected to attract millions of non-Jewish visitors in winter 2000–2001, as the second Christian millennium came to an end and the third began. Tourists who made it to Israel found some of their intended destinations off-limits because of the second *intifada*.

This discouraging sequence of events was received with ill-concealed glee by those American Jewish leaders who had never been enthusiastic about Oslo. Advocates for Israel whose pessimism was rejected as alarmist pointed to Oslo's failure as something ordained from the beginning, proving that hard-liners against the Arabs were right. AIPAC insiders expressed the same opinion, but only off the record.

At the close of the Clinton years, the Jewish-Democratic alliance appeared to have survived intact, but in fact it was deeply weakened internally. American Jews found themselves pushed by African American hostility, the culture war, and the discontents of Oslo into a new wandering in the desert. With bargaining for peace between the Israelis and Arabs apparently discredited, the stage was set for the triumph of a hard right-wing line in the Jewish leadership.

The election of 2000 brought George W. Bush to power, with an open disdain for the role of America as a broker of any kind in the Middle East and a notable reputation for Arabist sympathies similar to those of his father. Jews gave Bush 43 a marginally higher percentage of their votes—19 percent—than the 16 percent they had posted for Robert Dole, the Republican candidate in 1996. Bush 43 gained eight points over the ignominious 11 percent his father received from Jews in 1992. Democrat Al Gore and his running mate, Senator Joe Lieberman of Connecticut, obtained 79 percent of the Jewish vote.

The novelty of Lieberman, an Orthodox Jew, on the national ticket, considered a historic step by many of his coreligionists, would have helped rally Jews to the old Democratic stand. But the pro-Jewish reputation of the Clinton Democrats, including Gore, had been sufficient to temporarily conjure up the apparition of another happy anniversary for the Jewish-Democratic marriage. The Republican victory was contested, uselessly, in a Jewish stronghold: Florida. In one of the great comic moments of modern American political life,

George W. Bush prevailed in part because the "butterfly ballot" used in Florida so confused elderly Jews that almost 3,500 votes in Palm Beach County, which was normally a safe Jewish Democratic zone, had been cast for Pat Buchanan, running on the so-called Reform Party ticket. Clearly something was wrong with the system, but the results stood.

More important, however, would Bush 43 be good for the Jews?

CHAPTER 6

GEORGE W. BUSH AND THE JEWS

Before September 11

George W. Bush and his vice president, Dick Cheney, came to the White House in 2001 with several handicaps, as far as many American Jews were concerned. The president's father's tilt to the Arabs was not forgotten. Cheney was viewed as sharing such proclivities. Al Gore, the defeated Democrat standard-bearer, with Joe Lieberman as his running mate, was unequivocally devoted to the Jewish-Democratic alliance and support for Israel. The younger Bush had committed various gaffes during the election campaign. He had allowed himself to be photographed with Sami al-Arian, a Florida computer science professor and a leader, from the shores of the United States, of Palestinian Islamic Jihad in its violent assault against Israel. (Al-Arian was later tried on terrorist charges and ordered deported.) During the presidential debate with Gore, Bush had also stated, to the outrage of experts on Islamist extremism, that he opposed the use of "secret evidence" in terrorism investigations involving Arab Americans. Soon enough, and ironically, secret evidence would become a pillar of Bush policy in such matters.

On both sides of the Jewish street, domestic and Israelocentric, opinion about Bush early in 2001 was equally and resoundingly negative. Nobody thought Bush's cabinet would include Jewish representation comparable to that in the Clinton administration. This was at first as much a presumption by Republican neoconservatives as Democrats. Ari Fleischer, Bush 43's first press secretary, was seen by many Jews as a token Hebrew in the new administration. ADL expressed its now-habitual concern about conservative Christian influence on the Republican Party and Bush, and possible threats to separation of church and state. Liberal Jewish groups such as the Religious Action Center, headed by Reform rabbi David Saperstein, kept a close watch on Washington developments and harshly criticized Bush 43's commitment to "faith-based" charity—community relief through churches and other religious institutions. Faith-based charity was a central element of "compassionate conservatism," Bush 43's electoral platform.

When it appeared early in 2001 that Bush was serious about implementing federal support for faith-based charities, Jewish opinion was almost unanimously opposed to the concept. The most commonly stated fear involved the familiar anxiety over church-state separation: alarm that Christian charities, financed by government, would use their community assistance activities to proselytize. The quarrel over faith-based charities thus reproduced earlier liberal versus conservative arguments over school vouchers. Liberals, including many Jews, claimed that government would violate the establishment clause of the First Amendment by allowing parents with vouchers covering tuition fees to put their children in private and parochial schools. The Jewish split over vouchers further recalled an underlying grievance of the New York City education wars of the 1960s: declining public school quality. Some pious Jews, represented by the Union of Orthodox Jewish Congregations, or Orthodox Union (OU), supported vouchers, but their voice tended to be lost in the liberal roar.

Condemning faith-based charities, Rabbi Saperstein commented, "When President-elect Bush calls on churches, synagogues and

mosques to accept taxpayer money for their community-service programs, we hope their leaders will respond that America's religious
community is not for sale." Another concern lurked behind Jewish
and Democratic jeers at "faith-based" relief: that it would render a
sacred New Deal principle—the social welfare safety net—obsolete.
In truth, the latter suspicion was probably accurate; had faith-based
services effectively replaced government relief, American society
would have returned to the kind of voluntaristic solutions for poverty
and deprivation that existed before the Great Depression of the
1930s—and to most conservative Republicans, including some neoconservatives, that would have been fine.

Jewish irritability about the new president extended to international issues. The naming of General Colin Powell as secretary of state
met with Jewish enthusiasm as a sign of color blindness in the Republican White House. But Bush Republicans were feared as possible isolationists, and nobody among Jews had a clear perception of how far
Powell's known opposition to foreign intervention might extend.
Many Republicans had adopted isolationist rhetoric in criticism of
Clinton's humanitarian interventions in the Balkans. On the latter
issue, neoconservatives and the domestic Jewish groups, ADL and
AJC, along with countless rabbis, were united against the isolationists.
Most Jewish groups raised common demands for urgent action to res-
cue the mainly Muslim victims of Serbian aggression in Bosnia and
Kosovo. One thing had to be said for the Jews: they knew an attempt
at genocide when they saw it.

A much-discussed rivalry for the post of defense secretary
emerged between Paul D. Wolfowitz and former senator Dan Coats
of Indiana during the 2001 transition period. A favorite of the Christian right, Coats represented an extreme case of Clintonophobic isolationism. Coats referred to Bosnia as a "quagmire"—a term redolent
of Vietnam, and used in America only and exclusively to evoke the
tragedy of that war. Wolfowitz, until 2001 known mainly as a bright
but rather shy weapons systems analyst, favored Kosovo-style operations. Finally, however, neither won the prize. Coats ended up as an
ineffectual U.S. ambassador to Germany. Donald H. Rumsfeld was

named defense secretary—a post he had held under President Gerald Ford—and Wolfowitz became his deputy.

A veteran neoconservative, dating to his association with Scoop Jackson, Wolfowitz had been one of the leading members of Bush's "Vulcans," or foreign policy team, during the 2000 campaign. The Vulcans also comprised Powell; Rumsfeld and Dick Cheney, both former defense secretaries, the latter in the Kuwait war cabinet of Bush 41; Richard Armitage, a high Defense Department official under Reagan; Condoleezza Rice, a veteran national security expert, also under Reagan and Bush 41; and former secretary of state George Shultz.

The Vulcans functioned well as an advisory group to the Republican candidate in the contest with Gore and Lieberman, but significant differences were present, setting them off into two distinct factions. Powell's fear of internationalist initiatives, as head of the Joint Chiefs of Staff under Bush 41 and Clinton, was notorious. He had even opposed the military action in Kuwait that made him famous, to the outrage, notably, of Dick Cheney. At least figuratively, Bosnian blood stained Powell's hands, since he helped to successfully dissuade Bush 41 and delay Clinton from any effort to end the atrocities in the former Yugoslavia. After the Bosnian crisis became acute in 1993, Powell had an infamous exchange with Madeleine Albright, then U.S. ambassador to the United Nations, who asked forthrightly, "What's the point of having this superb military that you're always talking about if we can't use it?"

Powell, notable for an unctuous self-righteousness, later recalled, "I thought I would have an aneurysm." Powell was manifestly afraid of the big, bad Serbian armies, which consistently demonstrated that their chief military prowess consisted in rape, killing the elderly, firing antiaircraft weapons at civilians and especially children, and destroying holy sites, private homes, and public institutions. Powell invoked his service in Indochina as an explanation for his hesitation about committing any American troops anywhere. Thus the nightmare of Bosnia continued, even after Powell resigned from the Clinton team in 1993. Clinton finally acted in Bosnia in 1995—and again in Kosovo in 1999—and in neither case was a single American soldier lost in combat. Bosnia and Kosovo were not quagmires and were definitely not comparable to Vietnam. Powell's histrionics had done nothing but encourage the Serbs to act with continued impunity in their decade-long rampage of Balkan murder, rape, and pillage.

At first, Powell was expected to dominate the foreign policy of Bush 43's administration. But notwithstanding the illusion of amity among the Vulcans, he appeared from the moment of his nomination as secretary of state in January 2001 to be headed into a cockpit of ideological and bureaucratic infighting. Against him stood the harder conservatives, friendly with the neoconservatives and grouped in a phalanx around Rumsfeld.

Powell and Rumsfeld were separated by marked personal as well as philosophical differences. In contrast with Powell, the embodiment of isolationist reticence, Rumsfeld favored a vigorous exercise of American global power. Powell was intellectually mediocre, while Rumsfeld had steeped himself not only in the bureaucratic workings of the Pentagon and the defense industry but also in the world of conservative and neoconservative think tanks. He was among very few individuals who passed easily from one to the other: from the milieu of President Ford to that of Norman Podhoretz. This was, to cite another example demonstrating its rarity, a facility enjoyed by Lynne Cheney, who headed the National Endowment for the Humanities; but it was absent from her husband, Dick. Cheney, for his part, much preferred the tough, driven Rumsfeld to the diffident and petulant Powell. Indeed, given past tensions between Powell and Cheney, it immediately seemed likely that the Bush administration could harbor two rival foreign-policy centers that would balance each other uneasily, if at all. Nevertheless, Washington Jewish opinion, like Washington opinion in general, was vague about the Vulcans. Cheney and Rice were both considered captives of oil interests, and most observers assumed that, as Cheney had aggressively done in 1991, they would support any conceivable action to protect Middle East energy allies such as Kuwait. At the beginning of 2001, that was about as much as most Jewish sources would or could say about the Bush 43 foreign-policy team.

Some Washingtonians were paying closer attention than others. "Things are not shaping up as people thought. Foreign policy will not be entirely dictated by Powell," said Gary Schmitt, then–executive director of the Project for the New American Century (PNAC), and, at the time of this writing, a scholar at the American Enterprise Institute. PNAC was a "pocket think tank" supported by William Kristol, editor of the *Weekly Standard,* the main organ of the younger, Washington-based group of neoconservatives. The younger neoconservatives were soon to exercise an important influence in administration policy, and Arab apologists, Jew-baiters, radical leftists, and other neoisolationists would ascribe to PNAC a scope and potency far beyond reality. Indeed, after the 2003 Iraq war began, paranoia about PNAC would become so extreme that family members, and others associated with Kristol and his group, seriously worried about their physical security and that of PNAC personnel. In reality, PNAC was a limited organization run more like a department of the *Weekly Standard* than as a major Washington policy institution. Kristol's *Weekly Standard* editorials would pack more punch, and the importance of PNAC lay in them, not vice versa.

Powell and Dick Armitage, soon named as the former's deputy at State, shared a distaste for the intellectual manners as well as the internationalist activism of their fellow Vulcan Wolfowitz. Armitage had once been a close associate of Wolfowitz in the Reagan State Department but developed an openly contemptuous attitude toward him. Armitage was considered by Powell one of the "regular guys" who, like Powell, spent their weekends tearing down their cars while Wolfowitz preferred to read articles in *Commentary* (to paraphrase "a veteran of the first Bush administration" quoted without attribution in the *Washington Post*). This comment, reported early in Bush's first term, would prove remarkably pregnant with significance. Like his vigorous predecessor Reagan, who appointed the memorable Ambassador Kirkpatrick on the strength of an article in the neoconservative equivalent of the *Racing Form,* it turned out that Bush was more impressed with weekend *Commentary* readers than with people who liked to get dirty handling Volvo parts. Before the end of 2001, Wolfowitz and other Jews among the neoconservatives, *Commentary* fans all, would appear as powerful as any group of Jews ever to serve in American government, and with the backing of Bush and Rumsfeld, they would help decide American foreign policy.

In 2001, however, Powell still cut a formidable figure in Washington and around the country. Considered a hero of the Kuwait war and a political moderate, he won a 77 percent approval rating in a CNN/ *Time* poll taken around the time of his nomination to State, higher than any other figure on the Bush team. Differing opinions about Powell and Rumsfeld among Republican insiders, and the incipient rivalry between their camps, became even more complex when Wolfowitz joined Rumsfeld at Defense after being rejected by Powell for a position at State.

Wolfowitz was believed to hold strong pro-Israel sympathies, mainly because of his Jewishness. But although he wanted Israel to be safe, Wolfowitz was never an aggressive Zionist. Rather, the two teams—Powell and Armitage on one hand, Rumsfeld and Wolfowitz on the other—appeared to represent the alternative faces of a more traditional American policy: soft speech versus the big stick. The Jewish lobbies stood aside from these contradictions, which, to put it very mildly, became a great deal more significant than they appeared at the time, and were originally overshadowed by Bush's alleged Arabism. Many observers hazarded the belief that Bush intended to position himself between Powell and Rumsfeld, with neither having the upper hand. At the beginning, they were probably correct. Bush 43 was known as a politician who relished debate among his advisers, with competing strategies on offer, from which he could then choose.

As a second-level decision maker, Wolfowitz had excellent academic and diplomatic qualifications. A shy and scholarly man with an understanding of complex technology as well as political structures, Wolfowitz emerged from a background that hardly indicated just how exceptional his life would become. He was born in 1943 in New York. His father, Jacob Wolfowitz, was a noted figure in the theory of statistics who taught at Columbia University, Cornell, and the University of Illinois at Urbana-Champaign, with visiting professorships at other leading institutions. The family were survivors of the Holocaust, even though Jacob and his father had escaped before it began; they alone had emigrated from Poland to the United States. The extended family they left behind disappeared in the night and fog of Nazism. In 2003, Paul Wolfowitz, at a pinnacle of authority in the Pentagon, discussed this fact in a markedly subdued way with *Washington Post* reporter Thomas E. Ricks. He said only, "It was a fairly poor family in Poland," and when pressed about whether he knew the dates or place of their deaths, he said, "I really don't."

It might be argued that Paul Wolfowitz grew up in the presence of two kinds of human void: an emptiness of familial memory, and a vast system of abstractions, represented by his father's field of achievement. Perhaps in response to this background, Paul Wolfowitz burned with an uncommon imaginative flame.

Jacob Wolfowitz appears to have pushed Paul to study science and mathematics, since the father viewed the social sciences as "soft." Paul dutifully gained an undergraduate degree in mathematics and chemistry from Cornell but then struck out on his own to gain a master's and doctorate in political science and economics at the University of Chicago. There he studied under Albert Wohlstetter, a theorist of strategy, but also came to know the philosopher and intellectual historian Allan Bloom, a circumstance that led to claims that Wolfowitz was the model for the character of Philip Gorman in the novel *Ravelstein*, by Bloom's friend Saul Bellow. (Ravelstein was Bloom himself.)

In Bellow's account, Gorman is presented as a Defense Department official during the Gulf War of 1991. Bellow writes, purportedly describing Jacob and Paul Wolfowitz, "Gorman's academic father had strongly objected to the Ravelstein seminars in which Philip was enrolled. . . . 'Of course old Gorman would be too rigid to be grateful that his son did not go into business administration,' [Ravelstein] said. 'Well, Philip is now one of the [Defense] Secretary's closest advisers.

He has a powerful mind and a real grasp of great politics, this kid, whereas statisticians are as common as minnows.' "

But Wolfowitz's career was nothing meteoric. In the 1970s, he began as an assistant professor of political science at Yale University, then took a series of jobs in the U.S. Arms Control and Disarmament Agency before serving as deputy assistant secretary of defense (regional programs) under President Jimmy Carter. A short period at the Johns Hopkins University School of Advanced International Studies (SAIS) preceded postings, under Reagan, as director of policy planning for the State Department and assistant secretary of state for East Asian and Pacific affairs. During his latter service he helped effect the transition away from the Philippine dictatorship of Ferdinand Marcos. In calling for the United States to cease backing Marcos, he was a rare figure in the Reagan administration. From 1986 to 1989, he was U.S. ambassador to Indonesia, an experience that deeply affected him. His long stay in Jakarta brought him into contact with a pluralistic and moderate style of Islam (in the largest Muslim country on the planet) that led him into a real quest for comprehension of the faith of Muhammad.

His Indonesian assignment was followed by four years, under Bush 41, as undersecretary of defense for policy, reporting to then defense secretary Cheney. Between his departure from that post in 1993 and his appointment by George W. Bush, he returned to SAIS at Johns Hopkins as its dean. Wolfowitz often told friends and interviewers that the main influence on his development had been the removal of Marcos. As he said to Michael Dobbs of the *Washington Post*, "I actually thought it was the high point of my career. I never expected to do anything as interesting or as important." In the longer view of his life, however, the Philippines had led him to Indonesia, and the understanding of Islam he gained in the world's most populous Muslim country proved among his greater assets.

Wolfowitz, as an adamantine product of the Scoop Jackson/ Reagan tradition, was an unapologetic interventionist. But in the early period of Bush 43's administration, with isolationism widely believed to be the dominant philosophy, few thought Wolfowitz would dissent

from it. On one memorable occasion early in 2001, Michael O'Hanlon of the Brookings Institution, among Washington's preeminent
"policy wonks," in a discussion of the future of Kosovo, specifically
singled out Wolfowitz as someone in the Bush camp he believed
would be reluctant to support military remedies for humanitarian
crises. O'Hanlon appeared somewhat confused when reminded that
Wolfowitz, like other neoconservatives with whom he was associated,
had pressed Clinton for action in the Balkans.

While some saw Powell sharing authority with Rumsfeld, others predicted that Powell would end up playing a subordinate role to Rumsfeld. "Rummy" was and remains a consummate manager of the system
in Washington. But neoconservative Jews, AIPAC, and their Gentile
friends also approved the appointments of Rumsfeld and Wolfowitz,
if only because of their tough reputations. "It speaks extremely well
of Bush that he would choose Rumsfeld rather than someone who
would be no more than a cipher for Powell," said Frank Gaffney of the
Center for Security Policy (CSP). Gaffney and his small Washington
think tank were and remain minor but loud Gentile enthusiasts for
the militant wing of the Israel lobby. "In the end," Gaffney said,
"Rumsfeld and Wolfowitz could have greater authority than Powell."
The comment was extremely prescient.

   Although few would say so on the record, many in the Jewish leadership worried that Powell would be less pro-Israel than his recent predecessors at State. He was dovish while AIPAC, after the collapse of Oslo,
was hawkish. In addition, notwithstanding his early and open opposition to the Kuwait war, once combat began, Powell developed personal
associations with the Saudis and, by extension, other Arab leaders.

   A furor broke out over Powell's acceptance of a large speaking fee
at Tufts University from a lecture fund endowed by Issam Fares, a
politician associated with Rafiq Hariri, then prime minister of
Lebanon, who was assassinated in 2005. Fares, like Hariri, was said by
pro-Israel activists to have links to Hezbollah. The controversy

seemed to die down quickly. But Jewish skepticism about Powell's global perspectives was still heard, including his cautious approach to military engagement and his belief that American policy should be guided by American interests, defined narrowly, rather than a broad set of universal ideals or values.

With the new administration's foreign policy taking shape, leaders of the Israel lobby, as well as the domestic Jewish leadership, displayed a near-universal hesitation to voice criticisms that might limit future access to the incoming president or his secretary of state. "Nobody in the Jewish community wants to offend Powell," said one prominent Jewish figure. "His people are already defensive about the Tufts speech, and Jews do not want to be closed out for four years." Indeed, the Jewish leadership declined to probe Powell and proved reluctant to examine Bush 43 on Israeli issues—they were afraid they would find an Arabist wolf in sheep's clothing, or even a supporter of Palestinian claims.

Republican and conservative critics were equally loath to cross Powell, mainly because his Kuwait experience had left him with so impressive a public profile and his color provided the administration with credibility on race. Neoconservatives, however, repeatedly cited, as expressive of their concerns about Powell, an opinion essay in the *Washington Post* in 2000. It was written by Robert Kagan, a former Reagan administration foreign policy expert and another leading member of the Bill Kristol wing of younger neoconservatives. Kagan wrote, "Naming Powell may be good politics, but will it make for a good foreign policy? Not if past performance means anything."

Kagan, like others associated with Kristol, was and remains moderate in his enthusiasm for the Israel lobby and its agenda. Neither are they the sort of people who spend a great deal of time wondering whether American policies are good for the Jews; rather, they have emphasized universal, democratizing options that are good for the Jews because they are good for the world. A rising tide of stability and prosperity would raise the Jewish boat along with the rest. These younger Jewish neoconservatives sometimes disagreed with domestic

Jewish policies or Israeli tactics. Jewish neoconservatives did not and do not see eye to eye with ADL or AJC on relations with conservative Christians, about which the neoconservatives are much more optimistic than the *shtadlan* lobbies. Washington neoconservatives generally favor more, rather than less, religion in public life; they have not inherited the antireligious neuroses that their ex-leftist forebears among the neoconservatives occasionally displayed. Jewish neoconservatives in Washington were also more sympathetic to Ariel Sharon's turn to centrist solutions in Israel than their predecessors at *Commentary* or their peers in AIPAC.

Colin Powell, for his part, emerged from the Kuwait war in a role seldom seen in America for several generations: that of the Third World–style "political general" whose military standing had granted him a much bigger career in public life than he might otherwise have attained. The media were anything but hesitant to aver that race played a major part in Powell's rise. African American demagogues spoke unfairly when they accused Powell of being "white" or subservient in his outlook, but to many who observed him directly, unfiltered by media adulation, Powell seemed empty. His race, his manner of speech, and his "golf course" personality—nearly always referring to his subordinates and nominees by nicknames, with a veneer of extreme confidence—made him eminently valuable at administration photo opportunities. If ever there was a secretary of state for whom style was more significant than substance, it was Powell.

Powell could also be extremely charming to Jews, regaling them with tales of his teenage years as a "shabbas goy" hired by pious Ashkenazim in New York City, where he had been taken by his Jamaican parents, to turn electric switches and perform other tasks forbidden to Orthodox Jews on the Sabbath. A handful of Yiddish phrases he picked up also helped him when meeting with Jews, as, of course, did the long-established willingness of liberal Jews to consider the appointment of any black to a high position as a victory for all oppressed or formerly oppressed folk.

One could never imagine Powell emitting the venomous hatred

for Jews heard from "mainstream" black politicians such as Cynthia McKinney, the Georgia Democrat who regularly flailed at Israel as well as at President Bush in terms that led many observers to doubt her sanity. In 2002, for example, she delivered herself of the judgment that the chief executive and his administration had "personally profited" from terrorist attacks on the United States. Yet when he was paired with serious political operators and intellectuals such as Rumsfeld and Wolfowitz, Powell had nothing to offer but bluffing and clichés—just as he had when he tried to obstruct the intervention of American power in Kuwait and the Balkans.

It could be argued that Powell played his cards close to the vest, except that he had no cards save exhausted nostrums. Jewish leaders were willing to give him the benefit of the doubt if only to reinforce their benevolent reputation on racial issues, but aside from his criticism of direct American military action overseas, his attitudes could not be predicted. Kagan hammered at Powell's early lack of enthusiasm for the Kuwait war. "Like a majority of Senate Democrats (but not Al Gore)," Kagan wrote, "Powell wanted to limit the American response to economic sanctions. Like Pat Buchanan, Powell believed 'the American people do not want their young dying for $1.50 a gallon oil.' Defending Saudi Arabia and leaving the Iraqi army in Kuwait was the 'prudent option.'"

One could hardly imagine a more devastating parallel than that between the ameliorative Powell and the agitated Buchanan. For Jews, the Irish thug of the Chevy Chase public playground had become the most contemptible figure in American politics. Norman Podhoretz had reputedly said that if Buchanan were ever elected president, he would head for the mountains and counsel armed resistance.

Most important, Kagan pointed out a significant division between Powell and Cheney. "At the time [of the Kuwait war], Dick Cheney and other top Bush officials were aghast at Powell's timid response," he wrote. "As Brent Scowcroft writes in his memoirs [coauthored with Bush 41], 'I was frankly appalled at the undertone of the discussion, which suggested resignation to the [Iraqi] invasion and even adaptation to a *fait accompli*."

Kagan and other neoconservatives, however, perceived something that liberal Jews frightened of the Arabist Bush 41, hollow men such as Powell, and Republican isolationists seemed to ignore: George W. Bush was prepared from the beginning of his administration to deal firmly with Iraq. He is his own man, not his father's son, and wanted to complete the task Bush 41 left unfinished. Only weeks after Bush's inauguration, American and British jet pilots swooped down on Saddam's upgraded radar. This represented no departure from established policy toward Iraq. U.S. and British air forces had patrolled no-fly zones over Iraqi Kurdistan and the country's southern Shia Muslim area since the end of the Kuwait war, and 1998 had seen a brief but intense bombing campaign, known as "Desert Fox," against Iraqi targets. Raids on Iraq had continued through the end of Clinton's presidency. In effect, Bush had illustrated that he would not do anything new, that is, would not stop the pressure on Saddam.

The air strike also exposed the pitfalls of action against the Baghdad regime, for a troublesome issue intruded in the form of Chinese technicians on the ground, serving an Iraqi regime that most of the world considered an international outlaw. In the aftermath of the bombing, Pentagon sources said the action was carried out on a Friday, to avoid killing Chinese personnel assisting in the completion of a fiber-optic network serving the Iraqi antiaircraft system. The Chinese were mainly civilians, with some military officers alongside of them, but they did not work on Friday, the day of Muslim collective prayer.

According to the administration, Bush had authorized the Baghdad air raid because Iraq's improved radar endangered American and British pilots patrolling the no-fly zones. The strike gained immediate support from Democratic leaders, some of them prominently associated with the Jewish leadership, including California Representative Tom Lantos, a Hungarian-born Holocaust refugee. "I fully support the administration in this action and believe that the president acted appropriately," Lantos declared. In domestic politics Lantos has been a dependable liberal and mainstay of the Jewish-Democratic marriage. His support base comprises a declining labor movement, as well as the many folk nostalgic for sixties leftism in his northern California district. Lantos is both a convinced advocate of American intervention to protect human rights abroad and a major ally of the Israel lobby on the Hill.

Another Democrat, New York representative Gary Ackerman, sent a personal note to President Bush, congratulating him on the Baghdad air action. "Saddam Hussein should make no mistake about the resolve of the United States to prevent him from threatening our allies, our interests, or our aircraft and personnel," Ackerman wrote. His district is less ideologically leftist than that represented by Lantos; Ackerman has fewer issues from the liberal agenda to distract his attention but has been an even more prominent friend of the Israel lobby. Lantos and Ackerman have been two of the representatives that AIPAC has most consistently trusted to carry its agenda in Congress.

Despite widespread support for the Baghdad raid, some Washington analysts, including several leading Jewish figures, criticized American tendencies toward "coddling" the Beijing regime, the supplier of aid to Saddam. They accused China of supporting outlaw regimes (such as Iraq and Serbia) as well as other anti-Israel states, notably including Sudan, another topic of widespread Jewish commentary at the beginning of George W. Bush's presidency and thereafter. The Chinese energy company Petro-China had been deeply involved in attempts to bring Sudanese oil onto the world market.

Ruled by Islamist extremists, Sudan witnessed years of brutal civil war between its "Arab" north and its "Black" south, though most Sudanese are racially mixed. The "Arab" regime in Khartoum was repeatedly accused of killing up to 2 million people in its war against Muslims, Christians, and animists, of turning a blind eye to slave trading, and of assisting terrorists including Osama bin Laden. Sudan, like Iran and Saudi Arabia, had also devoted its energies to the exclusive establishment of radical Islamic law, or *sharia*—although in Sudan the *sharia* project had failed to gain much popular support. Sudan was and remains the running sore of eastern Africa.

Concern about Sudan had been notable among American Jewish activists for decades; Jewish community media and the domestic Jewish leadership expended great efforts against the Sudanese regime. Some Jewish leftists claimed that rather than terror sponsorship or *sharia* ideology, Sudan was targeted because it was considered useful to divert attention from the conflict with the Palestinians and, above all, to summon American Christian support. Still, the oppression suffered by the victims of the Sudanese regime could not be denied, and the United Nations, repeating its weak positions in the Balkans and Rwanda, as well as in many prior instances, allowed the Sudanese wound to fester.

The U.S. Holocaust Memorial Museum even held an exhibit on genocide in the African nation. But the Chinese connection kept coming up. "It is clear that the Chinese presence and intervention have greatly enhanced the ability of the Sudanese government to maintain their genocidal activities," said Reform rabbi Saperstein. He described the conflict in Sudan "as a 17-year civil war driven by an Islamist regime that has produced more victims than Rwanda, Bosnia, Kosovo, and Chechnya all together."

Roger Robinson, a former National Security Council official and associate of superhawk Frank Gaffney, had taken leadership of an economic boycott effort against Sudan. Based in the William Casey Institute, another minor think tank in Washington, Robinson said: "The revenues generated with the help of Chinese state-owned companies for the odious Khartoum regime are aiding and abetting terrorism, slavery and genocide." Given such comments, it was unsurprising to hear Robinson and others suggest that the Bush administration could gain dual support against Sudan from Jews and from African American leaders inflamed by the persistence of slavery in the Arab world. Some argued that Sudan would be paired with Iraq as a probable target of action by Bush. A few went so far as to suggest that Sudan could be positioned as the "apartheid issue" of the Republican ascendancy, similar to the role of South Africa for Clinton-era liberals.

The Christian right that backed Bush in virtual unanimity had long complained about Sudan. But some Jewish Washingtonians seemed to see greater importance in taking on China. "It's time to knock off the tolerance with the Chinese" on these issues, said a Jewish insider. "Everywhere we have a problem they are present. We should tell the Chinese, quit backing our enemies or we will ratchet up our support for Taiwan." The same advocate said that Russian support for anti-American policies around the world should also elicit a more aggressive response, including that of arming the Chechen resistance to Moscow.

But Jewish leaders were speaking with multiple voices on China. While the *shtadlan* lobbies, which concentrated on human rights issues, condemned China as well as Sudan, hard-liners associated with AIPAC assailed Sudan but defended the sale of Israeli weapons to China. China had earlier been injected into America's Middle East policy in spring 2000, when pressure from Congress and the Clinton administration forced Israel to cancel a planned sale of military aircraft to Beijing. The sale of four Phalcon early-warning craft had been considered a prospective coup for the state-owned Israel Aircraft Industries. It was abandoned on the eve of the Camp David summit, reportedly as a gesture to ensure American support for Israeli positions.

A month after the Iraq air raid, in March 2001, the American Israel Public Affairs Committee held its first Washington policy conference of the new Bush era, and officials of the Israel lobby left no doubt that the end of the Oslo peace process—the alleged disappearance of illusions about peace with the Arabs—had energized the organization. AIPAC convened with its members eager for confrontation with critics of hard-line Israeli policies. The conference, capped by an address by the newly elected Ariel Sharon and featuring Powell's first major talk on the Middle East, was one of the most spirited gatherings in the history of the lobby. "Membership is up, donations are up and people feel charged," said one AIPAC representative.

Nobel Peace Prize laureate Elie Wiesel set the tone for the three-day gathering with a speech on the opening day, his first ever to an AIPAC conference, in which he delivered a stinging attack on Jewish critics of Israel, some of the most prominent of whom were present. He called their critique of Jewish unwillingness to support the peace process, and their challenge to Jewish doubts about a Palestinian state, "anti-Semitism in Jewish leftist circles," and charged that they were often motivated by a "desire to please the outside world."

Wiesel declared that anyone "who uses their Jewishness as a context to attack or condemn Israel—that's something I'm against." He did not single out any critics by name, but many in attendance suggested that he was referring to small groups that continued to defend an Israeli-Palestinian compromise despite the resurgent violence of the second *intifada*. Most of these were seldom noticed, such as Americans for Peace Now and the Israel Policy Forum. They were liberal, and were simply defending the U.S. and Israeli position obtained during the Clinton era. Wiesel's comments were therefore viewed as deliberately provocative.

Sources close to AIPAC boasted repeatedly that the close of the Clinton era and the collapse of the peace process spelled the end of the Jewish doves' influence in Washington, which had never been as great as many of the doves wished it were. In reality, the doves were mainly gadflies, known only to Jews and ineffective with the American public, like many appendages of the Democratic-led coalition. The Israel Policy Forum declined to respond to Wiesel's statement. Americans for Peace Now said it remained "firm in [its] conviction that in the long run, achieving a negotiated, sustainable peace agreement is the only realistic option for Israel." AIPAC executive director Howard Kohr, protégé of Steve Rosen, praised Wiesel's "extraordinary" speech during his own address to the organization's banquet. Kohr denied that Wiesel's remarks might be called divisive, saying he had found them "unifying."

Sharon, victorious at the ballot box, and whose address followed Kohr's, delivered what was by contrast a relatively restrained message. While declaring to loud cheers that Jerusalem would "remain united under the sovereignty of Israel forever," and insisting that Israel "won't negotiate under the threat of violence," he also extended several olive branches to the Palestinian leadership. Noting that clashes greeted an easing of restrictions he had announced not long before, he said, "I know that patience is needed if we are going to try and fight terrorists." Moreover, he added, "I draw a clear distinction between terrorists and their supporters, on the one hand, and the general [Palestinian] population on the other."

Sharon's speech was interrupted every few seconds by more applause and cheers. The enthusiastic reception given Sharon and Wiesel contrasted with the chilly response offered to Joe Lieberman, so recently the great hope of Jewish Democrats, who delivered the closing address. After a hero's welcome, including two standing ovations before he even began speaking, Lieberman was met with a long silence when he mounted an articulate defense of "the Middle East peace process"—the first time the phrase had been uttered before the full audience at the event.

"There are many who say today that peace between Israel and the Palestinians is a fantasy," Lieberman declared. "I say to them what Theodor Herzl said: 'If you will it, it is no fantasy.'" Lieberman also delivered an indirect jab at Israel's economic and military blockade of Palestinian towns. "When I was born in 1942, Israel was shut tight by the British," he said. "We all know what the horrendous results of that 'closure' were," he continued, however, pointedly using Israel's term for its blockades in the occupied territories. "That must never happen again." Lieberman had the misfortune of defending the legacy of the Clinton administration in Middle East policy to an organization that wanted to leave that chapter of its history behind.

AIPAC itself left no doubt during the conference where its own priorities lay. Kohr, in an interview, said that one of the group's lobbying goals in the coming period would be to urge the Bush administration to "reassess the U.S. relationship with the Palestinians," including questioning U.S. aid and returning Palestinian groups to a State Department terrorism watch list. Kohr added, "With the violence continuing, there should be no business as usual."

As an opening shot in a carefully prepared campaign to lobby Congress for such a change, AIPAC publicized a letter sent to President Bush by four members of the House Committee on International Relations, asking him to consider, among other steps, charging the Palestinian Authority with responsibility for violence in Israel. Republicans Henry Hyde of Illinois and Ben Gilman of New York, and Democrats Lantos and Ackerman, signed the request. Hyde, a Gentile, and the Jewish Gilman (who has since lost his seat in Congress) were reliable friends of the lobby, regularly available to advance its proposals, no less than Lantos and Ackerman. To lay specific blame on the PA for uncontrolled terrorism would have been largely accurate, but was strongly resisted by Powell's State Department, which wanted to believe that the PA would soon stop the *intifada*.

An Israeli representative affirmed there was no contradiction between the prime minister's surprisingly moderate stance and AIPAC's hard-line view. The official suggested that the threat of American sanctions might help pressure the Palestinian leadership into returning to negotiations. "Maybe the international community should tell Yasir Arafat that if he behaves like Nelson Mandela he'll get positive reinforcement, but if he behaves like Saddam Hussein he'll be treated accordingly," the official remarked.

But the Bush administration had given no hint of any intent to harden its line toward the Palestinians. Powell, speaking to AIPAC several hours before Sharon, had offered what seemed a study in diplomatic language. He expressed a condemnation of "violence" without assigning specific blame for the bloodshed within the borders of Israel during the previous six months. At the same time, he pledged that America would not "strive for some arbitrary measure of evenhandedness when responsibility is not evenly shared." The argument for evenhandedness infuriated many Jews, who saw Israel as having just emerged from a sincere quest for conciliation, into which the second *intifada* had exploded irrationally. With Powell's every word being studied for clues to his attitude, this statement was seized on as a hopeful sign by Jewish leaders. AIPAC's Kohr, for his part, described the secretary's language as a repudiation of moral equivalence between Israel and the Palestinians, given that the latter were clearly perceived as the instigators of conflict.

During his address, however, Powell also stated that Washington remained committed to precisely the concept that Israeli hard-liners had long condemned: "the formula of land for peace." Introducing Powell, AIPAC president Tim Wuliger—an Ohio businessman and another characterless functionary—praised him for affirming, in congressional testimony two weeks before, that the United States considered Jerusalem the capital of Israel. The administration had, however, since backed away from that position, issuing a statement that "there's been no change in U.S. policy [from the Clinton era] . . . this is an issue to be resolved by the parties in negotiation."

Late in March 2001, several new Bush administration appointments were announced. They included, most notably at the time, Douglas Feith, named undersecretary for policy in Rumsfeld's department, and Daniel Kurtzer, a career diplomat appointed U.S. ambassador to Israel, replacing Martin Indyk. These choices enhanced the impression of a split between Defense Department hawks and the doves that were dominant, although not in total control, at State.

Feith was the lightning rod in the new group. A Reagan-era deputy assistant secretary of defense for negotiations policy, he had most recently worked as a lawyer in his own firm, Feith and Zell. Well known among the Israel lobby's tougher partisans, Feith would become one of four (later five) undersecretaries serving in the Defense Department. Daniel Pipes, director of the Middle East Forum and an outstanding critic of Islamic extremism, praised Feith for "a clear understanding of the issues and forces of the Arab-Israeli conflict and especially its historical context. He is good at analogies. One that especially struck me was his argument that just as the British government of Chamberlain was obliged to apologize for the actions of the Nazis and the Nixon administration had to sweep Brezhnev's mischief under the rug, so the governments of Israel in the Oslo era were obliged to ignore the trespasses of the Palestinian Authority."

Awaiting confirmation, Feith would state only that he was among those on record in favor of arming the Iraqi opposition—in retrospect, a considerable point. Feith and Wolfowitz shared with Bush the view that the way to deal with Saddam was by getting rid of him. Their outlook posed a sharp contrast to the mood at State, which had unveiled a set of proposals for fine-tuning sanctions against the Baghdad regime, including a complicated list of restrictions on Iraq and incentives to Turkey, Jordan, and Syria to firm up an anti-Saddam coalition including other Muslim countries.

But from the beginning of Bush's tenure, Washington heard backroom debate over whether the United States might financially subsidize the Iraqi National Congress, headed by a banker, Ahmad Chalabi, to overthrow Saddam. Chalabi had long been the target of criticism, mainly emanating from the Central Intelligence Agency. Chalabi was charged, in conspiratorial undertones, with misuse of financial resources, a common claim in the murky world of CIA cash distribution to foreign opposition leaders.

Jason Isaacson, government and international affairs director of the AJC in Washington, described "a tension in the policy" toward Iraq. But Isaacson continued, "There's always a tension in Middle East policy. It's just more pronounced when the administration is new and feeling its way." Gary Schmitt described the administration's posture as "reflecting a polarization between the policy of containment and the policy of activism . . . But it's a serious policy debate, and they're trying to find a way."

In addition to Wolfowitz and Feith, other Jewish figures were named to posts at Defense and State. In the former, Dov Zakheim became an undersecretary, as comptroller of the Pentagon—a quiet man, known to his critics as the consummate bookkeeper and to his friends for his wit. Zakheim referred to himself as the only "Dov" (i.e., "dove") in the Pentagon. He had previously served as deputy undersecretary of defense for planning and resources, as well as in other Defense jobs under Reagan. Stephen Cambone—not Jewish, but a neoconservative—was appointed undersecretary for intelligence, a new post, in 2003.

At State, David Wurmser, like Feith a firm supporter of the Israel lobby—and spouse of the equally militant Washingtonian and Middle East expert Meyrav Wurmser—would become special assistant to John R. Bolton, who had been appointed undersecretary of state for arms control and international security. The permanent staff at State hated Wurmser and Bolton, particularly the latter. But neither the "lifers" at State nor Powell could block their appointments.

Four major Jewish figures were now in place in the administration of George W. Bush: Wolfowitz, Feith, and Wurmser, along with Richard Perle, a member of a purely advisory body, the Defense Policy Board. This quartet, who did not work closely together or share all views, would come to be labeled a "Zionist cabal" by the administration's enemies.

Wolfowitz was still little known, but the appointments of Feith and Wurmser demonstrated that George W. Bush did not share his father's alleged Arabist sympathies and that the anxieties of the Jewish lobby about such attitudes were much exaggerated. The assignment of Daniel Kurtzer to replace Martin Indyk as ambassador to Israel got mixed reviews among American Jewish leaders. U.S. ambassador to Egypt since 1997, Kurtzer would, once in the Jewish state, suffer some of the ethnic insults hurled at Indyk. Kurtzer had been sent to Cairo from a post as acting assistant secretary of state for intelligence and research. While some might construe designating Kurtzer, an Orthodox Jew, as U.S. ambassador to Egypt to be a deliberate insult, such were the choices made during the post-Sadat era, when Egypt maintained diplomatic relations with Israel while receiving large quantities of American aid.

Kurtzer had also served as first secretary of political affairs at the U.S. embassy in Tel Aviv in the early 1980s, then as a member of the State Department's policy planning team, and as a deputy assistant secretary of state for Near Eastern affairs. In the latter post, Kurtzer was one of the architects of American contacts with the Palestinian Authority in the late 1980s.

"On one hand, as a diplomat [Kurtzer] has the experience, the knowledge, the professionalism that's needed," said Abe Foxman of ADL, who frequently worked with Kurtzer on human rights issues in Egypt. "What it means for the administration's policies is something else. It may confirm Bush's rejection of a hands-on policy, in that if the president were more committed he would have chosen someone closer to him."

According to the AJC's Isaacson, Kurtzer had been "a thoughtful ambassador and analyst of the U.S. relationship with the Arab world, and played a formative role a decade ago in conceptualizing the peace process." However, Isaacson admitted that Kurtzer had a reputation as an "Arabist" that made him controversial. In Israel, Ambassador Kurtzer reportedly criticized the state's policy of spending more on settlements in the West Bank than on the health needs of the handicapped. Israeli legislator Zvi Hendel, from the floor of the Knesset, responded sarcastically, "Irrespective of the fact that this is a representative of a foreign country, who can be Jewish or a jewboy, religious or not religious, the state of Israel should not ignore the intervention of a little jewboy who represents the U.S. . . . . I think that if we were a proud state, we would point this out to him and to the country that sent him, because I have no doubt that American support for Israel and the Jews is a thousand times greater than Ambassador Kurtzer's empathy." Morris Amitay, a former AIPAC director, argued that it would be better that the United States not send Jewish ambassadors to Israel, since they would feel obligated to show excessive fairness to the Palestinian side.

Neither Indyk nor Kurtzer should have expected that once they were in Israel as U.S. ambassadors they would be vilified by elements in the Jewish state and in Jewish Washington. Early in 2004, the same invective was heard again: Israeli settlement leader Adi Mintz called Kurtzer a "Jewboy" and accused him of influencing the United States to press Sharon for withdrawal of Jewish settlements from Arab-majority territories, in exchange for peace. "[Kurtzer] is a Diaspora Jew who arrived here, attends conferences of the left, and makes speeches in which he denies the legitimacy of the settlers' movement," Mintz complained.

Kurtzer persevered in his vision, since he saw "no conflict what-soever" between being an Orthodox Jew and being a diplomat. "Not only is there no conflict between my religious observance and my pro-fession, I believe the two are complementary," he wrote in a Yeshiva University magazine. "I hope the success I have enjoyed in my career is convincing to those who are thinking about public service that one can be observant and do one's duty to country." This slight ambigu-ity, and slightly pleading tone, should have troubled those who noticed it, for why should religious piety clash with service as an American diplomat?

Kurtzer may have been dissatisfied with his position in Israel, but he continued to occupy the embassy post until late 2005, when he was replaced by a Gentile, Richard Jones. The change received almost no national media attention in the United States. Nearly all of Jones' senior Foreign Service career should have stamped him as an Arabist *par excellence,* with postings in Iraq, Kuwait, Lebanon, Saudi Arabia, and Tunisia. He was, however, a nonentity.

For his part Feith, the opposite in sentiments to Kurtzer, also did not enjoy unanimous admiration in Washington. Some said privately that Powell's State Department team was strongly opposed to Feith's appointment, following on continued sniping at Wolfowitz.

Lewis Roth, assistant executive director of Americans for Peace Now, commented, "At the ideological table, Feith sits to the right, and in the context of the Bush administration it's clear that between com-passion and conservatism in the Middle East, he comes down for the latter. We're hoping that more moderate voices in the administration will be able to counterbalance his influence."

Thus, notwithstanding the months of American Jewish and Israeli angst about Bush 43's alleged Arabism and isolationism, the appoint-ments of Wolfowitz and Feith to the Pentagon marked the beginning of an entirely new era in American Jewish history. In these events, at least, a divorce from the Democrats and a new marriage to the Repub-licans appeared to be potentially very good for the Jews, even as the *shtadlan* leaders dithered over Bush, nostalgic for the days of Clinton's patronage.

But to some even the ascent of Wolfowitz and Feith in the Pentagon allegedly sent mixed signals about President Bush's Middle East
agenda to Jews. One obstinate Washington Jewish insider pointed to
"a fight for the soul of the administration in terms of Middle East policy ... This administration wants to define itself as what the Clinton
administration wasn't. But it's unclear what that new policy would be.
It could be a very positive approach, creating a constructive and positive regional policy. But it could find America at odds with Israel, in
a negative situation." The statement was a banal expression of the
insider's own incertitude, reflecting loyalty to the Democrats. Even
with Wolfowitz and Feith at the heights of American leadership, the
anguish caused by the second *intifada* and persistent fear that Israel
might be abandoned by Republican isolationists heightened the disquiet about the future habitually present in the Jewish leadership. In
addition, it still appeared that Jews would inexorably defend the New
Deal heritage. Soon, however, all would change utterly.

CHAPTER 7

✡THE SILENCE OF THE LOBBIES

September 11 and the Jews

"September 11, 2001, changed everything."

This phrase has become so banal as to even be somewhat distasteful. Yet it was true, especially in politics. In the aftermath of the horrific hijackings and the fire and smoke that billowed from the Twin Towers and the Pentagon, essential relationships would be recast. The administration of George W. Bush would be greatly emboldened in the use of American power in the world.

When 9/11 occurred, Western experts on Arab and Islamist extremism were cautious about too quickly identifying suspects. Daniel Pipes of the Middle East Forum was called on the afternoon of September 11 by Voice of America in Washington, which had no capacity for covering local breaking news, such as the attack on the Pentagon. Pipes, notwithstanding a false reputation spread by radical Arab and Islamist advocates as an excitable and irresponsible accuser, declined to speculate on the origin of the attacks until substantial evidence was available. Although al-Qaeda was obviously the prime suspect, Western governments were also reluctant to make hasty allegations.

As the days went by, New Yorkers and Washingtonians contended with the psychological blow of large-scale terrorism on American shores. The firm words of President Bush and the understanding that, unlike Clinton, he would not merely "sue" the perpetrators reassured Americans. There was also grim comedy in seeing stalwarts of Democratic anti-Americanism join their Republican colleagues on the Capitol steps in a shaky rendition of "God Bless America." Who could ever have predicted that one of the worst exemplars of immobile Democratic leftism, Senator Barbara Mikulski of Maryland, would one day imitate Kate Smith? Within two weeks, the concept of "Islamofascism" was being discussed and comparisons with the Second World War advanced among media commentators.

But many journalists, in dealing with the crisis, turned out to be incapable of abandoning attitudes suddenly obsolete. Steven Mufson wrote in the *Washington Post*, "If the culprits for the attack turn out to be linked to Osama bin Laden, the Saudi businessman accused of plotting terrorism against the United States from bases in Afghanistan, the war could pit the United States against much of the Arab world, put moderate Arab allies such as Egypt and Jordan in tenuous positions, place Israel at greater risk and imperil vital oil supplies." Not one of these predictions turned out to be correct. The 9/11 horror was greeted with joy by vagrants in the Arab street but by alarm on the part of most Arab rulers, and it discredited Saudi Wahhabism, which inspired the terrorists, among millions of ordinary Muslims. Jihadism declined in Egypt and made no immediate appearance in Jordan. Risks to ordinary Israelis remained significant, as visible throughout the second *intifada,* and then diminished. Oil supplies were unaffected. And even after three years of the soon-to-come Iraq war, Muslim discontent with America was greatly exaggerated in the American and British "liberal" media. Indeed, one of the main effects of the Iraq intervention was to accelerate demands for change in Saudi Arabia—the key to the whole Muslim world because of its control of Mecca and Medina.

American liberal media came to resemble the Holy Roman Empire, which was neither holy, nor Roman, nor an empire. Newspapers such as the *New York Times,* magazines including the *New Yorker,* broadcast enterprises such as National Public Radio, and the boring comedy writer Al Franken and the pseudo-intellectual Arianna Huffington among others were anti-American and illiberal and exemplified demagogy, not journalism. British media were worse: they attempted to outdo American leftist loudmouths by being more disloyal, less ethical, and so admiring of Islamist totalitarianism as to remind one of Lord Haw-Haw, the Nazi propagandist who broadcast from Nazi Germany to Britain during the Second World War. The time was long past when the BBC could be considered anything but a mouthpiece for disaffection, demoralization, and defeatism.

In the turmoil after 9/11, Jewish leaders were no less dazed than other Americans. Much discussion of whether the terrorists would win was superficial, since they had already won the first round. They had demonstrated that the West was too open, relaxed, and compromised, above all by Saudi influence, to anticipate attacks on itself, and that even the American Jews, with the presumptive help of the allegedly omniscient Israelis, were helpless to predict an assault that everyone in the Muslim world knew was coming. When the perpetrators of September 11 were identified, the most shocking detail was that fifteen of the nineteen hijackers were Saudi subjects—that is, neither Palestinians nor Iranians nor anyone else expected to have so deep a hatred of the West. Indeed, Saudis were considered America's best Arab friends. The news of their involvement was as startling to AIPAC and other Jewish groups as to most Americans.

Twenty years had passed since the AWACS fight in 1981. In the succeeding Middle East peace follies, especially after the Kuwait war, U.S. politicians, impelled by American energy companies and other business interests, acted aggressively and relentlessly to quiet Jewish suspicions about Saudi Arabia, and to convince AIPAC and other Jewish representatives, including Israeli politicians, that the Saudi monarchy was a moderate Arab state. Saudi Arabia could indeed take moderate positions in Middle East regional politics, but because of its

Wahhabi ideology it could not be a moderate Islamic power. Unless it was to break with Wahhabism, the Saudi state could never return to mainstream and traditional Islam, which is no more fanatical in its essence than Christianity or Judaism.

Yet in the 1990s, the Saudi ambassador to Washington, Prince Bandar, had conducted an extensive campaign to win over Jewish as well as Gentile opinion in the United States. This included invitations to professional wailers at the Western Wall such as Martin Peretz, then owner of the *New Republic*, who visited the kingdom in 1991. Peretz recalled in 2002, "When I applied for a visa, my Saudi hosts suggested that on the line marked 'religion,' I answer 'Christian.' I explained that my ancestors died rather than abjure their faith. 'What about leaving the line blank?' Again I said, 'No.' Then I was asked to procure a new passport, one without those irritating Israeli entry stamps. (Again I said, 'No.') The irony is that I was invited in large part because the kingdom wanted certain American Jews (American Zionists, in fact) to visit. They had an anti-Semite's—that is to say, a wildly exaggerated—estimation of the power Jews wield in the United States. And they wanted to speak to that supposed power."

Saudi foreign affairs adviser Adel al-Jubeir, briefly a fixture on U.S. television after American anger over 9/11 began to disturb the Saudis, had allegedly visited so many local Jewish communities in America that he accumulated a notable menorah collection. The Saudi outreach was amazingly successful; not all American Jewish leaders were as cautious or cynical as Peretz claimed a decade later to have been when he went to the kingdom. In 2000, an AIPAC media representative was asked to compare the threat of Iran and Libya to Israel and the West with that represented by Saudi Islam, and irritably denied that the Saudis were anything other than moderate. "We don't believe in conspiracy theories," the AIPAC employee insisted.

The identification of Saudi Arabia as a potential partner for peace in the Middle East was a commonplace in top American Jewish circles, which remained fixated on Iran. Sharon adviser Dore Gold, incredibly enough possessing academic training on Wahhabism, admitted that Saudi Arabia and Wahhabism had not been "on the

Israeli radar." A discussion of this oversight was one the *shtadlan* lobbies and AIPAC understandably preferred to avoid. They were also as unprepared to answer claims that Jews were mainly responsible for Arab terrorism because of their influence on Western policy as their forefathers had been unprepared to answer propaganda sixty years before that Hitler's grievances were caused by the Jews. Both charges were false. America had consistently tried to serve as a neutral "honest broker" in the Middle East, as illustrated by Suez and Reagan's response to Israeli actions in Lebanon. Saudi Arabia had more influence in Washington until 9/11 than Israel. George W. Bush would be the first American president to call for a Palestinian state.

As time passed, AIPAC and other Jewish groups seemed to remain paralyzed by the effect of September 11. Jews could not break out of their anxiety that the American alliance with Israel would be blamed for the deaths of more than 3,000 innocents in New York and Washington. Primitive elements of the Arab and Muslim societies reinforced these apprehensions, first by celebrating the attacks in the miserable Palestinian towns, unforgettably recorded on news videos, then by spreading rumors that September 11 had been perpetrated by Israel and that Jewish workers in the Twin Towers had been warned ahead of time not to come to their offices.

In reality, the timing of the terrorist attacks, before nine in the morning, ensured that many victims would be service workers, since numerous regular clerical and management employees would not normally turn up before 9:30 or 10 A.M. Many of the dead were Muslim immigrants. But Arab and other Islamist rumor-mongers, abetted by neofascist agitators in the United States, disseminated claims that Israeli agents either were involved in the attacks or had foreknowledge of the conspiracy.

Prince Nayef bin Abd al-Aziz, the Saudi minister of the interior, widely viewed in the Muslim world as the least-evolved troglodyte among the Wahhabi rulers, was early to repeat this charge. Nayef well deserved his reputation among Muslims as the Darth Vader of the Saudi royal family. Such rubbish about 9/11 was and remains believed by a share of the Muslim world, more out of embarrassed denial than out of conviction. This contributes in some part to the positive horror in Washington of drawing any parallel whatever between September 11 and terrorism against Israel. But *shtadlan* caution and White House vacillation were accentuated by the Democratic grip on Jewish politics.

September 11 united all loyal Americans, including Bush and the Jews, at least temporarily. Disagreements between the administration and the domestic Jewish lobbies over such policy matters as faith-based charities were swept aside. Bush 41's alleged Arabism was forgotten. Bush the son, not the father, was in charge. President George W. Bush emerged as a better friend of Sharon while remaining cautious in his handling of Israeli-Palestinian issues.

By the psychological distress they inflicted, the atrocities of September 11 brought home to the entire American public, once and for all, the brutal reality of Islamist terrorism. If ever the American Jewish leadership and AIPAC had an opportunity to make their case for Israel's democratic role in the Middle East, it was then. Yet something remained absent from the broader American and Jewish response to the horror. The *shtadlan* lobbies, AIPAC, and even President Bush stayed notably inert about Israeli involvement in what would come to be known as the global war on terrorism. From the time this war was proclaimed by the United States and operations against al-Qaeda and the Taliban commenced in Afghanistan, Israel has never been formally or even informally included in any aspect of it. And the silence of the lobbies has been profound; the *shtadlan* spirit has been reinforced by contempt for Bush and Jewish inveiglement with the Democrats.

Saudi responsibility for September 11 and Israeli affliction in its wake are realities of the war on terrorism seldom acknowledged in Washington, notwithstanding gestures toward Sharon by Bush and hallucinated rumors about Israeli involvement in the Iraq war, spread by speculative journalists such as the shameless Seymour Hersh. The Israeli and AIPAC obsession with Iran as the sole consequential threat to security also helped keep Israel "out of the game," to use a favorite cliché of intelligence operatives.

The position of the Jews after September 11 was uncertain, and could be compared with that a century before, facing tsarist Russian violence; in the 1930s, against the Nazis; and in 1948, when Israel was established. But the very success of the American Jews and Israel had left them vulnerable, for a new, but really very old, reason: recognition of their importance, rather than their weakness, made them and their Gentile allies excessively cautious, even when Israeli advocates and AIPAC seemed at their most militant. The paradox is a stunning one. The AJC's Hy Bookbinder had it right during the AWACS fight: in the *shtadlan* mind, "if we lose we lose and if we win we lose." Fatalism should not be a Jewish trait.

The Iraq intervention, beginning in 2003, brought about a new mainstreaming of anti-Jewish prejudice in America, in propaganda about a "cabal" that allegedly had taken over the Pentagon, the "secret agenda" of the neoconservatives, the allegedly nefarious role of the philosopher Leo Strauss, and many more peculiar things. The America First hysteria of 1939–41 reappeared, once again with major support from the left; indeed, isolationism in 2006 is more a phenomenon of establishment Democratic liberalism, based in media, academia, and the *lumpen* policy class, than of a business element comparable with the old rightist upper crust of the 1930s.

More important differences were visible between past paranoia about the Jewish lobbies and the myth of the "cabal." The claims about the "cabal" were adopted by a considerable stratum of American opinion that previously considered itself as far as anybody could be from crude prejudice, above all from Jew-baiting. The assault on the "cabal" was not vague, but quite pointed. It named the names of purported Jewish manipulators in the administration and ascribed to them esoteric motives in the effort against Saddam: above all, the protection of Israel.

Cabal is defined in the *Merriam-Webster Dictionary* as "the artifices and intrigues of a group of persons secretly united to bring about an overturn or usurpation especially in public affairs; *also* : a group engaged in such artifices and intrigues." It is a matter of separate interest that the dictionary traces the word to the Hebrew Kabbalah, the Jewish school of mysticism. Whatever its origin, *cabal* seemed especially fit for the use of Jew-baiters.

The trope of the alleged cabal had other distinctive characteristics in the twenty-first-century American context. It reproduced the Jew-bashing frenzy that had been seen in Europe for centuries, but had never previously appeared in America. Individual Jews had been alleged to have untoward influence over presidencies such as that of Franklin Roosevelt, but nobody considered sane had previously launched the libelous notion that a conspiratorial Jewish node had seized control of foreign policy from within the government. Allegations of a neoconservative takeover in Washington were even more dangerous for public tranquillity than past insinuations about Jewish "dual loyalty." Wolfowitz was the highest official accused of involvement in the "cabal," followed by Feith, although much of the most lurid propaganda in this vein centered on a man with no real role in government, Richard Perle.

In the first months after the terrorist attacks, however, there was relatively little such talk. The sewers of America had yet to discharge their packs of Jew-baiting demagogues.

But radical Arabs and Islamists in the United States and abroad, with the help of a few leftist and rightist gutter agitators, did their best to focus attention on blaming the Jews for September 11, and dim-witted "serious" intellectuals were also drawn to sympathy for the mass murderers. One among these vile types was the late authoress Susan Sontag, who reportedly enraged her own son, David Rieff, by writing in the New Yorker, within a few days of September 11, "The disconnect between last Tuesday's monstrous dose of reality and the self-righteous drivel and outright deceptions being peddled by public figures and TV commentators is startling, depressing. . . . Where is the acknowledgment that this was not a 'cowardly' attack on 'civilization' or 'liberty' or 'humanity' or 'the free world' but an attack on the world's self-proclaimed super-power, undertaken as a consequence of specific American alliances and actions? . . . In the matter of courage (a morally neutral virtue): whatever may be said of the perpetrators of Tuesday's slaughter, they were not cowards."

The al-Qaeda attack on America was followed by some of the worst incidents of the second *intifada* in Israel, including the assassination of Israeli minister of tourism Rehavam Zeevi by the Popular Front for the Liberation of Palestine (PFLP), a Marxist group, on October 17, 2001; the suicide bombing of a Haifa bus, in which fifteen died and a hundred were injured, on December 2; and the Netanya hotel blast by Hamas on March 27, 2002, leaving twenty-eight Jews celebrating Passover dead. Israel responded almost immediately with military cleanup actions against the headquarters of Yasir Arafat in Ramallah. Palestinian radicals occupied the Church of the Nativity in Bethelehem, and then came several days of Israeli antiterror operations in Jenin, in the northern West Bank. On May 7, 2002, a Hamas suicide bombing at a social club in Rishon Letzion killed sixteen people. Five weeks after that, Israel began the erection of a security barrier paralleling the borders of the West Bank, intended to impede the infiltration of terrorists into the Jewish state.

As these incidents filled world headlines, recusant leftists in Europe and America, as well as extremists in Arab and Muslim countries, rallied to the anti-Israel terrorists. A year after September 11, petitions by faculty members at some fifty law schools and universities called for divestment from Israeli firms and American businesses supplying Israel's defense needs—an illegal campaign to support the Arab boycott against the Jewish state. At San Francisco State University, expressions of crass anti-Semitism by Muslim students had been common for at least a decade. There, pushing and shoving accompanied hateful rhetoric at campus demonstrations against Israel, and the local Jewish Community Relations Council hired a security consultant for the protection of Jewish institutions. The year 2002 also saw the commencement of a boycott against Israeli academics on Western campuses.

African American Jew-baiting, meanwhile, was revived apace. Cynthia McKinney, the Georgia Democrat campaigning for reelection to Congress in 2002, enlisted none other than Louis Farrakhan to her cause. Farrakhan raved, "That nation called Israel never has had any peace in forty years and she will never have any peace because there can never be any peace structured on injustice, thievery, lying and deceit and using the name of God to shield your dirty religion under his holy and righteous name." McKinney herself outraged the whole country by sucking up to Saudi prince Alwaleed bin Talal. Alwaleed's comments suggesting that protest against American foreign policy was responsible for September 11 caused New York mayor Rudy Giuliani to reject a $10 million donation from the Saudi magnate for the city's reconstructive work after September 11. McKinney's father blamed her defeat in 2002 on "J-E-W-S," further declaring, "Jews have bought everybody." (Except for his family, apparently.) McKinney (reelected in 2004) is widely described in mainstream media as unpopular with Jews only because she criticizes Israel, as if her tone were mild and chiding rather than wild and inciting.

A similar message of hate came from the ludicrous Amiri Baraka, who had somehow wangled a position as poet laureate of New Jersey. He cited McKinney as a source of wisdom when he offered an exercise in bad verse titled "Somebody Blew Up America," with the lines

> *Who knew the World Trade Center was gonna get bombed*
> *Who told 4,000 Israeli workers at the Twin Towers*
> *To stay home that day . . .*

The *New York Times* protested, in typical *shtadlan* fashion, that Baraka should not be "censored," as if the state of New Jersey, which accounted for a considerable number of 9/11 victims, had no responsibility to uphold basic standards of decency out of respect for, if nothing else, community sentiment, let alone simple truth. But the literary poseur was finally removed from his post.

These events caused some Jews, and some who counted themselves the Jews' best friends, to warn of a worldwide revival of the lethal anti-Semitism of the 1930s. Leon Wieseltier, literary editor of the *New Republic,* ridiculed the New York Jewish critic Nat Hentoff, who declared memorably that he would not now be surprised to hear public address systems in Manhattan broadcast orders for Jews to assemble and await deportation. Wieseltier condemned as "ethnic panic" any and all comparison of the year 2002 with the 1930s and the menace of Hitlerism and Holocaust. In 1939, he noted, there was no Jewish state at all, much less one possessing nuclear weapons. But Hentoff, however silly he might sound, was more in the right than Wieseltier. The Jew-baiting of the Depression decade was about to reappear in a more repellent form, right here in America.

Early in 2002 President Bush met with Ariel Sharon, referring to him as "a good friend" but avoiding a specific linkage of the war on terror to Palestinian violence in Israel. Numerous observers wondered if Jewish votes, as well as Jewish money, might not switch to the Republicans—finally, after so many decades' endurance of the Jewish-Democratic alliance and so many yearnings for a divorce. But the *shtadlan* lobbies and AIPAC could not get closer to Bush without endangering their alliance with the Democrats, and that they were unwilling to do, regardless of their higher responsibility to defend Jewish interests.

Into the void of this *shtadlan*-decreed silence stepped Paul Wolfowitz. The younger neoconservatives represented by him and Bill Kristol seized the initiative on American policy in the Middle East from the Israel lobby and its *shtadlan* peers, as well as the Arabists at State. In doing so, the second generation of neoconservatives acted with daring that had been absent among their forebears in the Reagan era, such as Jeane Kirkpatrick. But Reagan, unlike Bush 43, had not had to fight a real war, and did not give the neoconservatives free rein.

Wolfowitz had never been very assertive about his Jewishness, on top of which he was extraordinarily open to Islam. In his doctoral dissertation he had opposed nuclear proliferation in the Middle East, including the Israeli atom bomb, and he was a reader of the Qur'an during his tenure in Indonesia. After 9/11 and the renewed Palestinian violence, he remained independent in his views on Israel. In 2002, then still a somewhat minor figure to the broader public, he spoke to a rally of Mort Klein's ZOA in Washington. When Wolfowitz declared that Palestinian grievances had to be addressed, he was booed by the assembled hard-liners. It was a humiliating moment that did no credit to ZOA. Wolfowitz's name soon became synonymous with the charge of Israelocentric influence in foreign policy. Yet the truth is that when he acted on the Middle East, preparing the way for intervention in Iraq, he did so for universalist and democratizing aims, rather than narrow Jewish ethnic goals.

Since the beginning of the twentieth century, American Jews had seen a series of Moses-like figures lead them in a migration back and forth across the American political landscape. Oscar Straus had brought the Jews under the banner of the Progressive Republicans; Felix Frankfurter took them into the New Deal, with the irreplaceable help of Dubinsky; Al Shanker stiffened their capacity for self-defense in the urban maze. After September 11, Wolfowitz knew what needed to be done. In helping craft an offensive against Iraq that could advance democracy in the Muslim world, Wolfowitz in 2001 was the best thing to happen to the American Jews since the days of Dubinsky. They should have been proud of him. And yet he remained a man who would literally shrink behind a pillar at a Washington reception, not out of fear but out of shyness, and most of Jewish Washington consistently ignored him.

In the end, perhaps the Jewish lobbies and AIPAC were correct to stay unobtrusive about September 11. The American people saw the experience as a Pearl Harbor–style attack on the American mainland, a devastating act of war, not as something comparable to a bombing in Israel. And the American people wanted a crushing blow delivered to whatever power most represented the radical Islamist enemy.

Saddam Hussein had been the main global focus of American worries since the beginning of Bush 43's administration. In subsequent polemics, much effort was expended to falsely suggest that Bush 43 had never thought much about Iraq until a climactic meeting of top advisers was held at Camp David on September 15, 2001. This was and is nonsense.

Still, at that conclave, Wolfowitz and Colin Powell reportedly clashed over the priority of action against Saddam's regime. Afghanistan, al-Qaeda's shelter, was already a chosen target for American military power. But Wolfowitz took the lead in arguing that the problem went beyond one isolated and impoverished Central Asian country and that effective action in response to terrorism must extend to Baghdad.

This was no novelty for Bush. But Wolfowitz posed the issue in stark terms. "I think the president made it very clear . . . that this is about more than just one organization, it's about more than just one event," he said later. "And I think everyone has got to look at this problem with completely new eyes and in a completely new light."

The probable connection between Saddam and al-Qaeda became a topic for extended, overwrought controversy as incompetent Western journalists and bought-off policy experts did their level best to turn Iraq into Vietnam. These sad characters tried to impose the highest possible standard for evidence in the matter. Reporting directly after the September 15 meeting at Camp David, the *New York Times* noted that both Cheney and Rumsfeld seemed to have downgraded the relevance of Iraq. Cheney denied that the administration had evidence of Saddam's complicity in September 11, and Rumsfeld was purported to have agreed to leave Iraq out of plans for early action, although he continued to express concern about it.

By contrast, according to the *Times,* Wolfowitz had engaged in a "tense exchange" with Powell, who complained that an assault on Iraq and Saddam would "wreck" the presumptive coalition needed for action in Afghanistan. When Wolfowitz spoke about "ending states" that enabled terrorists to act, Powell replied, "We're after ending terrorism. . . . Ending terrorism is where I would leave it and let Mr. Wolfowitz speak for himself." Powell's wisecrack was inappropriate, and historically obtuse. Had the United States in the Second World War, Korea, or the Balkans merely "ended" the flights of Axis, Communist, or Serbian planes, the movements of tanks, and the firing of weapons? Hardly. The Nazi regime had been ended, along with the fascist remnant in Italy. Japanese imperialism had been ended; the Japanese were deprived of the right to have an army. The North Korean invasion of South Korea had been ended, and South Korea blossomed as a major Asian economic power. Serbian domination over Kosovo had been ended along with the bloody terror wreaked against the Albanian majority. But in Kuwait, thanks in part to Powell, Saddamite aggression had not been cleanly ended in 1991, thus requiring its final end in 2003.

Wolfowitz's emphasis on Baghdad implied, soon enough, far more than mere punishment of a regime backing terrorists. Having helped remove Marcos from power in the Philippines and served in Indonesia, he understood the fundamental problem of the Muslim world: lack of democracy—meaning absence of entrepreneurship, accountability, and popular sovereignty. His vision, which would repeatedly be criticized as excessively idealistic, included a special role for Iraq—among the most educated and dynamic of the Arab states—as the key country for the spread of democracy in the region. In fact, his position was not idealistic (or ideological) at all; it was purely pragmatic. The United States, by the removal of Saddam, the most brutal of the Arab dictators, could demonstrate two things: that it would strike at a leading rogue state known for its sponsorship of terrorism and repression, and that it would no longer countenance dictatorships.

While the Wolfowitz doctrine gained credibility within the administration, and America prepared to liberate Iraq, *democracy* suddenly became a dirty word for polemicists of both the radical left and the isolationist right. Soon a wide, turbid stream of anti-democratic argument appeared in American media. Never before had American public opinion been bombarded with so much verbiage discounting the very idea that democracy could be exported to, or even nurtured on, foreign soil. The appeasement spirit of America First was abroad in the land.

History would be rewritten by anti-Bush talk show commentators and op-ed authors, who clamored to prove not only that the Arab and Islamic countries were impervious to democratic change but that the successful transformations seen in Germany and Japan after World War II were completely unique and irreproducible. Examples much closer to that of Iraq, such as South Korea and Taiwan, both of which had reached extraordinary levels of prosperity and stability with little more than an American military umbrella protecting them, were ignored by critics of the administration.

Wolfowitz made clear that the side effects of democratization, even including new expressions of anti-Americanism, comprised a risk worth taking. To Michael Dobbs, a *Washington Post* reporter, Wolfowitz described American rejection of change in the Arab world as "a formula for eventual catastrophe." In an interview with Jim Lehrer of PBS's *NewsHour* only six days after the terrorist attacks, Wolfowitz implicitly called for a new, activist turn in the Middle East. "The policies of the last twenty years, whether you think they were carried out effectively or ineffectively, obviously don't work," he said, describing the view that America should protect and reward its corrupt friends among regional rulers and should avoid pressing for reform. More important, he concluded with comments about Islam that indicated he, more than anybody else in the administration, really understood something about Muslims and really meant it when he said, "One of our greatest allies in [this] struggle has got to be the hundreds of millions of Muslims who do not believe that [September 11] was the face of Islam."

Nevertheless, Wolfowitz was soon labeled an aggressor against the peace of the Islamic world, in a campaign paralleled by similar attacks on Princeton academic Bernard Lewis, who became an adviser to Rumsfeld, and Middle East expert Daniel Pipes. All were slandered as Islamophobes and Arab-bashers. The literary critic Edward W. Said had made the main topic of his career the denunciation of Lewis' alleged misrepresentations of Islamic history, and Pipes was considered a Satanic figure by Arab Americans because of his extensive and authoritative denunciations of radical Islam. But Bush himself shared the enthusiasm for democracy. The president's policy speeches on the Middle East and particularly the Iraq intervention would eventually become heavily weighted with arguments in favor of the political transformation of the region.

But was the Iraq war good for the Jews? The leaders of the lobbies, AIPAC even more than ADL and AJC, seemed unable to decide. Israel and AIPAC were obsessed with Iran, and tended to downgrade Iraq just as they ignored Saudi Arabia. Some Jewish figures agreed with the argument that Muslims could not become democratic. Opinion among many right-wing Zionists held that democratization of the Palestinian Authority and of Arab societies in general could easily prove more rather than less dangerous to Israel. As of February 2006, with the victory of Hamas in the Palestinian elections, this argument gained more traction.

But did Wolfowitz counsel action on Iraq out of primary interest in Israel, as his critics alleged? The answer is no. Iraq had cooperated with every rogue state on the planet, from Serbia and Belarus to North Korea and Cuba, in facilitating terror. Saddam had further worked with Saudi Wahhabis to implant their jihadist version of Islam in Kurdistan, whose people refused to join the Ba'ath party. Iraq had also incited terror, shot Scud missiles, and threatened nuclear war against Israel. To bring down Saddam could clear the way to democracy in the Middle East, which could be good for Israel. Some things in the world might be good for Israel and America, while others might be good only for Israel but not for America—such as the previously mentioned option of selling Israeli weapons to China. But who could argue that nothing good for Israel could be good for America? Only irreconcilable Jew-haters, those leftists who had grown to despise "conservative Israel" in contrast with "progressive Israel," and prostituted Arabists. In a war against Islamofascism, Israel should have been an indispensable ally. The fight against Nazism and Communism was a defense of universal civilization, of which the Jews are a supremely valuable element. The same is true of the struggle against tyranny and terror in the lands of Islam.

The Iraq intervention was not primarily conceived as a means to assist Israel, regardless of the impact on America; rather, it was intended to support America by expanding democracy, notwithstanding the bad effects (such as Scud missile attacks) it might have for Israel. Numerous Washington Jews began to repeat a view described by Martin Indyk: Where once it was believed that resolution of the Israel-Palestine confrontation was the prerequisite to peace and development in the Middle East, it was now seen that real improvement in Israel's position would come at the end of a process, not the beginning. In the shorthand phrase that circulated in Washington at this time, "The road to Jerusalem runs through Baghdad." (The argument paraphrases the Bolsheviks, who believed the revolutionary road to London ran through India.)

Even that attitude, which somewhat downgraded Israel as a Middle Eastern priority for America, became shocking for the stupid. General Anthony Zinni, a Powell pal who imagined himself a great global strategist, expressed his horror at this notion in remarks before the radical-leftist Center for Defense Information. In the idiom of drinkers at the bar in an obscure American Legion hall, Zinni pontificated: "I couldn't believe what I was hearing about the benefits of this strategic move. That the road to Jerusalem led through Baghdad, when just the opposite is true, the road to Baghdad led through Jerusalem. You solve the Middle East peace process, you'd be surprised what kinds of other things will work out." But what intellectual insight into the Islamic world did Zinni possess that would encourage him to make such sweeping pronouncements? And how could he not recognize that this opinion was among the oldest and emptiest clichés in the American discourse? Exhorting Bush to "solve" the Israeli-Palestinian dispute was a recipe for running U.S. foreign policy aground on the same shoals that scuttled Clinton's efforts.

Wolfowitz and other neoconservatives led the way in preparing for combat with Saddam, while the Jewish lobbies lagged behind, their *shtadlan* mentality apparently incurable. On September 20, 2001, a detailed call for action against Saddam was issued by Bill Kristol's Project for the New American Century, signed by forty-one conservative and neoconservative figures, ranging from Kristol himself to Francis Fukuyama, Norman Podhoretz, Jeane Kirkpatrick, and Martin Peretz and Leon Wieseltier from the *New Republic*. Not one figure from the mainstream American Jewish organizations supported the statement. Nobody representing AIPAC, the ADL, or the AJC appeared among the names.

The PNAC document, in the form of a letter to Bush, stated, "We agree with Secretary of State Powell's recent statement that Saddam Hussein 'is one of the leading terrorists on the face of the Earth. . . .' It may be that the Iraqi government provided assistance in some form to the recent attack on the United States. But even if evidence does not link Iraq directly to the attack, any strategy aiming at the eradication of terrorism and its sponsors must include a determined effort to remove Saddam Hussein from power in Iraq. Failure to undertake such an effort will constitute an early and perhaps decisive surrender in the war on international terrorism."

The letter called for nothing more than "military and financial support to the Iraqi opposition," with U.S. forces establishing a "safe zone" inside Iraq as an opposition operational base. But it added, "American forces must be prepared to back up our commitment to the Iraqi opposition by all necessary means."

Soon thereafter, the *Weekly Standard* carried an article signed by Kristol and Robert Kagan, whose name was also affixed to the PNAC letter. Titled "The Right War," it cited Bush's address to Congress a week after the events of September 11, in which the president "made clear that taking decisive action against Saddam does not require absolute proof linking Iraq" to the terrorist atrocities in New York and Washington. The Kagan-Kristol article was even sharper than the PNAC letter in that they demanded, "if necessary . . . using American military force to complete the tragically unfinished task begun in Operation Desert Storm a decade ago."

The Kagan-Kristol article also cited a notable precedent for the call to action in Iraq. In 1998 Clinton had been urged to take strong action against Saddam in a letter signed by Rumsfeld, Wolfowitz, John Bolton, and numerous other figures who would occupy leading posts in the administration of George W. Bush. At the heights around Bush, the stage was now set for intervention in Baghdad. However, the road to war in Iraq would prove a longer one than might have been imagined. Eighteen months went by between September 11, 2001, and Bush's announcement that the United States was prepared to act against Saddam with or without the authorization of the United

Nations. The march through the international institutions, with the United States attempting to gain a consensus for what seemed to many ordinary people around the world, including Muslims, to be a commonsensical plan—the removal of a bloodthirsty, fascist dictator—was arduous and tedious.

Still, a more elaborated basis for unilateral action appeared necessary, and was laid in June 2002 when Bush announced in a speech at West Point that American strategy would now be based on a doctrine of "preemption," that is, anticipation of aggression rather than reaction to it. American power might with considerable justification be used to avoid a potential threat becoming real, he said, declaring that "security will require all Americans . . . be ready for preemptive action when necessary to defend our liberty and to defend our lives." This somewhat basic notion had been articulated in classical literature by the phrase "if you want peace, be prepared for war."

Jew-baiters soon attached Wolfowitz's name to the preemption doctrine, pointing to a 1992 draft document, "Defense Planning Guidance," developed internally in the Pentagon. The text, which had caused an uproar when it was leaked to the media, and was ordered by then Defense Secretary Cheney to undergo revision, was controversial at the time mainly because of its emphasis on U.S. preeminence after the Cold War and its argument that "our first objective is to prevent the re-emergence of a new rival." But the draft also included language committing the United States to "the spread of democratic forms of government and open economic systems." And to the fright of some, it indeed envisioned U.S. policy carried out without recourse to the UN, based on future coalitions that would be "ad hoc assemblies" in response to specific crises, and without expectation of permanence after such crises. Thus, the draft argued that "the United States should be postured to act independently when collective action cannot be orchestrated," or in an emergency.

Bush was prepared to act in Iraq without UN backing, as Clinton had acted in the Balkans. The difference between the two was only that Saddam had not yet overtly embarked on a fresh campaign of fascist crimes comparable to those committed in the former Yugoslavia by his ally, the late Slobodan Milošević—whose Muslim-killing regime depended on Iraq for oil, reciprocated with direct military assistance. When opponents of Bush's plan for the removal of Saddam demanded "a smoking gun" comparable to Milošević's attempted genocide, their adversaries would argue there was no time to wait for the gun to smoke, that is, for Saddam to carry out new massacres, invasions, or terrorist assaults. That was the point of preemption.

Except for Wolfowitz, few senior Bush administration officials would specify, prior to Saddam's overthrow, that the Iraqi dictator should be removed simply for the betterment of the region and the world. Still, in a speech before a Los Angeles conservative audience, introduced by publicist David Horowitz on November 22, 2002, Wolfowitz noted the president had affirmed that "building a just and peaceful world beyond the war on terrorism, and particularly in the Muslim world, has got to be part of [the] goal."

The democratization strategy did not dominate the discourse of the Bush administration until after the main campaign in Iraq was concluded. The question of Saddam's weapons of mass destruction (WMD) and the search for courtroom-level evidence of terrorist support by Iraq seemed more urgent. The Bush administration found itself, absurdly enough, compelled at the beginning of the twenty-first century to justify its success in overturning an atrocious dictatorship. Debates over both issues, but especially over WMD, became especially vituperative in Britain and the United States, where media and political commentators insisted that if the WMD threat could not be proven to have been as grave as Bush and British prime minister Tony Blair argued, the war was illegitimate. London-based critics of the intervention forgot that their involvement in the Second World War had been predicated on saving Poland from German invasion, not on removing the fascist regimes from Europe, much less curbing Japanese imperialism in the Pacific, which became a common military aim of the British and Americans. And Poland had not come out of that war with the borders it had at the beginning of the conflict.

Not until the year 2003 came to a close would Iraq as a factor for democratization in the Arab and Muslim world replace WMD and terrorism as the main argument, repeatedly enunciated by Bush himself, for war against Saddam. Unfortunately, as the administration reached a position of greater moral clarity on the issue, democracy, at least in terms of its global expansion, became even more a target of contempt on the part of the political class in the West. European and other voices complaining that the war was about oil now protested that the democratization strategy represented wholesale and irresponsible adventurism. (Similarly, the chancelleries of London and Paris, 140 years before, had swung from support of the antislavery cause to fear of slave insurrections after Abraham Lincoln announced emancipation.)

Wolfowitz was, to reemphasize, a hawk on the use of American military power rather than on the narrow security needs of Israel. But these facts, along with his genuine understanding and sympathy for Islam, did not prevent him from undergoing an exceptional degree of obloquy from antiwar activists and their sympathizers in various media venues. This "high-tech lynching" (to borrow the accurate phrase once used by Justice Clarence Thomas) was based exclusively on Wolfowitz's Jewish background and his neoconservative associations. The domestic Jewish lobbies, previously supersensitive to any manifestation of anti-Semitism, seemed incapable of grasping the vicious nature of the outcry against Wolfowitz and his associates.

Paradoxically, the sudden increase in public Jew-baiting among Americans, with the pretext of war in Iraq, did not dissuade numerous Jewish liberals and leftists from marching in "peace" parades. Some American Jews took to loudly denouncing the Jewish lobby. Indeed, in contrast with the totalistic image of a homogeneous ethnopolitical bloc conferred on them by Arabs, neo-Nazis, paranoiacs, and Jew-haters in general, Jewish opinion was divided on Iraq, and the Jewish-Democratic alliance acted more to fragment the Jewish view of the intervention than to make it consistent.

Some prominent Jewish Democrats—including Michigan senator Carl Levin—were so outspoken in their obstruction of the Iraq intervention that they were labeled "Jews for Saddam" by one observer. Once the war had begun, other Jewish Democrats maintained support for it through difficult periods—such as Joe Lieberman, who emerged as more of a hero to Republicans than to his own party, and who was often mentioned, as early as 2003, as a possible successor to Rumsfeld. But Wisconsin senator Russ Feingold also opposed the Iraq intervention. Feingold's weird mental convolutions had led him to propose, in 2000, a U.S. government apology for alleged "injustices" done to a small number of ethnic German Nazi sympathizers—the same trash polluting Madison Square Garden in 1939—because they were interned during the Second World War. Feingold was joined in the "Jews for Saddam" faction of the U.S. Senate by Barbara Boxer of California, the late Paul Wellstone of Minnesota, and Ron Wyden of Oregon, all offspring of the Democratic-Jewish marriage.

Did the *shtadlan* American Jewish lobbies or AIPAC contribute publicly, overtly, and loudly, as would have been appropriate, to the understanding of democracy as a goal in the Middle East? Hardly. Wolfowitz and Iraq were feared by much of the American Jewish leadership as embodiments of risk. But did the lobbies spring to the defense of Wolfowitz, Feith, Wurmser, Perle, or Kristol when they were libeled in the court of media opinion for their alleged Zionist deception in driving America to war? Not at all. The ADL, AJC, and AIPAC acted as if they had never heard of Wolfowitz or the rest. Had they really cared about fulfilling their role as Jewish defense agencies and as America's pro-Israel lobby, they would at least have soundly and thoroughly condemned the Jew-baiting attacks on the neoconservatives and warned against the introduction of such poison into mainstream American discourse.

Judaism does not possess a term like *crusade* or *jihad* referring to a religious war. In that, Jews are lucky. Yet if there has been any American Jewish leader who inculcates a crusader or jihadist spirit in dealing with Jewish issues, it is ADL's Abraham Foxman. As previously noted, when Mel Gibson released his movie *The Passion of the Christ,* which presented a traditional Christian account of Jewish treatment of Jesus, Foxman went on a rampage. He said of Gibson, "I think he's infected, seriously infected, with some very, very serious anti-Semitic views." That was Foxman at his mildest when dealing with Gibson. But when asked about Jew-baiting of the neoconservatives, who were alleged to have started the Iraq war and sacrificed thousands of lives for Israel's purposes, Foxman reacted with uncharacteristic diffidence. "This claim is out there," he said. "We were pointed out at the beginning, and it's easier to blame us when things go bad. We knew that if things went wrong, they will look for someone to blame. The more protest, the more politicizing of the issue, people will be sloppier and will not be careful in what they say." The cinematic "passion" of Gibson was, in Foxman's mind, a serious threat to religious civility in America—but the vicious attacks on the neoconservatives were the consequence of mere sloppy thinking. Here Foxman acted not only as a self-abasing *shtadlan* functionary but as a worshiper at the Democratic altar, since the Jewish marriage to that party—it can never be repeated enough—would not permit leaders of the lobbies to forcefully support Bush's and Wolfowitz's initiatives.

But was it not the case that the Jewish people had more than once refused to harken to the voices of their prophets? Wolfowitz could lead the American Jews out of their *shtadlan* environment and into participation in a great experiment in world transformation. But neither the domestic lobbies nor AIPAC would listen to him or even, once the time came, adequately defend him—or in AIPAC's case, themselves. Certainly, most Jewish Democrats, who retained the heaviest political weight with the domestic lobbies, were unprepared to offer a forthright position in favor of global democratization or a principled defense of Wolfowitz and other neoconservatives against Jew-baiting propaganda. Democrats had once been America's greatest proponents of internationalism. But they had sunk into an isolationist pit much deeper than that inhabited, in their time, by the McGovernites. Finally, Gallup Poll data shows almost three-quarters of Republicans, and less than half of Democrats, now sympathize with Israel rather than the Palestinians. The Democrats are no longer good for the Jews, or for America, or for themselves.

The liberation of Iraq was largely theorized by Wolfowitz, Kristol, and Bernard Lewis as a project with almost nothing directly to do with Israel. Of course, the trio saw benefit in the removal of Saddam as a supporter of extremism. But more important, these men saw Iraq as a keystone country, a "fertile crescent" that, thanks to its resources, high level of education, and history, could be an engine of rapid progress, with ramifications including:

- The beginning of a political transition in Saudi Arabia, including a break with the ultra-extremist Wahhabi sect
- Peaceful regime change, i.e., a similar transition, in Iran
- Disengagement of Lebanon from Syrian occupation

These countries represent more than enemies of Israel; they are also leading powers in the Arab and Muslim world. To change them would be to change the planet.

New outbursts of Palestinian terrorism in 2002 made Bush more publicly sympathetic to Sharon than he previously had been, yet Israel was still scrupulously omitted from virtually all U.S. and British calculations of how to deal with Iraq. But that did not diminish the flood of Jew-baiting against the neoconservatives. The lack of self-awareness on the part of those who purveyed such shameless libels was remarkable. Few of them, from the isolationist right to the radical left, seemed to have the slightest insight into the vicious slurs they disseminated far and wide.

In hostile commentaries about the "cabal," the "not very Jewish" Wolfowitz, as he was described by one who knew him well, was intimately linked to personalities much more involved with pro-Israeli lobbying, such as Feith, who had been active in right-wing Zionist circles for many years, and Perle, another activist for militant Israel. In reality, Wolfowitz and Feith had completely distinct tasks in the Pentagon, and Perle was no more than an outside consultant. But in 1996, Feith, then still working in his law firm, and Perle, a fixture at the American Enterprise Institute, were involved in discussions that produced an innocuous document, "A Clean Break: A New Strategy for Securing the Realm." Anti-Jewish conspiracy theorists leapt on this brief text as an alleged "blueprint" for intervention in Iraq. Yet although "A Clean Break" had been produced by a conference attended by Perle and Feith and was addressed to Israeli hard-liner Netanyahu, in it Iraq played a distinctly secondary role, which was one reason those who referred to it seldom actually quoted from it. Finally, "A Clean Break" was used by Jew-baiters for the same purposes once served by the "Protocols of the Elders of Zion."

"A Clean Break" included one apparently inflammatory phrase: "This effort can focus on removing Saddam Hussein from power in Iraq—an important Israeli strategic objective in its own right," but that rather offhand comment was set within a complicated analysis of Syrian and Jordanian aims that did not mean much with the passage of time. In 1996, Syria was a much bigger target in the minds of conferees than Iraq, which led the enemies of George W. Bush and the accusers of the "cabal" to issue constant charges that the intervention in Iraq would be followed, almost immediately and with no substantial pretext, by a war against Syria.

"A Clean Break" was a policy summary suitable for the time of its writing, rather than a long-range blueprint for transformation of the Middle East. Its recommendations for change were mostly moderate, including diminution of U.S. aid to the Labor Party–based socialist economy in Israel. Further suggestions included investment in the Jordanian economy, urging the Israeli government under Netanyahu to make an official visit to Jordan, and offering the Jordanian king improved security means against Syrian pressure. These were not adventuristic or even provocative proposals; some might even call them Arabist, given their tendency to find ways to cooperate with Israel's neighbors.

Other participants in the conference that produced "A Clean Break" included James Colbert of the Jewish Institute for National Security Affairs (JINSA)—yet another minor Washington think tank, but as big as AIPAC in the minds of Jew-baiters; Charles Fairbanks Jr., an expert on Central Asia and the Caucasus; Jonathan Torop of

WINEP; and David and Meyrav Wurmser. Wolfowitz had nothing at all to do with it, although his name was attached to it by Judeo-phobic forces on both the left and the right. Before, during, and after the Iraq war, he was habitually described as head of the "cabal," and "A Clean Break" was treated as a road map for the "cabal." The document was, finally, fully comprehensible only to specialists in Middle East politics, but that did not prevent politically illiterate, anti-Jewish fanatics from depending on it as their sole item of evidence. As always, Jew-baiting profited from ignorance and innuendo. It was pathological to imagine that because in 1996 the overthrow of Saddam was called "an important Israeli strategic objective in its own right" the 2003 intervention in Iraq was purely motivated by Israeli demands.

At the same time, Bush was clearly sincere in his commitment to a road map that would secure a Palestinian state. Politically, this perspective represented the sharpest possible turn by Bush away from the attitude of disengagement from the Israeli-Palestinian conflict he had enunciated during his presidential campaign. The course of events, not Jewish or Arab influence, had moved him.

Bush had other problems involving Jews. After September 11, certain leaders of the Christian right, who associated their "end times" theology with defense of the state of Israel, envisioned a planetary conflagration uniting Christians and Jews against Muslims. Christian demagogues perceived the war against terror as an opportunity to press their agenda as possessors of "the truth about Islam." Some were bumptious clergymen such as Franklin Graham, son of Rev. Billy Graham, who proclaimed ignorantly, "The God of Islam is not the same God of the Christian or the Judeo-Christian faith. It is a different God, and I believe a very evil and a very wicked religion." This position has never been held by Jewish authorities, who since the great Islamic age have recognized that Islam is the same revelation as that heard by Jews. Evangelists such as Graham and various bigoted amateur experts whose names do not bear citation arrogated to themselves not only a bogus expertise on Islam but also a superior understanding of the challenges of statecraft and war faced by the Bush administration.

After 9/11, this, as much as their fantasies about Armageddon, drove some elements of the Christian right to wave the Israeli flag—much more than the proselytizing ambitions ascribed to them by ADL's Foxman. Unfortunately, this dangerous gambit was greeted with enthusiasm by a significant section of the Israeli right. Sharon had previously made numerous public statements welcoming the Christian right into the Jewish camp, as had Podhoretz and other neoconservatives, as well as AIPAC, before him. In opening the tent to Christian extremists, Jewish hard-liners seemed intent on closing off any dialogue with Muslim believers, which Wolfowitz (and Bush) desired.

American support for Israel had never been greater, but it remained more conditional than ever. The "cabal" was fictional, and, notwithstanding the lies spread throughout the world, most of those who purportedly belonged to it played little if any role in promoting anti-Muslim attitudes. A war could not be won in Iraq if it was declared to be a crusade against Islam. There was no way around that. Bush had, right after September 11, once used the term *crusade* in a way that elicited squeals of protest from Islamist extremists and leftists. They claimed he incited the religious offensive the Christian right wanted. But he had not repeated the usage, and a prominent Iranian diplomat admitted that the president's mention of the word, commonly used in the West outside a religious context, should not be considered so seriously.

Like Bush, Wolfowitz continued to voice his sympathy for a Palestinian state, and his colleagues in government kept a measured calm about other Israeli issues such as the country's new security barrier, while focusing on Iraq. Of course, the Arab, radical Islamist, and leftist constituencies in America construed such a low-key approach as approval of radical Zionism; nothing short of total capitulation to Palestinian terror would satisfy such critics. As late as March 2003, questioned by Arizona Republican congressman Jim Kolbe about the role of an Israeli or Jewish cabal directing the summits of American power, then Secretary of State Colin Powell repudiated the very possibility of its existence. American policy was not, Powell said, "driven by any small cabal that is buried away somewhere," but rather reflected our national interest. In 2005, Rumsfeld put the case more directly when asked about improper Jewish influence in administration policy making: "I suppose the implication of that is that the president and the vice-president and myself and Colin Powell just fell off a turnip truck to take these jobs."

Some journalists were convinced they knew what the "cabal" was and what it was up to. They included James Atlas, who wrote in the *New York Times Magazine* on Wolfowitz and his alleged mentorship by Leo Strauss, and William Pfaff of the *International Herald Tribune,* who warned readers against the malign influence of Strauss and Trotsky. But these neoisolationists were hardly isolated. Wolfowitz and Feith remained, predictably, the main targets of this libel campaign, with Perle attracting special but inconsistent attention.

The once-staid *Christian Science Monitor* treated neoconservatism as it might have dealt with a criminal conspiracy: mug shots of the leading figures in the first and second generations of the movement were offered on its Web site. They ranged from Podhoretz to Kagan, linking to potted biographies. To the *Monitor*, neoconservatism was an urgent issue for every American citizen to learn about. And the *Monitor*'s description of the phenomenon was anything but measured. Neoconservatives, the paper warned in an unsigned feature titled "Neocon 101," argued that "the U.S. must do whatever it takes to end state-supported terrorism. For most, this means an aggressive push for democracy in the Middle East." The *Monitor* went on to caution that "even after 9/11, many other conservatives, particularly in the isolationist wing, view this as an overzealous dream with nightmarish consequences." Who would have thought, a century before, that Americans would be taught in their mainstream media that democracy resulted in nightmares? This was the idiom of Mussolini, if not Goebbels.

The result of this demagogy was a predictable witch-hunt. Democrats and leftist media hacks looked for a victim, and their gaze landed on Perle. Seymour Hersh, the journalist who had proven he was not too proud to retail Soviet apologetics to the American public in the case of the shot-down Korean Air flight 007, claimed intimate knowledge of the alleged cabal. Indeed, according to him, the members called themselves by that title, in an apparent surfeit of arrogance. Hersh made himself the personal scourge of Perle, accusing him of serial indiscretions and ethics violations. Pat Buchanan took up the cry, launching Perle's candidacy for the role of an American Dreyfus in the *American Conservative,* a pulp magazine he founded. Buchanan demanded that Perle be removed from the unpaid post he held with the purely advisory Defense Policy Board.

Perle *did* resign as the chairman of that board, to dampen accusations of misconduct in a commercial transaction involving the Global Crossing communications firm. He thus deprived the anti-neoconservative lynch mob of the capacity to refer to it as "Perle's board"—the implication being that it was his private political tool for advancement of the agenda of the "cabal."

To anyone with a capacity for logic, the realities of American power and its employment in Iraq, and even the details of neoconservative involvement therein, discredited any claim that the Jewish lobbies or AIPAC had a determining role in the Bush administration's policy. Nothing better expressed the shrinkage of the lobbies' role in American Middle East policy and the ascendancy of Wolfowitz and his neoconservative associates—sans "cabal"—than the emergence of a new attitude toward Shia Muslims, who had long been castigated by Israelis and American Jews as the extremist foot soldiers of Khomeini and Hezbollah, even during the liberation of Iraq.

The disturbing ease with which democracy had become an object of sneers by the Western intellectual elite was seldom noted even by the most militant defenders of the Iraq intervention. Jewish neoconservatives and Israel were reproached with wanting to revise the maps in the Middle East, under the guise of promoting democracy. The leading Saudi-financed lobbyist, James Zogby, dismissed the vision of democratic Arab states as a childish fantasy; scholars scattered throughout the liberal campuses and think tanks rejected the notion almost without discussion.

The radical left and the "old right"—better called neofascists— coalesced on a platform of public, paranoid loathing of the Jews and the democracies. The nadir of this campaign was doubtless reached when Eric Alterman wrote in *The Nation** of the presumptive diffi- culty, had she been alive, in explaining to his grandmother that the warmongers in Iraq were Jews, and that Likudniks had seized control of the U.S. government. Others were less polite; a controversial aca- demic, Paul Buhle, scribbled in the Jewish leftist organ *Tikkun*, "It is almost as if the anti-Semitic Protocols of Zion, successfully fought for a century, have suddenly returned with an industrial-sized grain of truth."

Scorn for democracy did not appear out of nowhere. Stalin had made a pact with Hitler in 1939, and had revived Jew-baiting in Russia in 1948. The intellectual soil for the new growth of this noxious plant had been prepared since the onset of the death agony of Soviet Communism, when the concept of a "Red-Brown" alliance was first bruited about. In this schema, fascists and leftists would unite on a common platform of hostility to the United States, hatred of Jews, fear of economic restructuring, and protest against globalization. To Russians, this merely restored the anti-Jewish cultural habits seen from the pogroms of 1903 to the discrimination that began again in 1967. With Communism in ruins, democracy was to be viewed as a pure sham, hiding superexploitation by multina- tional interests. Stalin had loved this political weapon. He had planned a complete break with the Western left and their Jewish pro- clivities, as well as a new alliance with German ex-Nazis, when he launched the frame-up of the Jewish Kremlin doctors just before his death. But the first recent public expression of this political oddity consisted in a sudden surrender of sections of the French radical left

---

* One of the last articles by Trotsky, written just before his slaying in 1940, was titled "The Reptile Breed of *The Nation*."

to Holocaust revisionism, and to a Jew-baiting vocabulary about the Middle East, in the early 1980s. Later examples included neo-Nazis and anarchists marching together in antiglobalist demonstrations.

The left had once championed globalization against autarkic and protectionist economics; socialism had been conceived of as the victory of a planetary, human identity. Frederick Engels, the collaborator of Marx, had written that socialism would come about through the arrival of a single world market. But a massive reaction had emerged against market reforms at the end of the twentieth century. Along with the association of the ideological left with the seventy-year Russian debacle, and the later leftist habit of blindly defending Milošević in Serbia and Saddam in Iraq, this made the liberal *lumpen* intelligentsia unexpected admirers of existing national borders and ethnic particularism . . . except in the case of Israel.

Stalinism, in its vision of "socialism in one country," had embodied an autarkic mentality not unlike that of Nazi Germany and Fascist Italy, even as it controlled an international movement. This, as much as common designs on Poland, brought Stalin and Hitler together in the years when Senator Wheeler and Pete Seeger twanged the same evil tune. Two generations later, the same young people who loved world music, in which styles from the Western Hemisphere, North Africa, South Asia, and other regions merged, hated the world market that had allowed it to exist. All collective memory of the left's globalist past was abandoned or erased as legions of marginalized activists formed up to attack the specter of U.S. hegemony.

Neither leftists nor even most conservatives who favored Bush's action against Saddam could conceive of an *inevitable* triumph of entrepreneurship, accountability, popular sovereignty, and other foundational concepts of a democratic order in the Arab and Islamic countries. The global process that Wolfowitz had helped start in the Philippines, with Marcos deposed, and which continued to drive the former deputy secretary of defense during his tenure in the Pentagon, could not leave the Middle East untouched. Based on the rise of the middle class through local capitalism, democracy had come to prevail, as noted earlier, in previously authoritarian countries such as Portugal, Spain, Greece, South Korea, Taiwan, Chile, Mexico, and Indonesia, generally without violence.

In addition, of course, the former Soviet-dominated Baltic states, as well as Poland, the Czech Republic, Hungary, and Slovenia, had completed a transition to democratic stability. If Communism had failed to hold back the tide of modernization and capitalism, surely Arab nationalism, local variations on state socialism, the Islamo-fascism of the Saudi Wahhabis, and the Iranian theocracy could not do so. Human nature does not change. What Stalin could not prevent, bin Laden or Mahmoud Ahmadinejad, the hate-monger president of Iran, certainly would not.

The march of the Middle East into the modern world might have been, once upon a time, called bourgeois revolution. But however it was labeled, it would not be obstructed. Almost blindly, the Bush administration had been transformed into the artifice of such a change, even as Wolfowitz himself discreetly declined to be described as a "revolutionary." He and other neoconservative Jews, like so many of those who came before them, fought for humanistic, liberal, universal values, not for a particular ethnic agenda.

CHAPTER 8

✡THE AIPAC SCANDAL

Proof of a Conspiracy?

AIPAC had a narrower perspective than the neoconservatives. According to various sources, in 2004 when the AIPAC spy scandal broke, U.S. authorities had been investigating the lobby for some two years, impelled by suspicion that the organization was serving as an intelligence-gathering front for Israel. Some would laugh at the obviousness of such a claim; others would insist that AIPAC was too smart to act with such crudity. But the case of Lawrence Franklin, a Gentile and minor official at the Pentagon, AIPAC policy director Steve Rosen, and lobby Middle East expert Keith Weissman was a potential media catastrophe, comparable to no other event in the lobby's history. In 2005 the Israeli newspaper *Haaretz* reported, "Since the investigation began, AIPAC's ability to maintain good ties with U.S. administration officials has suffered." By then, the Washington offices of the lobby had been raided by federal agents.

The crucial event had occurred when FBI personnel observed

Franklin as he disclosed "information" to Keith Weissman during a meeting in July 2004 in Arlington, Virginia. "The information" Franklin communicated was in reality a hoax, created by the federal authorities as bait for AIPAC. The bogus intelligence concerned alleged Iranian intentions to kill Israeli agents who were purportedly operating in Iraqi Kurdistan. Franklin warned Weissman that the information was "highly classified Agency stuff" and that Weissman "could get into trouble by having the information," according to the federal indictment. Franklin met with Rosen and Weissman several times before and after the July 2004 meeting and repeatedly discussed classified national security information he had gained in his Pentagon job.

The mess behind these details was so incredible it lent itself to the mixing of metaphors. As the process unfolded, the principals would turn and flip on each other in a show worthy of the dolphins at Sea World. Then it all began to resemble a Japanese monster film, with lawyer-predators flailing at one another as Tokyo burns.

First, it emerged that Franklin was cooperating with the FBI when he met Weissman in July 2004. Franklin had originally been approached in August 2002 by Rosen, who called the Pentagon seeking an Iran expert. Franklin harbored a concern about Iranian influence in Iraq as did AIPAC, and made himself available to the AIPAC duo.

But Franklin was also personally vulnerable. He was well known for eccentric work habits at the Pentagon and especially for taking documents to his home in West Virginia, in violation of regulations. He was so notorious for his sloppy attitude toward classified files that once he was discovered by the FBI to have transferred information to AIPAC, there seemed to be no chance Franklin could disengage himself from legal action against the lobby. The final indictment of Franklin, Rosen, and Weissman alleged that AIPAC had been getting information out of the Pentagon since 1999. The indictment also mentioned another U.S. government official, "GO-2," who briefed Rosen on secret matters but who would not be charged. The *New York Times* identified "GO-2" as David Satterfield, a Foreign Service professional appointed senior adviser on Iraq by Secretary of State Condoleezza Rice in May 2006.

Soon enough AIPAC, which at first claimed stoutly that it would stand by Rosen and Weissman, turned on them. In March 2005, they were fired by the lobby for "conduct that was not part of their job, and beneath the standards required of AIPAC employees." Howard Kohr, who was Rosen's protégé, discharged his mentor.

Rosen then flipped on AIPAC, and his side informed Jewish Washington—and the whole American Jewish and Israeli galaxy—that he was prepared to drag other AIPAC officials, and U.S. officials up to Secretary Rice and National Security Advisor Stephen Hadley, into court to force out of them evidence of something everybody who knew the lobby believed. That is, Rosen was not a maverick or loose cannon, acting on his own when he received classified information from Franklin. Rosen was the personification of AIPAC. His defense was that in soliciting information at the Pentagon he acted with full knowledge of the organization's top leaders, and his actions were business as usual for the lobby. Few could believe any claim otherwise. But Rice, Hadley, and Satterfield worked at State, not Defense. It was unlikely that material from Larry Franklin would fall into the same class as briefings at State, even if the latter touched on secret topics.

Arguments in defense of Rosen and AIPAC's unauthorized access to classified information would, however, be late in coming: that they were normal lobbying activities, and protected under the First Amendment guarantee of petitioning for redress of grievances; that prosecution of AIPAC would threaten journalists who reported on leaks from government sources. But neither corporations, lobbies, nor media were ever encouraged to play fast and loose with Pentagon national security information, especially with Rumsfeld in the saddle. Contracts and policies could be fought over like raw meat torn apart by hungry wolves. But on such sensitive matters, the Pentagon had something in common with Las Vegas: the culture of the building held that what happened there stayed there.

Once accused, AIPAC and Rosen had lawyered up—both at least twice. AIPAC hired Abbe Lowell, one of Washington's legal Godzillas, to represent Rosen. Yet after Rosen was fired, AIPAC cut off payment of Lowell's fees (which had reached almost a million dollars in the year between August 2004 and August 2005). Rosen threatened to sue

AIPAC over his dismissal. Rosen and Weissman even retained an unnamed specialist in employment law. The organization already had Washington legal mastodon Nat Lewin advising it. The FBI investigation of Rosen and Weissman was said to have been so serious that Lewin was required to gain a special security clearance before reviewing it, and after examining the evidence, Lewin recommended the discharge of the lobby officials. AIPAC also hired Jamie Gorelick, former deputy attorney general in the Clinton administration and another legal heavy, for representation in the controversy over the legal fees.

One AIPAC insider described Rosen's attitude after he was dumped as "like Samson, trying to bring the house down on everybody." But anybody with the slightest ability to read character should have understood that Steve Rosen would not take kindly to disloyalty from the organization and the individuals whose activities and careers he had nurtured. He had drunk deep of power in Washington, while responsible to no elected authority. It was an intoxicating and addictive experience. Now his drug of choice had been taken away.

Israeli diplomat Naor Gilon, the recipient of Franklin's information, had meanwhile been recalled from Washington. No Israeli diplomat would be available for the trials, thanks to diplomatic immunity. As a compromise measure, Rosen and Weissman offered to make Israeli government representatives available for depositions, in which the Israelis would explain that their relationship with AIPAC was not improper. But since the Israelis would not agree to appear as trial witnesses, the proposal was rejected by the U.S. prosecutors.

Larry Franklin, represented by yet another Washington legal raptor, Plato Cacheris, would plead guilty to three charges: conspiracy to communicate national defense information, conspiracy to communicate classified information to an agent of a foreign government, and unlawful retention of national defense information. The last charge was based on discovery in his residence of eighty-three sensitive intelligence documents dating back some thirty years. That Franklin was a pack rat with Pentagon documents who could not help taking his work home was the explanation accepted by many who knew him. A humorously laconic comment, faintly reminiscent of dialogue from a

Quentin Tarantino film, appeared in the original complaint against him: "At no time was FRANKLIN's house an authorized location for the storage of classified US government documents."

In January 2006, Franklin received a sentence of twelve and a half years in prison. His punishment was based on an agreement under which he would testify against Rosen and Weissman in their eventual trial, while also retaining some military pension benefits; after he testified against them, his sentence might be reduced. Franklin argued throughout his proceeding that he had never intended to harm the interests of the United States, and U.S. district judge T. S. Ellis III, who also presided over the trial of "American Taliban" John Walker Lindh, recognized the truth of that claim.

But Judge Ellis declared, "It doesn't matter that you think you were really helping. That arrogates to yourself the decision whether to adhere to a statute passed by Congress, and we can't have that in this country." Since Franklin's fate remained dependent on his testimony against Rosen and Weissman, he was left free until their trial, which was to begin in August 2006. He was reduced to working as a parking valet at a racetrack, tending bar, and occasionally lecturing on terrorism and the history of Asia at a small West Virginia college. He had slid a long way down from his position at the Pentagon.

Rosen and AIPAC faced an even steeper and more destructive plunge. Jewish Washington kept quiet through the early period of the AIPAC scandal. Some seemed to be holding their breaths for months at a time, as if trying to set a sports record. The inconceivable had happened: AIPAC had stumbled and fallen badly. Rosen could face prison, which seemed unspeakably terrible. Some voices in the community wondered if AIPAC might not be ordered to register as a representative of a foreign government, not much different from any other foreign lobby, with a legal status equal to that of the American-Uzbek Chamber of Commerce and comparable entities. AIPAC itself was chastened, and also held its tongue; at the end of its May 2005 policy conference, the Israeli national anthem, "Hatikvah," was not intoned.

That was a shocking first for the organization, although the singing was reinstated in 2006. The *Forward* quoted an AIPAC delegate from northern California, Harvey Gilbert, who described the absence of "Hatikvah" from the 2005 proceedings as "the most significant and telling event of this conference." Gilbert elaborated, "AIPAC wants to become an American organization, not a Jewish organization, not the kind of organization that Jews support from the heart."

Nevertheless, the 2005 AIPAC conference boasted the leading participation of Condoleezza Rice, Richard Perle, and California Democratic representative Jane Harman, as well as the presence of half the members of Congress, representing both parties. Rice stressed the commitment of the Bush administration to Palestinian democratization, but the conferees were distracted, as the Rosen case remained a major topic of speculation. Howard Kohr briefed participants in such a manner as to indicate that whatever Rosen, his former patron, had done, AIPAC would conduct its affairs with a full commitment to "transparency, accountability, and . . . effectiveness." Delegates to the event privately expressed their anxiety over the unknown, namely, how far the FBI would take its inquiry. Rice and Cheney appeared at the 2006 AIPAC policy conference, but the delegates were still anxious over the Rosen affair.

But regarding controversies involving prominent Washington Jews, the concurrent Jack Abramoff lobbying scandal and prosecution of I. Lewis "Scooter" Libby occupied the attention of the local and national media much more than the AIPAC affair. Abramoff, who unethically exploited Indian gambling to enrich himself, was not a figure of whom Jews could be proud. But the media preferred him to Rosen as a target, because Abramoff was a supporter of the Republicans, while Rosen had worked both sides of the street—for example, he was alleged to have earmarked information received from Franklin for a reporter at *The Nation,* as well as the *Washington Post.* For his part, Libby was the target of exaggerated media attention as well as the usual Jew-baiting slurs handed out by neo-Nazis, isolationists, and other gutter inhabitants who preached against the Iraq war, because of his alleged role in the media uproar over the sleazy ex-ambassador

Joseph Wilson and his CIA spouse, Valerie Plame. But few Jewish or Gentile Americans feared that Abramoff or Libby (whose Jewishness was uncertain to many people) would incarnate or encourage anti-Semitic paranoia. By contrast, Rosen and AIPAC had, it seemed, the power to fulfill the dreadful fantasies of Jew-haters and Israelophobes.

Knives that had been hidden but kept sharp for many years came out with the news that Rosen was in trouble. AIPAC without Steve Rosen was difficult to imagine; one commentator described it as self-decapitation. But self-decapitation is suicide. Was the pro-Israel lobby committing suicide? The lobby owed Rosen a great deal for the twenty-three years in which he had driven the organization to the top of the Washington system of influence. Rosen had accomplished this by relentlessly pursuing AIPAC's contacts with the executive branch rather than cultivating legislators, as earlier lobby leaders had done.

But loved Rosen was not. When he was fired, the *Forward* used such terms as "secretive, Machiavellian . . . confrontational and abrasive." Many in Jewish Washington were glad to see him go, for he embodied a stereotypical aggressivity the *shtadlan* leadership and prior AIPAC chiefs had tried to expunge from the image of American Jews. One source who refused to be named described Rosen and AIPAC as guilty of "overreaching." The Rosen scandal was said by another top American Jewish leader to be a "cancer" in the lobby.

The combination of a federal sting operation and incaution by Rosen had brought the Israel lobby to the brink of disaster. The allegation of dual loyalty among pro-Israel American Jews could be powerfully and perhaps permanently mainstreamed. With the *shtadlan* groups such as ADL and AJC still headquartered in New York and focused on domestic issues, American Jews might, at least temporarily, have to trust the goodwill of the dominant Gentile political class in Middle East policy. But liberal Democratic Jews would not grant such confidence to the Bush administration and other Republicans.

The damage to the lobby could end up being more psychological than practical, at least as far as the needs of Israel were concerned. A guilty verdict and jail sentence against Rosen or Weissman would leave AIPAC badly blemished. But Israeli leaders seemed rather diffident about AIPAC's problems. If it was certain that AIPAC needed Israel, it was not so clear that Israel, in the final reckoning, needed AIPAC. Israeli leaders and diplomats did not defer to AIPAC; rather, when Israeli politics swung, as it tended to do, back toward peace-oriented solutions of the problems between the Jewish state and the Arabs, the lobby had struggled to adapt to the new line. In most cases, the Israelis themselves seemed perfectly happy to deal with the United States on a government-to-government basis without requiring the services of an elaborate lobbying group.

What had really happened here? Some Jewish advocates alleged a CIA/FBI anti-Semitic conspiracy. The widely respected Barry Jacobs, Washington director of strategic studies for the American Jewish Committee, broke the habitual silence of the AJC about such matters to publicly declare that resentment in the CIA and other intelligence agencies over the supposed alliance of neoconservatives and the pro-Israel lobby to prosecute war against Iraq "and possibly also Iran" was "behind the investigation." Such discontent was common among the spooks. The CIA was enraged at the neoconservative initiative in Middle East policy and, as shown by the mental disintegration of the former CIA expert on bin Laden, Michael Scheuer, who had turned into an extreme public Israelophobe, the vaunted intelligence professionals viewed the Jewish neoconservatives and the pro-Israel lobby as the same, which they were not at all. The CIA, itself in a state of moral breakdown, could not strike at Wolfowitz, but it could fire at AIPAC in the mistaken expectation that the ricochet would damage the neoconservatives. To some in the CIA, all Jews were alike, and to hit one was to hit all. Such had never been true; had it been, the *shtadlan* lobbies and AIPAC would have better defended the Jewish neoconservatives against the libels that rained down on them.

But let us first look at Larry Franklin. Historians of espionage speak of recruitment by MICE: money, ideology, compromise (usually sexual), and ego. Money and compromise seemed to have played no role on the wayward road Franklin took, but ideology and perhaps ego were driving forces in his decision. Franklin had visited Israel and viewed the Jewish state as an indispensable American ally. He was a minor Pentagon figure who might well have wanted more recognition; he sought AIPAC help in attempting to move to the National Security Council. But he had also come to share a peculiar myopia affecting the Jewish leadership: the inability to perceive any serious enemy for Israel and the Jews other than Iran.

Even before Rosen contacted him in 2002, Franklin had, independently of any AIPAC association, become briefly involved in an abortive attempt, late in 2001 and early in 2002, to establish a back channel for high-level U.S. communication with Iran. The operation centered on Manucher Ghorbanifar, an Iranian arms dealer and "informant" considered unreliable by Western intelligence agencies. But the Ghorbanifar effort was found unproductive and was stopped at the order of the U.S. embassy in Rome as well as the CIA and the NSC. Franklin would also meet, independently of his relationship to Rosen and Weissman, with an unnamed foreign diplomat, presumably an Israeli.

American Jewish, Israeli, and general Western concerns about Iran are legitimate. The Khomeinist system of clerical rule (a heresy in Islam) has proven unworkable, and Iran elected the bizarre demagogue Mahmoud Ahmadinejad to its presidency. In addition, it has been truculent about gaining nuclear capacity. For a quarter century, the Khomeini regime and its successors made an uncompromising stand against Israel the chief point of their ideological rivalry with Saudi Arabia for putative leadership of world Islam. The Iranians assisted Palestinian Islamic Jihad, a murderous terror group, and Hezbollah, the Shia militia in Lebanon, for years. But Iran was by no means the main source of Islamist violence in the world—that distinction belongs to Saudi Arabia's Wahhabi cult, which impels al-Qaeda and its brutal terrorists in Iraq, while also funding the Al-Aqsa Martyrs Brigades and Hamas in their suicide-bombing campaigns in Israel. In addition, U.S. policy toward Iran was a matter of dissension even at summits of American power, and among the neoconservatives themselves. Some favored negotiations with Iran's leaders, or encouraging the Iranian masses in their disaffection with the clerical regime, rather than direct confrontation.

Rosen's original intent in contacting Franklin had been to harden the position of the White House in the debate over Iran.

But the single-minded focus on Iran, before 2001, had distracted American Jews and important elements of the U.S. government from the looming danger of al-Qaeda. One only had to do the math—Iran could rally extremist Shias to its platform, but Shia Muslims account for no more than 15 percent of Muslims worldwide. By contrast, Saudi Arabia sought to radicalize and recruit for armed jihad the hundreds of millions of Sunni Muslims across the globe. In addition, Iranian attempts at politicizing global Shiism had failed, while the Saudi-Wahhabi strategy for recruitment of Sunnis to terror had increased worldwide bloodshed, culminating in the events of September 11, followed by attacks in places from London to Bali and the bloody offensive by the late Abu Musab al-Zarqawi in Iraq. By trying to fit every problem with radical Islam into a Procrustean bed imagined in Tehran, American Jews and Israelis had left the world unprepared for the realities of a real struggle against Islamofascism.

The fixation on Iran, embodied in Rosen and Weissman and echoed by Franklin, was old news for AIPAC. The eyes of American Jewish leaders, from cautious *shtadlan* representatives to the hard guys in AIPAC, from comfortable Democrats to ambitious Republicans, long remained on the Iranian threat. For this reason, they also failed to understand the greater potential of Iraq for the neoconservative system of analysis. Success in Iraq, to emphasize, is more likely to positively, rather than negatively, affect Iran's necessary process of reform.

Jeffrey Goldberg had it right in a *New Yorker* article in which he recalled his observations of Rosen and Franklin. He had seen Franklin in Washington late in 2002, at a banquet held by the Jewish Institute for National Security Affairs (JINSA) to honor Wolfowitz. Conversation should have been occupied with the impending intervention in Iraq, which was then Franklin's area of responsibility. But as Goldberg wrote, "Franklin did not seem especially concerned with the topic at hand. As we stood outside the banquet hall, he said that Iran, not Iraq, would turn out to be the most difficult challenge in the war on terror."

But Franklin, unlike Rosen and Weissman, had seemed able to compartmentalize: a useful character trait in a clandestine agent, a revolutionary activist, or a military functionary. Franklin, who frequented the Iraqi-American "Shia-cons," i.e., influential Shia Muslims who, like the neoconservatives, backed the United States in Iraq, kept his eye on the task at hand: lining up support for the intervention. Every element in his demeanor indicated that he believed in this mission. In his meetings with Shia clerics, he seldom mentioned Iran, which was probably wise, because nearly all of them were and are soft on Tehran. They rejected the Khomeini scheme for clerical rule in politics, but they were not against Iran as a leading Shia power. Indeed, of the clerics Franklin met with, one repeatedly showed Hezbollah videos from Lebanon in his mosque. Another had given interviews in which he appeared to legitimize suicide terror bombings and approve of Holocaust denial by Ahmadinejad (whom some disgruntled Iranians, reflecting the global corruption of political language, referred to insultingly as a "neoconservative").

Franklin spent a great deal of time in 2003 and 2004 shmoozing at the Washington conventions of the Universal Muslim Association of America (UMAA), a new organization founded to promote the interests of Shia Muslims in America. Shias had never participated in the "Wahhabi lobby" coalition of radical Sunni organizations that dominate American Islam—led by the Saudi-financed Islamic Society of North America (ISNA) and the Hamas-front Council on American Islamic Relations (CAIR)—and by 2003 many American Shias believed the time had come to assert themselves politically. American Jewish groups, however, looked at Shias, with their Khomeinist reputation, with great distaste, notwithstanding their importance in the approaching Iraq conflict. Throughout the Iraq war Shia Muslims, including the Shia-cons, and the American Jewish groups, although they might have been considered natural allies in supporting the democratization effort in Iraq, eyed each other gingerly, if at all.

A contact of Franklin and the main wheeler-dealer in UMAA was a Maryland urologist named Parvez Shah, a Pakistani Shia by origin.

Every foreign freedom movement the United States has supported since the end of the Second World War, from the South Korean defense against North Korean aggression to the Iranians, has had its Parvez Shahs: not-very-distinguished ethnic politicians who believe they can hire their people out as policy cattle, in exchange for notoriety or wealth. Parvez Shah is completely unlike the Iraqi politicians supported by the United States, but in the American milieu from which Shia support for the Iraq intervention emerged, he imagined himself a power to contend with.

UMAA was confounded by the presence within it, in addition to the Shia-cons, of "Sha-habis," i.e., Shia Muslims who followed the dictates in the United States of the Saudi-backed Wahhabi lobby. The presence of "Sha-habis" in their community was especially grating to the Shia-cons because the Saudi-Wahhabis promote virulent hatred and violence against Shia Muslims, as represented by al-Zarqawi in Iraq. The struggle against Wahhabi influence in American Islam represents the domestic front in the war on Islamist radicalism.

Still, Shias remain a minority in American and worldwide Islam, a situation that can only leave them disadvantaged in the face of the Saudi-Wahhabi conspiracy. Unlike Sunni Muslims, who are often politically passive and easily manipulated, Shias consider dissent and controversy within their ranks to be positive values. It was for that reason, above all, that they had not previously established a major community organization in North America. Most important, they bore a deep loathing for Saddam's regime and an extraordinary desire to see the Shia holy cities of Karbala and Najaf liberated. Thus, even many American Shias who condemned Israel and criticized U.S. policy toward Iran were prepared to support the Bush plan for the liberation of Iraq. Yet the administration was slow, if not inert, in assessing, mobilizing, and otherwise utilizing them in the transformation of Iraq or as allies against the influence of Wahhabism.

In part, the problem was one of ignorance, but it was compounded by Shia phobia and by the widespread presumption, turned into an article of faith by AIPAC and other Jewish groups, that Shia radicals, even if they were few, were more dangerous than Sunni extremists, who were and are very many. In 2006, three years after the invasion of Iraq, American Shia leaders still waited in frustration, in Washington and New York, for meetings with leading American officials that never took place. The U.S.-led coalition and its representatives in Baghdad had difficulty in maintaining good relations with Shia leaders on the ground there, and could apparently see no value in seeking better communications by liaison with Shias in the United States.

Perhaps American official ambivalence toward Shias was justified by their pro-Iranian tilt. But when Larry Franklin, in 2003–2004, cultivated the company and counsel of Iraqi American Shia clerics to pursue administration policy in their native country, did he understand that they were mainly as pro-Iranian as he was anti-Iranian? When he attended a 2003 memorial for the slain Iraqi Ayatollah Baqir al-Hakim, in Crystal City, near the Pentagon, did he grasp that Baqir's faction was the most pro-Iran? There is no evidence that he ever considered the possibility, or that he reported to anybody on the Iranian sympathies of American Shias. He compartmentalized: his job was to line up Shias for the Iraq action, and he did so. There is also no indication that he understood that even among the Iraqi Shia clerics who were educated in and looked nostalgically on Iran, Arab-Persian rivalries were still extremely deep. In private some Iraqi Shia clerics would declare their hatred of the *ajam,* an Arab word for foreigners that is used as a hate term against Iranians.

Perhaps the walls of Larry Franklin's compartmentalized mind were broken down by the Iranian obsession of AIPAC and Rosen. They could not grasp or accept the direction American policy had taken: to keep the Iraq and Iranian issues separate as long as possible, and to depend on the goodwill of Iraqi Shia leaders such as Ayatollah Ali Sistani, even though Sistani was also close to Iran—as were Ahmad Chalabi and other Iraqi Shia leaders.

That American Jews were and remain so much more concerned with Iran than any other threat partly explains, along with Democratic influence, why by the end of 2005 a majority of them opposed the Iraq war but said they would support armed action against Tehran.

The unstable Ahmadinejad did not help the situation with his vile Holocaust-denying comments.

Yet the common wisdom of the Jewish and Israeli leadership— that all members of the ruling Iranian clerical class were equally evil— was comparable to the immense mistake of the German Communists of the 1930s, who declared that the Nazis were no worse than the governing socialists. The art of politics is that of making, rather than confusing, distinctions, and in staunchly refusing to distinguish between diverse personalities among the Iranian and Iraqi Shia clerics, Western opinion, and certainly Jewish opinion, made a serious strategic error. One would imagine that, since he possesses an advanced academic degree and is a speaker of Farsi, Franklin would understand these differences; indeed, that it would be his job to track them. But Franklin appeared oblivious to such issues when they took the form of a living, pro-Iranian Shia cleric from the United States, as opposed to "the mullahs" of Iran as an abstraction.

As previously noted, FBI agents had fabricated the main item of information that Franklin proffered and toward which Rosen lunged in July 2004 like a hungry hammerhead—the false report that Israeli agents in Iraqi Kurdistan had been targeted by Iranian agents. Curiously, the claim that Israeli agents were operating in Kurdistan had been put into print, along with a windy commentary, by the shlockmeister of disinformation, Seymour Hersh, in *The New Yorker,* a year before the story was retailed by the FBI to Rosen. Hersh described Israelis training Kurds for raids into Syria and Iran. There is no evidence that such forays ever took place. Hersh got the fairy tale from Vincent Cannistraro, a former federal security official with the regrettable habit of exaggerating his past responsibilities in the counterterrorism field. Cannistraro had also, bizarrely, offered to testify on behalf of the infamous "blind sheikh" Omar Abdel-Rahman, plotter of the first World Trade Center bomb attack in 1993—but his testimony was rejected. The Cannistraro-Hersh story may have been recycled in laying the foundation for busting AIPAC. By summer 2006 the tale had sunk to the pages of the neo-Nazi press, where it always belonged.

The Jewish Telegraphic Agency (JTA), a news service respected for its professionalism and independence, revealed under the bylines of veteran reporters Ron Kampeas and Matt Berger that the FBI had "apparently" recorded a conversation on July 21, 2004, between Rosen, Weissman, and *Washington Post* reporter Glenn Kessler. In the colloquy, the AIPAC leaders said Franklin had passed information to them because their "connections" at the White House were better than his. This was, at the very least, a provocative suggestion, considering that the Pentagon, which employed Franklin, is considered an institution at the supreme heights of power. Did Franklin buy into the Jew-baiting stereotype of AIPAC as a controlling force in the life of the republic, superior to the Defense Department in its command over U.S. policy? Did Franklin think Rosen was more powerful than Rumsfeld, his own boss? Or that Rumsfeld was weak on Iran? How could he have thought either thing? Rumsfeld had consistently denounced Iran in the strongest terms employed by any Bush 43 cabinet officer. Kessler was said to have been included in the conversation because Franklin wanted knowledge of the Iranian danger widely disseminated. Supposedly, the three men kidded each other about the possibility of legal difficulties over the sharing of information, with Rosen joking that "at least we have no Official Secrets Act," along the British model, in the United States.

According to the JTA, Rosen was well known for his scoffing attitude about American legal restrictions on classified information. While the United States punishes the *disclosure* of secret information, its standards have been more ambiguous about the *receipt* of classified matter. Nevertheless, the JTA suggested that the comment to Kessler about the absence of an Official Secrets Act would indicate an awareness that the shared information was for restricted access and that possession of it by Rosen was illegal.

The veracity of the information transmitted was not important. What counted was that it had allegedly been passed by Franklin to Rosen and then to the Israeli embassy. But strangely, when Franklin appealed for funds to support his legal defense, he turned to some of

the same American Shia leaders whom he had met at the beginning
of the Iraq war, and who were still as soft on Iran as any Iraqi Shias
could be. Is it really possible Larry Franklin did not know this? Was
he simply confused, in a fog about geopolitical reality?

At the end of May 2005, someone acting on Franklin's behalf
transmitted the following e-mail:

05/31/2005 09:35 PM

xxxxxxxxx@highstream.net

To: xxxxxxxxxx@aol.com, xxxxxxxxxx@earthlink.net, jsirrs@xxx.com,
mowaffakalrubaie@yahoo.co.uk, xxx@xxx.mail.virginia.edu,
xxxxx@xxxxxx.xxxxx.xx.xx, xxxxxx.xxxxxx@xxxxxxxxxxxxxxxxxxxxx,
xxxxxxxxxxxx@hotmail.com [names redacted by Stephen Schwartz]

Subject: Larry Franklin's Defense

Dear friend of Larry Franklin,

Larry Franklin is resisting the charges made against him and welcomes any
support you can give him. To give financial support, please make checks
available to the Larry Franklin Defense Fund, P.O. Box 333, Kearneysville,
WV 25430.

XXXXXXXXXX [name redacted]

Two names have been left in clear type here, those of Mowaffak al-
Rubaie and Julie Sirrs. Al-Rubaie has served as national security minister of Iraq and is a Shia political figure with close ties to Iran through
his role in the Khomeinist Iraqi Da'wa party. But was not al-Rubaie precisely the kind of Iranian-influenced Iraqi Franklin was so concerned
about? Julie Sirrs is a former Afghanistan expert for Franklin's past
employer, the Defense Intelligence Agency. A year before the message
was sent out, she was editing the *Terrorism Monitor* issued by the

Jamestown Foundation, a Washington outfit considered by many to be a front for the U.S. intelligence agencies. Sirrs was a good editor of Jamestown's material but was replaced by a questionable youth from Britain, Mahan Abedin, who made the periodical a mouthpiece for Sa'ad al-Fagih, a Saudi associate of Osama bin Laden. Al-Fagih has been named as a terrorist financier by the U.S. State Department. The Jamestown Foundation also stood out for its promotion of Israel-baiting CIA renegade Michael Scheuer, and publishes a weekly on Chechnya edited by a Christian fanatic named Larry Uzzell.

Most Americans would find it peculiar that an organization believed to serve the interests of the American intelligence agencies would embrace a bin Ladenite like Sa'ad al-Fagih. The convoluted thought patterns, inconsistencies, and instability present in the "hall of mirrors" environment of the CIA and similar enterprises seemed to be reproduced in the Jamestown Foundation; indeed, such contradictions in the latter's activities appeared as a convincing item in the argument that Jamestown had such links. Scheuer, for example, had gone from work as the CIA's bin Laden expert to a public advocacy for the view that the al-Qaeda leader would sincerely abide by a truce if the West would simply leave him alone and withdraw from Afghanistan and Iraq.* Other recipients of the message request-

---

* Full disclosures: The author of this book published articles with Jamestown on radical Islam in the Balkans, Central Asia, and Nigeria. In addition, it must be observed that Scheuer and a number of other neocon-baiters seemed to have drawn back, at least partially, from their strident rhetoric after the publication of the Mearsheimer-Walt pamphlet against the Jewish lobby. One of the first of the anti-Israel chatterers to indicate that Mearsheimer and Walt had gone too far in their smear tactics was none other than Noam Chomsky, who argued that U.S. global economic and political goals, rather than the Jewish lobbies, dictated American policy on the Middle East. For his part, Scheuer, after many months of unrestrained and virulent attacks on Israel, suddenly announced in April 2006 his hope that Mearsheimer and Walt would repeat their efforts, but this time deal with the Saudi lobby, which Scheuer acknowledged as "probably more dangerous to the United States than the Israeli lobby." Scheuer's meanderings seemed to reveal nothing so much as an intellectual disorientation that had overcome the CIA.

ing contributions for the Franklin defense included a leading American Shia-con. So what was really going on in Larry Franklin's head?

While Jewish Washington mainly kept its silence as the Rosen trial approached, in New York, communal journalists and other Jewish figures stirred the pot of suspicion and doubt about the future of AIPAC. The organization's members had responded to the Rosen case with an exceptional upsurge in donations. Like any other such group, AIPAC could, in an immediate crisis, count on many of its longtime supporters around the country for emergency aid.

But among Jewish leaders, recriminations became more convoluted. Where Rosen had once been subjected to scarifying comment because of his arrogance and overeager tactics, AIPAC and Howard Kohr were, two years after the investigation was made public, metaphorically flogged for abandoning Rosen.

Neal M. Sher, a predecessor of Howard Kohr as AIPAC executive director and Clinton appointee as a "Nazi-hunter," exploded in print at the end of January 2006. Writing in a New York Jewish weekly, Sher blasted AIPAC with the worst of all criticism: it had gone *shtadlan* and was "in peril of becoming a modern-day version of the ancient court Jew." The accusation was hyperbolic, to say the least. AIPAC had never been *shtadlan* and never could be, since it did not claim to embody the domestic concerns of American Jews. Sher (a partisan Democrat) accused AIPAC of being driven by "an almost blind deference to the positions and wishes of the Bush administration" in dismissing and criticizing Rosen and Weissman. That claim was simply ridiculous. AIPAC had never been deferential to the administration; at the end of 2005 it stridently assailed Bush for insufficient militancy on Iran. The lobby described the cautious approach of the administration in handling the Iranian nuclear problem as "disturbing" and "dangerous." Predictably, the Bush administration, which had a fire to put out in Iraq, was little interested in starting another—notwithstanding the entreaties of Iran hawks and the conspiracy blather of neocon-baiters.

Sher averred a much more serious motive for AIPAC to turn against Rosen and Weissman: the federal investigation of the pair had produced evidence dating back to 1999, so the feds had been watching AIPAC for quite a few years. *Haaretz* reported that the FBI was determined to complete a serious investigation of AIPAC encompassing the overall operations of the lobby and not merely the Franklin case. The Israeli paper quoted an official twice interviewed as a witness by the FBI; the source was said to be "astounded by investigators' intimate familiarity with AIPAC." The *Forward* disclosed that FBI agents had interviewed Uzi Arad, former head of the research section of Mossad, the Israeli intelligence agency, and, according to Arad, asked him about his relations with Franklin. The FBI was apparently engaged in a fishing expedition, since no evidence of links between Franklin and AIPAC prior to Rosen contacting him in 2002 were turned up. Eventually, Bureau agents in search of AIPAC leads would be reported to have sought access, on the basis of a disreputable report, to the papers of Jack Anderson, the muckraking writer who died at the end of 2005. The agents cast a wide net, also allegedly interviewing former AIPAC chiefs Tom Dine, Morrie Amitay, and Neal Sher, as well as ZOA's Mort Klein, about Rosen's ability to pay for his defense and his prospective employment.

Some observers argued that AIPAC's difficulties were caused less by the Franklin affair than by its slowness in adapting to political changes in Israel. Ariel Sharon had turned to the center, and Jewish settlements would be withdrawn from Gaza. In its militant mode, AIPAC was allegedly resistant to the new Israeli politics. But AIPAC's long-established habits of secrecy, symbolized by the Franklin blowup, were also said to have undermined its standing with the Bush administration. *Haaretz* claimed that the presidential staff and the Departments of State and Defense had adopted a policy of discretion in their encounters with AIPAC, since they knew that the FBI was tapping the lobby's telephone traffic and surveilling its e-mail. Even the Israeli embassy was reputedly keeping a distance from the lobby.

Sher, however, had no compunctions about dragging Howard Kohr, the current AIPAC executive director, into the spotlight and underscoring his protégé status with Rosen, whom he accused Kohr of abandoning. Sher also blamed fealty to the Bush White House in

AIPAC's failure to support the Saudi Arabia Accountability Act of 2005, which had been introduced by Senator Arlen Specter, the Jewish Republican from Pennsylvania. Its first cosponsors were Senators Evan Bayh, Susan Collins, Tim Johnson, Patty Murray, Russ Feingold, and Ron Wyden.

The bill's text stood as an inventory of evidence against the kingdom and its role in enabling Islamist terrorism. The Saudi Arabia Accountability Act summoned the rulers of the kingdom to comply with United Nations resolution 1373, calling on states to refrain from supporting terrorism, to combat terrorism, and to deny safe haven to financiers and planners of terrorism. As the home of Wahhabism, Saudi territory has been a rich field of targets for serious counterterrorism.

The Saudi Arabia Accountability Act quoted the Council of Foreign Relations (CFR), which concluded almost three years before that Saudi Arabia is the main source of al-Qaeda backing and that Saudi officials have refused to take serious action to end it. In 2004 the CFR emphasized, in language incorporated in the bill, that not a single Saudi funder of terrorism has been arrested, tried, or otherwise "publicly punished." The bill went on to cite reports critical of Saudi behavior, issued by the U.S. 9/11 Commission, the human rights monitor Freedom House, and the U.S. Commission on International Religious Freedom. It referenced 2003 Senate testimony on Wahhabism in which David Aufhauser, then general counsel of the Treasury Department, called the Saudi state the "epicenter" of global terror financing. It also noted that the Saudis subsidized half the annual budget of Hamas, as part of a $4 billion outlay to Palestinian extremists since the beginning of the second *intifada* in 2000.

Above all, the Saudi Arabia Accountability Act emphasized the Saudis' lack of effective commitment to U.S. efforts against terror. Saudi foot-dragging in investigating al-Qaeda recalls Saudi obstruction of U.S. inquiries into the 1996 bombing of the Khobar Towers, in which nineteen American service personnel died. Even after September 11, the Saudis prevented U.S. officials from interviewing terrorist suspects in Saudi custody, including a Saudi subject knowledgeable about plans to inject poison gas into the New York City subways.

But failure to combat terrorism is only part of Saudi mischief. The Saudi Arabia Accountability Act condemned the indoctrination in hatred pursued by Wahhabis in mosques and schools on U.S. soil, as well by clerics on the kingdom's official payroll at home. The bill had already been introduced into the House of Representatives with the backing of twenty-four members, from Republican Dan Burton of Indiana to Democrat Henry Waxman of California. If passed, it would express a congressional consensus that Saudi authorities must immediately cooperate in a complete and unrestricted manner with the U.S. government in the fight against terror and permanently close all charities, schools, and other organizations or institutions that support terrorism, whether inside Saudi territory or abroad. The latter provision would include cutting off payments to the families of suicide bombers in Israel.

In case the Saudis might not get the message, the bill provided for sanctions, including a bar on exporting special military technology to the kingdom—twenty-four years after AWACS—and restriction on travel by Saudi diplomats outside a twenty-five-mile radius of their embassy and consulates in Washington, New York, Houston, and Los Angeles. Certification of Saudi compliance would rest with President Bush. But the Bush administration showed little interest in the legislation. Bush was dissatisfied with the Saudis, but he was going to play Texas-style, without communicating anything to his opponent in public. The Saudis, on the other hand, were terrified of the new legislation.

The combined House-Senate effort to make the Saudis behave like a normal and respectable country came late but remained urgent. Five years have passed since September 11, 2001; fifteen of the nineteen terrorist pilots on that day were Saudis. This is a fact no American is likely to forget or forgive. As this book goes to press, Saudi clerics continue to incite their followers to kill Shia Muslims, non-Wahhabi Sunnis, and the forces of the new Iraqi government, along with Americans and others in the ranks of the U.S.-led coalition in Mesopotamia. The day the Saudi Arabia Accountability Act was dropped in the Senate hopper, June 7, 2005, a Saudi subject, Fahd Nouman Suweilem al-Faqihi, stood trial in Jordan for an attempted bombing at the border of that country and Iraq. The week before, the State Department named the Saudi kingdom and three other Gulf states as the worst offenders of international laws against human trafficking. And the suppression of Christian, Hindu, Buddhist, and Jewish as well as non-Wahhabi Muslim worshipers inside the kingdom continued.

There were two curious things about the Saudi Arabia Accountability Act. One is that the *shtadlan* organizations and AIPAC did not support it, scoffingly referring to its passage as an impossibility. Only Mort Klein's Zionist Organization of America backed the legislation enthusiastically. But so did Saudi Muslim dissidents, who looked toward the demand for Saudi transparency by the United States as the fulcrum of social change in the kingdom and of progress in the global Islamic community, or *ummah*. To blame the scarcity of official Jewish support for the bill, as Neal Sher did, on the Bush administration was silly.

But if some part of Sher's diatribe was typical Democratic partisanship, he also forecast a very real possibility: because of Rosen, AIPAC could be compelled to file under the Foreign Agents Registration Act, or FARA. Most American Jewish leaders admitted that, at least in their minds, they had always deferred to Israeli opinion—a suggestion that was not completely accurate during the Oslo period. But they acted as if their status as a lobby, which might require them to comply with registration laws, was a sudden discovery. According to Sher, registration would be AIPAC's "death knell."

How could any of this be good for the Jews? AIPAC had almost willfully missed the point of global democratization, the basis of neoconservative policy under Bush. It was difficult to avoid three conclusions:

- AIPAC's narrow concern with Iran had warped its judgment.
- Rosen had been snared precisely because of the fixation on Iran.
- Franklin was a pawn in an assault on Jewish Washington by the latter's enemies.

In such a situation, could it be that the Jewish defense and advocacy groups had outlived their usefulness? Jewish interests would have
been far better served by a wholehearted commitment to the neoconservative effort in Iraq—which could be decoupled from the problems
of Iran, if not utilized as a force for progress in Tehran. Wolfowitz had
left the Pentagon, but democracy was slowly consolidating in Iraq and
bourgeois revolution was appearing, as a tiny flower needing maxi-
mum protection, in such nearby countries as Lebanon.

Yet few in AIPAC or the broader Jewish leadership were prepared
to study the lobby's debacle in these terms. The intervention in Iraq
was conceived for the betterment of the Iraqis, America, the Bush
administration, the world . . . and, only secondarily, the Jews. But the
truth remained: the *shtadlan* Jewish leadership and AIPAC had little
role in advancing that policy.

One Jewish appointee of George W. Bush who did not support the
neoconservative policy of Middle East democratization was Dov
Zakheim, who resigned his post as comptroller of the Pentagon in
2004. An Orthodox Jew, Zakheim had frequently been targeted by the
cruder Buchananites as a member of the alleged "cabal." But he had little in common with Wolfowitz and others like him. On his resignation,
Zakheim said, "I am proud to have been part of President Bush and
Secretary Rumsfeld's senior Pentagon team for the past three years. . . .
It has been an exhilarating, albeit extremely demanding experience.
[W]e have addressed the many concerns arising out of the War on Terror and Operations Enduring Freedom, Noble Eagle and Iraqi Freedom, including winning both military and financial support from the
international community for operations in Afghanistan and Iraq."

After his resignation, however, Zakheim went public with a harsh
criticism of the administration's position. Zakheim delivered his cau-
tionary speech before the national conference of World Affairs Councils of America in Washington on January 28, 2005—only eight days
after George W. Bush's second inaugural, with its inspiring call for full
democratic transformation in the Middle East.

Zakheim's criticism was a buffet of clichés, drawn from less-than-
authoritative sources, about Islamic society, which he claimed could

not sustain a democratic transformation. "The Neo-Wilsonian notion that somehow America is the best vehicle for spreading democracy," he declaimed, "or even that it is in America's interests that the Middle East be politically 'transformed' in the near term, may be as fanciful, and indeed, as counterproductive, as was Woodrow Wilson's own vision nearly a century ago. . . . We must consider whether democracy is always superior to other forms of government. We must consider whether democracies are always peace loving. . . . And, perhaps most important of all from America's vantage point, we must consider whether we can be certain that democratically elected governments will support American interests—because in truth, it is not merely democracies that we seek to support, but, far more important, friendly democracies. The two are not identical. And the choice between unfriendly, or even hostile democracies, and friendly, or even supportive authoritarian regimes is not a foregone conclusion in favor of the former."

Zakheim blamed the pluralistic Ottoman Empire for the current chaos in the Middle East. He apparently did not know that an open style of Islam dominated the Ottoman caliphate and continued under the secularist regime of Mustafa Kemal, which became the modern Turkish republic. Yet the self-anointed expert went on to mouth a series of confused misapprehensions that could not even be called half-truths. They included the meaningless demand for an "Islamic Reformation," demonstrating that Zakheim knew nothing of the historical difference between Christian and Islamic civilizations. Zakheim even recycled the classic Arabist and Islamist claim that "For Arabs in general, Muslim or Christian, American support for Israel— in the absence of an agreement between Israel and the Palestinians— is the cause of deeply held resentment." That for many Iraqis, Saudi subjects, and other Arabs, the Israel issue was subordinate seemed beyond Zakheim's ken.

Zakheim's warnings vanished almost immediately from public attention with the heartening news of the successful election in Iraq early in 2005. Michael Rubin, a former Pentagon official, later told the *Forward* in an e-mail, "Zakheim's objections to the 'neocon' idea of tying foreign policy to human rights and democratization took quite a blow when Iraqis marched to the polls two days after his speech. . . . Friendly dictators may be better than prickly democracies for businessmen, but not for American national security. Friendly dictators can also backfire. Isn't that the story of Washington's relations with Baghdad? Consistent betrayal of people's democratic aspirations can also turn ugly. Take Iran: In 1953 and 1979, American officials sided with a friendly dictator over the will of the people, and just look at where that got us. We shouldn't make the same mistake three times."

The trial of Rosen and Weissman approached inexorably through a late Washington winter in 2005–2006. Lawyers for the two former AIPAC officials insisted that enforcement of the law in their case would have the often-evoked "chilling effect" on journalistic and other use of leaked information. The federal authorities rejected all such arguments with decisive, even rude language. On February 22, 2006, U.S. Deputy Attorney General Paul J. McNulty signed off on responses to several procedural motions filed by the defendants. McNulty is a tough professional whose determination in pursuing Islamist extremists had become well known when he succeeded in putting a group of especially dangerous al-Qaeda sympathizers, known as the "north Virginia jihad network," behind bars in 2003–2004. Indeed, some observers of the AIPAC case had sniped that because McNulty was so efficient in prosecuting radical Muslims, he might be expected to take a soft line on Rosen and Weissman.

That expectation was incorrect. McNulty and his prosecutorial team dealt with Rosen and Weissman in strict, even shocking terms. McNulty contemptuously dismissed attempts by the defendants to claim the statute under which they were charged was so vague they did not understand it. The prosecutors' brief commented acidly, "Two highly educated men (both defendants hold Ph.D.s) who made a living discussing foreign policy issues related to a region of the world . . . that an ordinary person understands is vital to our national security cannot credibly claim ignorance" about the meaning of security laws.

Instead, McNulty and his team hammered at Rosen and Weissman as "intent on willful evasion" of the law. Furthermore, McNulty and his associates bluntly rejected any First Amendment protection for Rosen and Weissman. The prosecutors pointed out that the AIPAC representatives were not journalists and could not claim the constitutional right of press freedom. As federal attorneys, McNulty and his associates further stipulated that "a prosecution under the espionage laws of an *actual* member of the press for publishing classified information leaked to it by a government source, would raise legitimate and serious issues and would not be undertaken lightly, indeed, the fact that there has never been such a prosecution speaks for itself."

The prosecutors' responses were plain and simple: Rosen and Weissman, as well as AIPAC, their employer, were "lobbyists representing for all practical purposes the interests of a foreign country.... Most, if not all, of the ordinary spies now sitting in jail could advance the same argument" as those put forward by the defendants. "Ordinary spies"—AIPAC had never before been put anywhere near such company in a U.S. government document. In later arguments, the prosecutors would go further, citing against Rosen the case of the Soviet spy ring headed by Julius Rosenberg and precedents involving other Russian agents. In attempting to introduce Israeli witnesses into the proceeding, Rosen and Weissman hoped to show that actions in favor of Israel "were always seen by Israel to benefit the United States." In the view of the prosecutors, this argument added to the guilt of the defendants in that it showed information being passed to a foreign state. The prosecutors noted that the law makes "no distinctions between allies or enemies, friends or foes" in barring transmission of information to foreign governments. Judge Ellis himself assumed a biting tone with Abbe Lowell, asking in one hearing if the attorney would apply the same standards to defendants with ties to Iran and similar motivations in seeking policy change.

As the unexpectedly harsh Washington winter ended, only one thing seemed certain: AIPAC, the King Kong of the lobbies, teetered on the edge of its demise.

But if we move from the idiom of popular culture to that of

divine revelation, we may be reminded of the servant of the prophet Elijah, who warned him, after searching the skies seven times, of a "cloud no bigger than a man's hand, rising from the sea"—and soon "the skies grew dark with clouds and wind, and a heavy rain fell" (1 Kings 18). With the case of Steven J. Rosen and Keith Weissman, a new era in the history of American Jews, their politics and their lobbies, had begun. The future would necessarily be clouded, if not stormy, thanks neither to theological differences among Jews, nor to a fresh pattern of immigration, nor to controversies over ideology or social vision. Even U.S.-Israeli policies would count for little, compared with the coming of the worst possible consequence: a public trial, in which numerous contradictions facing American Jewish leaders were bound to be exposed. In deciding what is good for the Jews, discretion and audacity would, more than ever, remain in conflict.

WORKS CONSULTED

Note: Some material by the author that was first published in the *Forward*, *National Review*, the *Weekly Standard*, *Commentary*, and *Investors' Business Daily* is included in this book.

Alteras, Isaac. *Eisenhower and Israel: U.S.-Israeli Relations, 1953–1960*. Gainesville: University Press of Florida, 1993.

Andrew, Christopher, and Vasili Mitrokhin. *The Mitrokhin Archive II*. London: Allen Lane, 2005.

Baldwin, Neil. *Henry Ford and the Jews*. New York: Public Affairs, 2001.

Bellow, Saul. "In Memory of Yetta Barshevsky," www.marxists.org/history/etol/document/1930s/yetta01.htm.

Carlson, John Roy. *Under Cover*. New York: Dutton, 1943.

Court documents in *U.S. vs. Rosen, Weissman*.

Cohler-Esses, Larry. Interview material on www.lukeford.net.

Farrell, James T. *Tommy Gallagher's Crusade*. New York: Vanguard Press, 1939.

Feingold, Henry L. *Zion in America*. New York: Hippocrene Books, 1974.

Freedman, Samuel G. "The Long Goodbye," *New York*, August 10, 1998.

Goldstein, Judith S. *The Politics of Ethnic Pressure: The American Jewish Committee Fight Against Immigration Restriction, 1906–1917*. New York: Garland Publishing, 1990.

Eshkol, Levi. *State Papers*. New York: Funk & Wagnalls, 1969.

Hertzberg, Arthur. *The Jews in America*. New York: Simon & Schuster, 1989.

Kahlenberg, Richard D. "Hire Education: The Strike That Changed New York," *Washington Monthly*, January–February 2003.

Koch, Ed. Remarks on President Franklin Roosevelt, 2005, at: http://www.wymaninstitute.org/articles/2005-02-koch.php.

Kyle, Keith. *Suez*. London: Weidenfeld and Nicolson, 1991.

Maisel, Sandy L., and Ira N. Forman. *Jews in American Politics*. Lanham, MD: Rowman and Littlefield, 2001.

Mann, James. *Rise of the Vulcans*. New York: Penguin, 2004.

Marshall, Paul, ed. *Radical Islam's Rules*. Lanham, MD: Rowman and Littlefield, 2005.

Mearsheimer, John J., and Stephen M. Walt. "The Israel Lobby and American Foreign Policy," at: http://ksgnotes1.harvard.edu/Research/wpaper.nsf/rwp/RWP06-011.

Morris, Benny. *Righteous Victims*. New York: Vintage Books, 2001.

Orwell, George. "Second Thoughts on James Burnham," 1946, at: http://orwell.ru/library/reviews/burnham/english/e_burnh.html.

Parmet, Robert D. *The Master of Seventh Avenue*. New York: NYU Press, 2005.

Peres, Shimon. *Battling for Peace: A Memoir*. New York: Random House, 1995.

Peretz, Martin. "Veiled Threat," *The New Republic*, January 28, 2002.

Pipes, Daniel. "Democrats, Republicans, and Israel," *The New York Sun*, May 23, 2006.

Podair, Jerald E. *The Strike That Changed New York*. New Haven: Yale University Press, 2002.

Podhoretz, Norman. "The First Term: The Reagan Road to Détente," *Foreign Affairs*, Winter 1984/85.

Portnoy, Samuel, trans. *Henryk Erlich and Victor Alter: Two Heroes and Martyrs for Jewish Socialism*. Hoboken, NJ: Ktav, 1990.

Powell, Colin. *My American Journey: An Autobiography*. New York: Random House, 1995.

Roizen, Ron. "Herschel Grynszpan: The Fate of a Forgotten Assassin," at www.roizen.com/ron/grynszpan.htm.

Rosenstock, Morton. *Louis Marshall: Defender of Jewish Rights*. Detroit: Wayne State University Press, 1965.

Roth, Cecil, and Geoffrey Wigoder, editors-in-chief. *The Encyclopedia Judaica*. New York: The Macmillan Company, 1972.

Roth, Philip. *The Plot Against America*. Boston: Houghton Mifflin, 2004.

Siegel, Fred. *The Future Once Happened Here*. San Francisco: Encounter Books, 1997.

Tank, Herb. *Inside Job!: The Story of Trotskyite Intrigue in the Labor Movement*. New York: New Century, 1947.

Trotsky, Leon. "Trade Unions in the Epoch of Imperialist Decay," at www.marxists.org/archive/trotsky/works/1940/1940-tu.htm

——. *Writings 1938–39*. New York: Merit Press, 1969.

Truman, Harry S. Diary for 1947, Archives of the Truman Library at www.trumanlibrary.org.

* * * * *

Archives of *Commentary*, *Forward*, the *New York Times*, the *Washington Post*, and *Haaretz*.

INDEX

ABOUT THE AUTHOR

STEPHEN SCHWARTZ was staff writer at the *San Francisco Chronicle* from 1989 to 1999. Since 1992, he has contributed to the *Forward*, the preeminent Jewish periodical in America. In 2000–2001, he was *Forward* bureau chief in Washington. He has also been a frequent contributor to the *Weekly Standard* and a writer-expert for the National Endowment for the Arts. He resides in San Francisco, Washington, and Sarajevo.